Fighter with a Heart

Presented by:

Nihil Alienum Mihi

Great Steel Strike Committee

_____

Presented to:

George Higgins Labor Center

University of Notre Dame

Fighter with a Heart

Father Charles Owen Rice, 1937

FIGHTER WITH A HEART

Writings of Charles Owen Rice
Pittsburgh Labor Priest

EDITED BY
Charles J. McCollester

UNIVERSITY OF PITTSBURGH PRESS

Published by the University of Pittsburgh Press, Pittsburgh, Pa. 15260

Copyright © 1996, University of Pittsburgh Press

Manufactured in the United States of America

Printed on acid-free paper

ISBN 0-8229-3966-5 (cloth)

ISBN 0-8229-5619-5 (pbk)

LC 96-061126

10   9   8   7   6   5   4   3   2   1

Book design by Michael G. Maskarinec

A CIP catalog record for this book is available from the Library of Congress
and the British Library.

Nihil Alienum Mihi

All I have is a voice
To undo the folded lie,
The romantic lie in the brain
Of the sensual man-in-the-street
And the lie of Authority
Whose buildings grope the sky:
There is no such thing as the State
And no one exists alone;
Hunger allows no choice
To the citizen or the police;
We must love one another or die.

W. H. Auden
Outbreak of War, 1939

Charles Owen Rice signs articles or documents with his initials COR which means "heart" in Latin. The motto is his rendition from the Rice family coat of arms. It means: "Nothing alien (to me)." Heraldic texts give the Rice motto without the Mihi. The Auden quote is a selection from a compilation of some favorite poems provided by Rice near the completion of this volume.

Contents

Acknowledgments

First is Monsignor himself. He cooperated fully, answering questions about chronology, discussing history, identifying photos. However, he offered no opinions about my choices of text; suggesting no additions or subtractions. The selections and their organization are mine for better or worse.

Then there is Gerri Mullooly, Rice's faithful and supportive secretary. Besides helping Monsignor remain active, she has done much useful work for this project: copying, transcribing, checking dates and facts.

Fannia Weingartner was the experienced editor who fervently believed in the book and provided important advice and encouragement. Collaboration with Fannia on the *The River Ran Red: Homestead 1892* gave me an indication of how to coherently organize Rice's voluminous writings. Her passing at the midpoint of her work on the Rice book was a deep personal and professional loss. Her spirit marches on!

Michael Maskarinec took this complex montage of articles, editorial commentary, and photos and through layout and careful design made it work visually. Molly Rush corrected the manuscript; Marty Morand, Dave Demarest, and Monsignor George Higgins read and commented on the text, as did Alice Hoffman, Ramelle McCoy, and Heinz O'Donnell for the introduction. Richard Bobak did the photographic copy work.

The Pennsylvania Center for the Study of Labor Relations at Indiana University of Pennsylvania, under the direction of Martin Morand, provided employment and much support for this project. Two faculty senate grants assisted the early research and text selection. Cynthia Miller, director of the University of Pittsburgh Press, provided calm and steady guidance during the endgame.

Bill Serrin helped greatly both with encouragement and advice. Lynn Williams and Rose Trump read the manuscript and led the fundraising effort. Many people and organizations supported the project financially. I must thank particularly George Becker, Rich Trumka, and John Sweeney. The complete list of the project committee and supporters is printed at the end of this book. The list is a tribute to Rice's importance to the American labor movement.

Finally, I need to thank especially my wife Linda and our children: Karl, Rebecca (who helped with the typing), Sarah, Matthew and Maria. It is her love and their strength as a family that has made it possible for me to lead the life of an activist, worker, teacher, and writer. I am deeply grateful.

Introduction

Charles J. McCollester

☎ It was late in the evening at the rectory in Castle Shannon. After reading Monsignor Rice's papers for several hours, I had to catch the last trolley at the foot of the hill below St. Anne's Church. I knocked on his door to say good-bye.

Rice signaled me to enter while hurrying to the TV for the eleven o'clock news. The lead story concerned the British-Argentine war over the Falkland Islands.

"Come in lad," he said. He stared intently at the report of an Argentine air attack on the British fleet. "I have to see this. I hate to see those English lads die, but I love to see those British ships sink."

I recalled that incident as I completed work on this book. Compassion for people's suffering combined with a combativeness toward those deemed oppressive has been the hallmark of Charles Owen Rice's long and eventful career—fighter with a heart.

☎ During the spring of 1982 I was on strike. Following years of travel, political activism, and a doctorate in philosophy from the University of Louvain in Belgium, I was a machinist and a second shift union steward at the Union Switch and Signal plant just east of Pittsburgh. A six-month strike led to the company's decision (not revealed until three years later) to move the plant to Macon, Georgia. It also created the conditions for my election, in the fall of 1982, as chief steward of the union at the plant.

My discovery of Monsignor Rice began nearly four years earlier. Simultaneously with the arrival of the third of our five children, I was returning to the Catholic religion of my ancestors. On the Sunday after the birth of my daughter Sarah, I opened a *Pittsburgh Catholic* while waiting for mass to begin and to my surprise read an insightful column entitled "Zaire, Victim of Colonialism" (June 9, 1978). Educated in Belgium, I knew a good deal about the situation in the former Congo. Furthermore, in 1972 my wife and I had crossed Zaire and witnessed at close hand the political corruption and physical decay of that ill-fated land, Joseph Conrad's "Heart of Darkness."

That anyone in Pittsburgh knew about such matters impressed me, especially someone who wrote so well. I was to become increasingly intrigued by the man and his writings. In 1978, I unsuccessfully attempted to organize the small machine shop where I worked. I called Rice for the first time and he acted as a go-between with the owner. Shortly after, I was hired as a machinist (milling machine operator) at the Union Switch and Signal Company, which had been established almost one hundred years before by George Westinghouse.

During the course of the 1981 strike at Union Switch and Signal and at Westinghouse Air Brake conducted by United Electrical Workers (UE) Local 610, I began to examine the massive personal files that Rice had turned over to the Archives of Industrial Society at the University of Pittsburgh.

These files provide useful information on many social conflicts. I became particularly fascinated by Rice's public writings, which constitute a sprawling, complex chronicle of the town's labor and social history over the course of nearly sixty years.

The ironic twist of fate was that I, a Catholic labor union radical, had stumbled into employment at one of the few large facilities in the Pittsburgh area still represented by the United Electrical Workers (UE).

Only in time would I discover the importance of Charles Owen Rice to the history of that organization.

Charles Owen Rice was born in New York City on November 21, 1908. When he was four, his mother Anna's death in childbirth forced his father to send him and his elder brother back to Ireland, to Dundalk on the coast north of Dublin, to be raised by his grandmother, two aunts, and an uncle. He stayed seven years, gaining an acute political sensibility, a love of Ireland, and a lifelong sympathy for nationalist struggles against large and powerful overlords.

In 1920, Charles and his brother Patrick rejoined their father, Michael, a warehouse foreman for the A&P food chain in Pittsburgh, who had married his wife's older sister, Jennie. They lived in a substantial brick house on Bailey Avenue in Mt. Washington with Michael's brother Joe and his wife and daughter. Uncle Joe became a tough union organizer for the CIO and had an important influence on the young Charlie.

Mt. Washington overlooked Pittsburgh's Golden Triangle business district at the entrance to the heavily industrial Monongahela Valley. Just upstream lay Homestead, Braddock, and the other massive steel mills of the Carnegie empire that had been transformed into the giant U.S. Steel Corporation in 1901. Further upstream, along a tributary called Turtle Creek, sprawled the great Westinghouse domain. The Electric Valley joined the Steel Valley at the very spot where in 1755 the arrogant General Braddock led a combined British and American army to catastrophic defeat at the hands of a Native American and French force barely half its size.

Numerous manufacturing concentrations, specializing in aluminum, glass, railroad equipment, chemicals, steel fabrication, and hundreds of smaller businesses, spread out like branches along the valleys from Pittsburgh. The rivers were thick arteries hauling unimaginable tonnages of raw materials and processed products. Fueling the whole panoply of industrial production was the eight-foot-thick Pittsburgh seam of high-grade bituminous coal, a seemingly endless source of cheap energy to fuel the furnaces and power the machines of the region's mighty mills and factories. The rich Pittsburgh seam ran right under the Rice home, giving Mt. Washington its original name of Coal Hill.

The Rice boys attended St. Mary of the Mount parochial school until they graduated from high school. They cultivated their distinctly Catholic consciousness in a town dominated by Scots-Irish Presbyterians like the Mellons who came from County Tyrone, a scant eighty miles from the Rice family's ancestral digs. Old Judge Thomas Mellon despised the Catholic Irish, and his progeny continued to resist unions and Democrats with unflinching determination. Andrew Mellon, leader of the clan, was arguably the most powerful man in America during the 1920s; the secretary of the treasury under whom, it was said, three presidents (Harding, Coolidge, Hoover) served. The Mellons dominated an international financial and industrial empire that included Mellon Bank, Gulf Oil, Alcoa, Koppers, Carborundum, substantial holdings in U.S. Steel, Westinghouse Electric, and a constellation of supporting manufactories, utilities, and construction firms. They also ran the politics of Pittsburgh through their control of the local Republican Party.

A political landscape where Orangemen ruled by force and fortune while Irishmen were political agitators against the established order was a scene to which a politically astute Charlie Rice could easily relate and quickly orient himself. The Ku Klux Klan, very active and numerous in western Pennsylvania during the twenties, attempted several times to burn a cross above the city atop Mt. Washington. Once, confronted by local Catholics, they were forced to withdraw. Another time, Rice's father and his Uncle Joe ran down and demolished a cross that had been ignited on the hillside below their house. "The Klansmen had fled before they got there, but Papa and Uncle Joe did not know that and were prepared for a fight, both of them tough men physically."

Opposition to the hegemony of the Scots-Irish Presbyterian leadership in Pittsburgh was weak during the 1920s. Resistance was centered in the labor unions, the Democratic Party, and ultimately the Catholic Church, all struggling to advance socially against an apparently invincible power structure that tightly controlled both the economic and political life of the city. Second- and third-generation Irish were prominent in the leadership of the church, the party, and the unions. The defining political event of the era had been the famous Homestead battle of 1892. There the skilled craft unions, led largely by the Irish, saw their power broken by the very machines that they had erected, machines that increasingly supplanted skilled workers in the production process.

Organized labor's historic defeat at Homestead was reenacted on a still grander scale during the Great Steel Strike of 1919, when mostly Slavic workers endured a bitter four-month strike. Many of these strikers, especially the Slovaks, Poles, Croatians, Italians, and Slovenes, were Catholic; most strongly favored industrial unionism; and nearly all later found a home in the Democratic Party of Franklin D. Roosevelt and David Lawrence. They often accepted the political and religious leadership of the Irish, who were proficient in both the English language (unlike more recent immigrants) and the politics of resistance.

Paradoxically, the Catholic Church and the Democratic Party represented powerful institutions for both opposition to and assimilation into Pittsburgh society. This dual attitude toward the existing power structure was shared by Rice. While he could discern ancient foes holding the reins of economic control and had little love for capitalism, he also appreciated the freedom of religion and speech available in the United States and saw communism as an avowed enemy of religion.

Rice entered Duquesne University in the fall of 1926. His brother Pat would graduate from Duquesne at the end of that academic year and enter the seminary, setting an example for the young Charles. At Duquesne, Rice wrote for the literary magazine, was senior class president, and as the editor of the college newspaper was involved in several battles with the school's powerful football establishment. After his graduation in 1930, he accompanied his older brother Pat on a summer trip to Ireland where he made up his mind to become a priest. Upon his return, he enrolled in St. Vincent's Seminary in Latrobe, Pennsylvania.

The depression of the early 1930s ("Hoover's depression") brought Roosevelt and the Democrats to power. When the effects of the depression deepened in 1937, it was seen as Roosevelt's depression, and the urgency of vigorous action was felt acutely by the young cleric. Change was in the air, Roosevelt and the labor Democrats had swept the Republican machines from their stranglehold on the mill towns, and the CIO had conquered General Motors with sit-down strikes. U.S. Steel, anticipating massive British orders for armor plate in response to the rise of Nazi power, capitulated without firing a shot to the Steel Workers Organizing Committee on March 2, 1937, and signed a union contract. Despite the move of the historic steel industry leader in both production and anti-unionism to secure labor peace, the second rank of steel companies, Little Steel, led by Republic Steel's Tom Girdler, vowed eternal resistance. The Little Steel Strike that followed in the spring of 1937 would be broken on Memorial Day on a bloody field in south Chicago where ten strikers were shot down by Chicago police.

Influenced by Dorothy Day and Peter Maurin of the *Catholic Worker* and their popularizing of the papal and encyclicals' teachings on workers and the poor, Rice founded the Catholic Radical Alliance with two other priests and a small group of lay people. He quickly moved the agenda from education and the study of Catholic social teachings to direct and active involvement in the labor movement. His first appearance on a picket line was in support of an AFL union at the Heinz plant, and he worked with Cliff Caldwell and the AFL Meatcutters to organize the A&P store chain, but he quickly established himself as a vocal public apologist for the new Congress of Industrial Organizations.

Rice's importance in the early CIO drives is illustrated by his being selected to give the opening prayer at the first CIO convention, held in Pittsburgh in the fall of 1937. But he was much more than a friendly cleric trotted out to bless union gatherings. Very often he was a featured rally speaker, counseling nonviolence and urging adherence to the union cause. To workers and the general public, he implicitly carried the Church's sanction for industrial union organizing which was being attacked from many sides as communist inspired. His defense of the CIO as free from communist domination led him logically to struggle with the real influence of the Communist Party inside the CIO.

During the 1930s Rice focused his anticommunist efforts on the political arena outside the unions. He picketed gatherings of such Popular Front groups as the American League Against War and Fascism, asking why they did not oppose communist as well as fascist dictatorships. He debated well-known Communist Party spokespersons in large public forums. He was critical of Franco, but vigorously opposed left-wing activities that promoted American intervention on the side of the Republic in the Spanish Civil War. He believed that his outspoken anticommunist stance gave him credibility as a defender of the CIO, just as his fervent support for unionism gave greater force to his anticommunist attacks.

The issue of communism loomed large in economically depressed Pittsburgh in the 1930s, and Rice was often called upon to answer charges of communist domination of the CIO, especially from conservative Catholic clerics like Charles Coughlin and Fulton Sheen. Capitalism was deeply discredited by its own performance and communists provided dedicated cadres of union organizers. CIO President John L. Lewis used them to organize workers and they used him to gain legitimacy. The party line from 1935–39 supported a united front against fascism. This led the communists to seek alliances with a broad range of social forces and to throw their full weight behind the CIO organizing drive.

Rice's influence expanded as he put his journalistic know-how to work. He began publishing book reviews and occasional articles in the local Catholic paper in 1935, forming a long term relationship with the lay editor of the *Pittsburgh Catholic,* John Collins, whom Rice described as "a tremendous scholar and perfectionist." One of the oldest Catholic papers in the United States, the *Pittsburgh Catholic* was privately owned and independent of the diocese until 1955.

Rice promoted the paper assiduously. He also understood the importance of radio, having such radio priests as James Cox and the notorious Charles Coughlin as exemplars. He loved radio and with topics ranging from the devotional to the agitational, had a regular slot on several different stations for more than forty years. His broadcasts (primarily on stations WWSW and WJAS) made him a household name in the region.

Rice's credibility as a clerical spokesman was enhanced by his involvement with the St. Joseph's House of Hospitality. Inspired by the Catholic worker movement, the house was organized in 1937. While Rice profoundly admired Catholic worker leaders Day and Maurin, he was considerably more anticommunist and less pacifist than either of them. Unlike most Catholic Worker houses, which were small and spiritually intense, the Pittsburgh house was quite a large operation that fed up to 900 men and slept many hundreds. Rice publicized the needs of the facility in newspaper columns and radio broadcasts, gaining a reputation as the "pastor to the poorest" that somewhat deflected conservative religious attacks on him for his prounion activities.

While Rice situated himself inside a growing Catholic social justice movement, he was so energetic and forceful that he tended to dominate the Pittsburgh scene once he engaged himself. He merged the Catholic Radical Alliance into the Pittsburgh chapter of the Association of Catholic Trade Unionists (ACTU) in the late 1930s, but the Pittsburgh chapter remained in Rice's shadow, never developing as an independent force or fostering the lay leadership that it had in Detroit or New York City.

With the American economy improving after 1939 as Europe rearmed, many companies began to sign union agreements in order to buy labor peace. Rice's attention turned to the international scene as he gradually came to believe that the United States had to come to the aid of England against the Nazi threat. He became an effective and outspoken proponent of Roosevelt's support for England's resistance to German expansionism. He also began to speak out against anti-Semitism. His anticommunist sentiments were only fortified, however, by the signing of the Hitler-Stalin pact on August 23, 1939. He used political reaction to this event by labor activists and subsequent political flip-flops occasioned by the German invasion of Russia to identify local communists.

During 1940–41, Rice became directly involved in internal union politics over the communist issue. He focused on the giant union local at East Pittsburgh's Westinghouse Electric plant, United Electrical Workers (UE) Local 601. A bitter factional battle had erupted inside the local over communism, and a series of elections reflected an uneasy balance between left and right factions. Rice set up a labor school at St. William's parish and trained activists in public speaking, parliamentary procedure and labor history. He was sometimes attacked and praised by different writers in the same issue of the local's paper, the *Union Generator*. The struggle got particularly nasty and confusing as positions shifted and alliances changed; first, Russia was attacked by Germany on June 22, 1941, and then the United States was attacked by Japan on December 7, 1941.

While, with Rice's help, the left-wing leadership was defeated in union elections in late 1941, the Japanese attack and the wartime alliance between the United States and the USSR moderated internal union divisions. The wartime patriotism of the left helped them to regain control of the local by the war's end in 1945, as Rice himself moved on to other issues. He had been appointed the federal rent control director in Pittsburgh during the war, while remaining as resident director of the House of Hospitality. In 1946, the CIO, squeezed between wartime wage controls and escalating inflation, unleashed an unprecedented wave of industrial strikes that initiated the significant wage gains that fueled postwar consumer-driven prosperity. Mounting union power, however, generated increasing corporate and rural reaction that culminated in Congress passing the antilabor Taft-Hartley law in 1947.

Pittsburgh experienced this sequence of labor militancy followed by political reaction in an especially dramatic fashion during the Duquesne Power Company strike of 1946. While massive steel and electrical strikes were settled successfully by CIO unions in the spring of 1946, the independent former company union at the Duquesne Power Company held the city hostage later that year, plunging it into darkness and defying attempts by both Rice and Pittsburgh's mayor to mediate the dispute. Mayor David Lawrence gained national prominence for his tough stance toward the unions, while the strike helped to reduce the reservoir of public sympathy toward organized labor that had been built up during the heroic organizing struggles of the 1930s and the unions' all-out participation in the war effort.

At the very moment when public sympathy for unions was cooling, Stalin was lowering his iron curtain across Eastern Europe. The deepening cold war prompted the American Communist Party to adopt an increasingly confrontational attitude toward the foreign policy positions of Harry Truman's Democratic Party. Rice fervently believed that the communist tactic of trying to move the labor movement toward overt opposition to Democratic foreign policy would isolate and ultimately destroy the unions. Communist persecution of the Church in Poland, Czechoslovakia, and Hungary only whetted Rice's appetite for the struggle.

A key concern for Rice was the attitude of the president of the CIO and Steel Workers' Union, Philip Murray. A close personal friend and confidant, Murray had secured Rice's position as Pittsburgh's rent control director. Although a devout Catholic, Murray was reluctant to attack the communists because he recognized their services in organizing the CIO and did not want to divide and weaken the labor federation. Communist aggressiveness on both the international and national fronts helped Rice push him toward an outright break and full-scale battle against the party's influence inside the federation.

Internationally, the Greek Civil War, the imposition of Communist regimes in Poland, Hungary, Czechoslovakia, and East Germany, and the Berlin blockade, marked the end of the wartime united front. An aggressive policy of struggle was adopted by Communist parties worldwide. In the United States, this policy shift inspired the left-wing Progressive Party to split from the Democrats, which, combined with the Dixiecrat defections on the right, threatened the survival of the Democratic coalition and the erosion of labor's gains under the New Deal.

In late 1947, Rice launched his attack on communists in the unions with the first of a series of three influential articles in the nationally distributed conservative Catholic publication, *Our Sunday Visitor.* These articles triggered hundreds of letters from Catholic unionists nationwide, providing Rice with a grass-roots information network that he carefully cultivated. In the pages of the *Pittsburgh Catholic*, he closely chronicled the ebbs and flows of the anticommunist campaign in a dozen different unions. The central focus of his attention, however, was the United Electrical Workers with special emphasis on Local 601 representing workers at the giant Westinghouse Electric plant in East Pittsburgh.

Between 1948 and 1950, Rice, with the support of Philip Murray, coordinated the struggle to wrest control of the UE from its left-wing leadership. For some, this period constitutes the defining moment of Rice's career. He would always be that old "red baiter," despite any later espousal of progressive causes. He was indeed a ferocious political fighter who was all the more effective for aiming his bullets carefully. Rice always rejected the red baiter label for himself, reserving the title for those who applied the red label indiscriminately or as a club against political foes or unpopular causes. For his part, he labeled as communist only those groups or individuals whom he judged, through careful observation over many years, to have followed the political shifts of the party line.

Relatively few left-wing union activists openly espoused communism. This was partly a reflex action born of the Palmer Raid days of 1920 when the Justice Department deported immigrant radicals with little regard for due process or human rights. But the clandestine, underground character of the communist movement was also an important component of the mythic legacy of Russian bolshevism. The communists exhibited little faith in "bourgeois" democratic legal rights. The invisibility of a substantial portion of the party made it easy for both friends and enemies to either underestimate or overstate its role and power. To this day, some interpret the anticommunist movement as an establishment plot with virtually everyone labeled as red an innocent victim, while others portray party militants as the core of the labor movement whose elimination condemned the unions to sclerosis.

The truth is that there were communists and they were important in the labor movement. They were, however, far from dominant. Rice estimated that, at their peak, they controlled or heavily influenced a quarter of the labor movement. Even in those unions, such as the United Electrical Workers, where they were most powerful, actual party membership was quite small. Steve Nelson, Western Pennsylvania Communist Party organizer, estimated that the party had about one hundred members in the Turtle Creek Valley in 1948. These few members, however, occupied key positions of leadership in the electrical union as stewards and officers. They were respected trade union representatives who commanded a substantial following because they were effective shop floor leaders. They were also often supported by other activists who knew of, but did not share, their communist beliefs or organizational loyalty. However, the fact that they acted in a disciplined and concerted fashion caused many honest union militants to see them as a factional and destructive force. Their support for Soviet foreign policy, which was imposing communist regimes on Eastern Europe, made them increasingly vulnerable as the cold war intensified.

Rice rarely attacked individuals unless they were leaders who publicly espoused the party political line. He marked union people by their behavior at critical junctures: the Hitler-Stalin pact, the Nazi invasion of Russia, and the Progressive Party campaign of 1948. He concentrated his attacks on organizations which closely followed what he understood to be the party line. He could, however, be singleminded and relentless when on the political attack. He collaborated with the House Un-American Activities Committee, which held a hearing in August 1949, on the eve of crucial union elections in East Pittsburgh. Noncooperation with HUAC and McCarthy's Senate Committee by left-wing union leaders eventually led to several local leaders being fired by Westinghouse Electric and one by Westinghouse Air Brake in 1954.

After the UE was split and the International Union of Electrical Workers (IUE) formed in the fall of 1949 to take its place in the CIO, Rice began to soften his tone. He criticized McCarthy, but he remained largely on the sidelines as the juggernaut that he had helped to create rolled on to its tragic conclusion. The whole experience seemed to disorient him, as the labor movement lost its energy and he saw the anticommunist crusade come to its sordid end. Indeed, an ample measure of the labor movement's subsequent conservatism, which Rice would come to bitterly decry, was forged in the furnace of Pittsburgh's red scare that he had fueled and stoked.

In later years, he would apologize publicly for his overzealous pursuit of the struggle and his failure to reverse course emphatically and come to the defense of the victims of the antired campaigns once it became clear that the Communist Party's power was broken inside the union movement. His only significant union battle during the fifties was his support of a rank-and-file insurgency in the baker's union that eventually helped clean out a corrupted leadership. He was deeply affected by the death of his mentor, Philip Murray, and when an unfriendly Bishop Dearden took over the diocese, he went quietly into exile, leaving Pittsburgh for Natrona. When the Diocese of Pittsburgh took over direct control of the *Pittsburgh Catholic*, his column was dropped.

In 1958, Rice was named pastor of a large parish in Washington, Pennsylvania, and with the arrival of Bishop John Wright in 1959, he again became an important player in the life of the diocese. Wright valued Rice's labor ties and political experience. Restored to his position as a regular columnist in the *Pittsburgh Catholic*, he returned to action seemingly refreshed, once again articulating a positive Catholic radical response to the problems of the day, especially racism and the growing war in Southeast Asia. The late 1960s and early 1970s would witness his third period of sustained activism, a passionate engagement in movements for peace and social justice that sometimes alienated him from old friends and allies in the labor movement.

During the early 1960s, Rice was active in the National Association for the Advancement of Colored People and an early participant in the ecumenical movement seeking religious tolerance and dialogue stimulated by the Second Vatican Council. By the mid-1960s, he grew sharply critical of American foreign policy. He opposed President Johnson's invasion of the Dominican Republic and, in an influential column published in April 1965 that provoked heated reader reaction, Rice answered his own question, "Do we belong in Vietnam?" with an emphatic negative: "I do not fear that we will lose. I fear what we will do to win."

Rice then launched into a long period of sustained and active opposition to the war, both in Pittsburgh and at the national level. Nationally, he marched on the Pentagon and marched arm in arm with Martin Luther King, Jr., at the United Nations; locally, he appeared at countless teach-ins, rallies, and picket lines. Rice always wore his Roman collar, his presence on the front lines given added weight by the support of Bishop Wright and the uncensored podium offered his highly controversial opinions by the *Pittsburgh Catholic*.

At the end of 1965, he asked Bishop Wright to move him to an open parish in the African-American neighborhood of Homewood, putting himself into the center of an active black community in deep political turmoil. Rice used his unique vantage point to try to explain the black rage and rebellion that was engulfing America's streets to the white working-class "ethnics" who were the backbone of the Pittsburgh Church. He took up the extremely unpopular role of advocate for African-American prison inmates.

Given Rice's long association with labor, it was natural that he would be especially sensitive to the exclusionary practices of many unions. He repeatedly warned the craft-based construction unions about the harmful and dangerous consequences of their stubborn refusal to open their doors to qualified blacks. When the battle lines over access to construction jobs were drawn,

Rice chose to march with the blacks. He lost many old friends and allies and even saw the Labor Day march and mass canceled for many years because of the construction trades' displeasure with Rice's positions.

Rice maintained his interest in the union movement throughout the 1960s and 1970s, but increasingly he criticized labor's inflexibility on racial justice and its knee-jerk patriotism toward the Vietnam War. He began to be the defender and ally of union dissidents and rank-and-file reform movements inside the Steel Workers, Mine Workers, and other unions. He had the sad duty of burying his old friend Jock Yablonski, the Mine Worker reform leader, who was assassinated following an insurgent campaign for the union presidency.

By the mid-1970s, as the steam went out of the various social movements that had dominated his life for a decade, Rice left Holy Rosary in Homewood and moved to the suburban parish of St. Anne's, where his old friend Phil Murray lay buried. He began to write more retrospectively, reflecting often on his early life, reexamining in particular his anticommunist period. He became concerned with the paralysis that seemed to affect both the steel industry and its union. Once again, he alienated old friends by actively supporting the insurgent candidacy of Ed Sadlowski for president of the United Steelworkers' Union.

As the 1980s dawned, Rice provided support and encouragement to the Monongahela Valley insurgency of labor activists who tried to stop the wave of plant closings that eliminated 100,000 industrial jobs in the Pittsburgh region. Supporting calls for the use of eminent domain to staunch the flow of the region's manufacturing lifeblood, he railed against those local and national political leaders who permitted viable working-class towns to collapse virtually without response.

There was increasing bitterness in his writing as he watched the Reagan administration destroy the achievements of the New Deal that he had so ardently supported in his youth. Rice was particularly dismayed by the increasing conservatism of his Catholic flock. While he never wavered in his anti-abortion position, he continued to support liberal Democrats politically because he found their overall positions more congenial with the social teachings of the Church than those of the hard-line neoconservatives. His endorsement of Bill Clinton provoked dozens of howling letters of protest to the *Pittsburgh Catholic* by prolife advocates. He entitled one column "Catholic Republicans, Another Sorrow in My Old Age."

Charles Owen Rice, Pittsburgh's labor priest for more than sixty years, is an important figure both as activist and writer.

As the writer of weekly columns in the *Pittsburgh Catholic* and other journals, Monsignor Rice chronicled the dramatic evolution of Pittsburgh as one of the world's greatest manufacturing centers to a city in search of its soul. In the 1930s, he had articulated the Catholic Church's support for organized labor and the New Deal. His anticommunist campaign in the 1940s had helped define the character of trade union politics in the post–World War II period. In vocal opposition to the Vietnam War and active support for African-American struggles in the 1960s and 1970s, he had expressed a Catholic social philosophy that was politically radical while theologically orthodox. Deeply loyal to the institutional church, Rice never deviated in matters of faith or morals, reserving criticism solely for Catholic hospitals and nursing homes that resisted unionization.

His writings constitute an invaluable account of the struggles of workers and the poor.

☎ Texts for this book are drawn primarily from Rice's published writings; previously unpublished material is used only sparingly when needed to bridge subjects or provide an example of Rice's preoccupations during a particular time in his life. Sections of articles that seemed extraneous to the flow of the book or too distracting from major themes have been deleted. This is especially the case with Rice's writings of the late 1940s, which were often updates on a half dozen separate anticommunist union struggles; I chose to follow key stories, especially that of the United Electrical Workers in East Pittsburgh, with excerpts from numerous columns. In recent years, Rice has written extensively about his life. These writings, reflections on events that occurred thirty or forty years earlier, have been placed alongside pieces written at the time. I have written headnotes to connect sections in order to provide narrative flow or provide necessary background.

While the focus of this book is on Rice's writings about labor unions and the struggles for social justice in which he participated—in my judgment, the core of his historic legacy—I felt that such a focus had to be supplemented by writings revealing the inspiration he derived from his Irish family roots and his love for his church. Rice wrote copiously about Irish and Irish-American politics and a wide range of national and international events; I have included only a few examples. His feelings toward the Church were pastoral rather than theological or mystical, and I felt that his humorous articles best displayed his lifelong affection for the institution that sheltered him.

Charles Owen Rice defies easy categorization: compassionate and combative, ferociously dedicated to causes held dear yet willing to write about his nagging doubts, sure of his values and in the truth of his beliefs, but freely self-critical. The rich complexity of his career and writings have led some to see only contradictions; I have become convinced that there is deep integrity and a logical consistency to the man and his beliefs. That is the character I have known and to whom this book gives voice.

FIGHTER WITH A HEART

Father Michael; mother, Anna; sons, Charles and Patrick, 1910

CHRONOLOGY

☎ 1908
On November 21, 1908, Charles Owen Rice is born in New York City.

☎ 1913
Following the death of his mother in the spring, he is brought to Ireland to live with his father's family in the village of Bellurgan, near Dundalk, fifty miles north of Dublin.

☎ 1916
On Easter Monday, Irish independence from Great Britain is declared in Dublin, but the rebellion is forcefully suppressed and its leaders executed.

☎ 1920
Charlie Rice and his older brother rejoin their father who now lives in the Mt. Washington neighborhood of Pittsburgh. He attends St. Mary's of the Mount parochial school.

☎ 1926
He enters Duquesne University. Following graduation and a summer in Ireland, he decides to become a priest. In 1930, he enters St. Vincent Seminary in Latrobe, sixty miles east of Pittsburgh.

☎ 1931
Pope Pius XI issued the encyclical letter *Quadragesimo Anno* on the fortieth anniversary of Pope Leo XIII's *Rerum Novarum*. Both documents uphold workers' rights to organize and join unions.

☎ 1934
On June 17, he is ordained a priest in the Diocese of Pittsburgh and assigned as an assistant to St. Agnes Church.

Rebel Roots
1908–1936

1

Irish and Catholic (1987)

Irish roots nourished Charles Owen Rice from the soil of an oppressed nation. They endowed him with a combative nature, a fierce loyalty to family, to Church, and that paradoxical love for the English language that so many Irish writers exhibit. His background also gave him a particular perspective on Pittsburgh's elite and the politics of its working class.

My father was born in Ireland in 1873, the third of nine children, seven boys and two girls. The place was the townland of Bellurgan, which has an Upper and Lower Point. We were on the Upper, directly on the Bay. When the tide was in, it came up virtually to the front door. On a couple of occasions, it crossed the road and came right in the front door. The family was poor and farmed eleven acres. My grandfather was primarily a farmer, but he would supplement the family diet with fish and shellfish, caught or gathered by him and his sons. It helped that my grandmother was a good cook.

The way out of poverty was teaching. Papa was into it as a monitor in the local national school when he was recruited by the Irish Christian Brothers in his early teens. I am not sure of the date because I wrote none of this down when he was alive, but he was professed [took vows as a Brother] and spent ten years in India. Why the Christian Brothers pushed

him out was a mystery to him. Possibly it had something to do with his health, which was very bad, after bouts with yellow fever and smallpox.

In India he taught school in Calcutta and Darjeeling, and had many stories to tell.

His pupils were the children of the Irish members of the British garrison, which garrison was mostly Irish.

In characteristic Irish fashion, the Christian Brother connection was kept from Pat and me. I think I learned of it toward the end of my college days. Bellurgan was a small close-knit community when I was growing up there between 1913 and 1920. While visiting Ireland recently I had a discussion with a first cousin of mine, and I wondered why Papa's religious profession wasn't "thrown up" to us. All sorts of other things were in the course of the occasional bitter quarrels we had with our peers. "Ye were too young," she said. There were ground rules evidently, but I find it amazing,

3

in retrospect, that this ground rule was observed. . . .

After he got back to Ireland around 1900, [my father] spent a year recovering his health. For a while, he clerked in a grocery store in Dundalk. Then off to America.

His mother had some parting words: "Michael, if you are going to be good, you will often be lonesome." She also told him that she understood there were Irish policemen in New York (a resounding understatement), and when he got off the boat, he should ask one of them if he knew where there was a job for a young Irishman. It worked exactly as she predicted. There was an Irish policeman, a large, friendly one, who, when asked did he know where there was a job, said: "That I do, my boy. Go over there to that building that says James Butler, and since you are a tall, fine-looking Irish lad, they will hire you." He did, and they did.

The joke in Irish circles used to be that James Butler hired them off the boat, which is what happened.

Butler, an Irish immigrant himself, owned a racetrack, amassed tons of money, put up the money to start a religious order (of which his sister was foundress and Mother Superior), was a power in New York, a most prominent Catholic Irishman, and withal, a hard-hearted, tyrannical sonofabitch, Lord rest his soul.

In 1915 Papa left him for the A&P and was sent to Pittsburgh. Shortly he left the A&P for an executive position in a local grocery chain, and eventually retrieved us in 1920.

We had been sent to Ireland upon the death of my mother in 1913 and had seven formative years being raised by my grandmother and some aunts and uncles. That time, which has a golden hue about it in my memory, will have to wait.

"Irish and Catholic in the 1920s"
THE CRITIC
Spring 1987

The Irish Revolt (1991)

On Easter Monday, April 24, 1916, Padraic Pearse stood on the steps of the Four Courts in Dublin and read a proclamation of Irish independence from England which resulted in an insurrection that appeared to end in failure. England's response was massive force. Within a week the insurgents gave up their positions and surrendered. They had numbered less than 2,000.

The fight had been clean and the surrender was formal, but the defeated were dealt with as traitors. The leaders were men of distinction, among them were poets and educators (Pearse was both), but with indecent haste the British began summarily to court-martial them and shoot them.

Fifteen executions, spaced over nine days, did what the insurrection failed to do — rouse Ireland and, more than that, inflame Irish men and women around the world.

As William Butler Yeats was to write: "All was changed, changed utterly, a terrible beauty was born."

Before the Easter Rising, Ireland was peaceful and rather content because, although a World War was raging, and tens of thousands of Irish were fighting on the British side, the country itself was untouched and was prospering, doing well out of the war.

Besides, most Irish felt all right about England whose marvelous propaganda machine had demonized Germany. German barbarity was contrasted with British solicitude for democracy and for the rights of small nations, such as Belgium. Some cheek! as the Brits would put it.

I was in Ireland at the time and old enough to know what was going on. Incidentally, I remember seeing what the heart of Dublin looked like after being shelled.

That city, including its poor, was hostile to the rebels and jeered them as they were led away in chains. The Irish newspapers were nasty. Most of the clergy were opposed. Even the Vatican got in on the act — on the wrong side.

The executions were barbaric and stupid. This sort of British tactic had worked in the past to squelch the Irish — not this time. A strong political movement, known as "Sinn Fein," sprang up. Simultaneously a guerrilla war waged by the Irish Republican Army (IRA) met with such popular support that it could not be suppressed.

A fire storm of indignation swept America, affecting more than those of Irish descent. Mass meetings of tens of thousands were easily organized in our cities. England's counter terror, featuring the vicious Black and Tans, fed the flames and, eventually, there was peace and a treaty of sorts, which is another story.

The IRA guerrillas were tough and merciless and quite efficient. One could say that this Irish revolution wrote the book for the colonial uprisings which followed World Wars One and Two. Native informers were knocked off to deprive the occupying power of its eyes and ears. The revolutionaries also struck at the head of the snake.

My family in Ireland did not favor the Rising or the subsequent guerrilla action. I had to be reprogrammed by my father and my uncle Joe after I returned to the States in 1920. Since then I have not wavered.

The Rising and the guerrilla war which followed cost around 3000 lives, but that was less than a tenth of the Irish lives lost fighting England's battle in Europe.

My little townland of Bellurgan was in

> **"My** family in Ireland did not favor the Rising or the subsequent guerrilla action. I had to be reprogrammed by my father and my uncle Joe after I returned to the States in 1920."

Dundalk Bay and we had seafaring families. A member of one, Felix Byrne, was an officer in the British Navy. He cut a dashing figure in his uniform and had a way with kids. I doted on him.

Among my clear memories is the last time we saw Felix. His ship was berthed in Dublin and he told how, as he was standing on the bridge, a sniper bullet whistled over his head. He ignored the sniper and lit a cigarette. "Poor fools" he said of the insurgents. Shortly thereafter the Sub Chaser which he was commanding disappeared without a trace in the North Sea. I often think, who were the fools? The Irishmen, who died for Ireland; or the Irishmen, like Felix, who died for England.

The leaders in 1916 were idealists and among them were poets and educators. One of the poets was Joseph Mary Plunket, author of Cardinal (John J.) Wright's favorite poem: "I saw His blood upon the rose." Plunket was young and his talent would have matured into greatness. But he had signed the Proclamation and so was executed.

The rank-and-file volunteers of 1916 were quite youthful. James Stephens wrote of them:

"Be green upon their graves, Oh Happy Spring, for they were young and eager who are dead."

The IRA men and women of today claim to be true heirs of 1916, and they have a point even as they follow the terrible logic of revolution. I do not sanction all they do, but I understand.

"Jubilee of Irish Revolt May Stir Sparks"
PITTSBURGH CATHOLIC
April 19, 1991

Adventures in Uncle Owen's Library (1996)

Believe it or not, I learned Shakespeare in about the fourth grade in Ireland.

This was during the period after the death of my mother, when my brother Pat (RIP) and I were parked with grandmother and some aunts and uncles in the old country. It was intended by my father to be just a year or so, but due to the First World War, and the U-boat devastation of shipping, it stretched to seven.

We went to the local grammar school and got a fine education, owing partly to the high caliber of the principal, a man who was more learned than average because he had done some preparation for a college teaching career.

Irish schools of this sort had a man termed "the master," to teach boys, and a woman, "the mistress," to teach the girls and very small boys. They were often, as in our case, but not always, man and wife.

Some irreverent older boys would refer to our master as the Badger, and his wife, who had a facial mole, as the Turnip, always beyond their hearing.

The family name was O'Hare and they had a son the same age as my brother, who was intended for the priesthood and made it as a Marist. It may have been because of this lad, Eddie, that our curriculum was enriched.

I was a beneficiary because in this two-room school we heard what the others were being taught. If it were Algebra, for this urchin—nah! If it were Walter Scott, or Stevenson's Treasure Island—grand; if it were Shakespeare, for this urchin—very heaven.

Macbeth was the play the upper class, including my brother Pat and his pal Eddie, were being taught. I was supposed to be doing something else, studying perhaps, but I was transfixed by the traitorous Scotsman and his deadly wife. As a part of his teaching, the mas-

ter would do long stretches of the Bard. It was like hearing a good actor on the stage. The old Badger was very talented.

The image of Stevenson's Long John Silver throwing the knife into the back of a non-pirate gave me more and better nightmares than anything in Macbeth. Treasure Island is one of the very great adventure stories of literature, but the other samples of good literature that we were given left me cold.

The eldest of our family, my Uncle Owen, was the scholar and our house was packed with books, including one magazine which would devote a full issue to some classic. When we caught the flu and were confined for a month, I got through nearly everything. Not that I remembered the titles of the books or much about them, but my head was packed with references that have a way of coming out when appropriate.

Books on the Index were in Uncle Owen's library. The French bishops had all sorts of classic authors put on the deadly list. I read

Patrick and Charles in Ireland, 1919

them all and I cannot say that they did me or my faith any harm. They were wonderful reads, and bits and pieces of them were and are, part of my general erudition, such as it is.

It would be better for me as a scholar if I could place the sources and name the authors, but what the matter?

When we came to Pittsburgh fresh from Ireland, my brother really knew enough algebra and geometry to be graduated from high school, but he was lacking Latin and a modern language. He went into third-year high —it was April near the end of the school year. So next year he was a senior and then on to college.

Me, I had a deficiency other than not pay- ing attention. In Ireland I could not get alge- bra because I was not paying attention when the teacher explained what X was. I was near- sighted and getting worse, could hardly see the blackboard much less read what was writ- ten on it. Maybe that's why I missed X.

Kids in Ireland did not wear glasses and even in America specs were unusual, fragile and expensive.

I remember the gradual onset of my myopia because the day came when I could not see the aircraft that flew over our area in Ireland. Could hear, but not see. . . .

PITTSBURGH CATHOLIC
May 3, 1996

A Pittsburgh Home (1987)

Mighty center of industry and commerce, Pittsburgh in 1920 bore little physical resemblance to the Irish coastal village of Rice's youth. The political landscape was strikingly similar, however. A Scots Presbyterian elite dominated the economy, while the Irish fomented political and labor resistance.

Back we came to America, April 1920. A long, horrible ocean voyage. Although Papa had paid for second-class passage on the Celtic, we came steerage. During most of the long ten-day voyage, we were buffeted by storms and seasick.

Pittsburgh in 1920 was gritty and smoky. Some bright, winter days at noon you couldn't see a hundred yards ahead of you, but Pittsburgh was prosperous. Prosperous and Republican. There was a small Democratic opposition, mostly Irish, and Papa and Uncle Joe used to argue with them at wakes over Irish and American politics.

I had retained no useful memories of America, and started from scratch. The heat of the summer was awful. The strange accents and customs were puzzling. Ice cream cones were a delightful discovery. I missed going barefoot in the summer, the pavements were too hot.

School was totally different and I had trou- ble adjusting, partly because I had become ter- ribly nearsighted and it was six months before they figured out that I needed glasses. For Pat, things went swimmingly. His quiet personality endeared him to his schoolmates and he was both bright and studious. Interestingly enough, in everything but Latin, of which we learned nothing in the Irish National School, he was ahead of his American contemporaries.

Pity my poor stepmother, my mother's older sister, the eldest of six. Not so pretty as Anna, my mother. As Protestants from County Clare, they were better off than the Rices but not rich by any means. Forty acres is better than eleven, however. Their mother died young and Aunt Jennie helped to raise the rest; she was a workhorse and didn't like it a bit. She was the first of the family to emigrate. She got hold of the passage money by raising her own pig and selling it for five pounds, which paid her way.

Neither she nor my father ever discussed their actual voyages from Ireland to the United States. Was it grim or just uneventful?

About four years after the death of Anna, Papa married Jennie. If I ever knew the actual dates, I have forgotten them.

Papa remarried to make a home for us but he was an affectionate husband, and quite demonstrative for an Irishman, as he was demonstrative of his love for us two boys. No children to the second marriage.

Jennie was jealous, although she tried not to show it, of her younger and more pampered sister, and of the aunts and uncles who raised us and whom we, especially I, missed openly and terribly. I was so lonesome for everything about Ireland in those early years in Pittsburgh!

In addition, I was a skinny, restless, rather outspoken and tactless kid. Clumsy, also. I would not shape up. She would be furious at me, and I don't blame her.

The nuns in school had their problems with me. Not at all studious, I read everything I could get my hands on other than the required school books. In school, fidgety and talkative, I always brought home a poor report card. There was one mark called deportment, on that I generally got sixty, and my handwriting was as bad as the deportment. Writing was important because that was the day of the

Palmer Method when all school children, especially those in Catholic schools, were expected to write uniformly. You were to practice the various strokes and swirls and eventually receive a diploma — I never did.

School in America was miserable for me in those early days of my re-Americanization. Our own parish had no school so we went off a mile-and-a-half to St. Mary of the Mount, a huge parochial school in a lovely big parish that was an Irish Catholic ghetto sprinkled with Germans and having an Italian fringe. There were WASPs in the neighborhood, a distinct minority with a touch of minority psychosis.

At the start, I got along better with the mostly Protestant kids around Bailey Avenue than my schoolmates, and now I know why. School makes kids aggressive. Being put in with scads of other kids stirs you up. A child, especially a male child, will be meaner and more hostile in a school playground than he will be in his neighborhood. Same things for girls, mutatis mutandis.

Those sisters. All Irish, it seemed, more than forty of them stuffed into a convent too small, dealing with fifty kids in a classroom, some of the kids being rather tough. The nuns had to be strong, and they were. The parish knew what they were putting up with and revered them.

They were a special group, most of whom came from Scranton and they wanted you to learn, behave, and be a believing Catholic. On the last, I gave them no trouble, but I would not study, would not be quiet and could not sit still. Not great for paying attention, I would occasionally realize what was going on and I would ask an impudent question. They were always telling me how much nicer my brother was, which was true, and wondering why I couldn't be like him. That raised no resentment in me, nor did it cause me to do better.

The nuns would say, "He could do better if he tried," but one sweet nun said, "Poor fel-

Patrick, his father Michael, and Charles on porch of
Bailey Avenue home in Mt. Washington, Pittsburgh, 1921

low, he is doing the best he can." I was mortified and put on a spurt to show her I had the potential, then I slackened off and went back into my dream world.

In the beginning, especially since I had undiagnosed myopia and couldn't read the blackboard, I was a bit withdrawn and docile. After I got glasses, life got better and I changed.

Although the Master in Bellurgan had been stern and demanding, and occasionally caned us, I was used to him. For all sorts of reasons, at first, the teaching nuns scared the hell out of me. In Ireland I had had nothing to do with nuns, saw them only from afar, and had a reverential awe toward them. Meeting them face to face and witnessing them cope with their impossible teaching situations overpowered me.

In Bellurgan our male teacher was dealing with only 25 or 30 of us in 4 grades and I hadn't many contemporaries, so mass parochial education took getting used to.

We were taught our religion in Ireland and taught very well. It was a totally Catholic environment, a different learning and teaching atmosphere.

It used to be said that American teaching in general was women-dominated, and that was in all the schools. Certainly at St. Mary of the Mount that was so. The priests would come in with some regularity, and I saw more of them on a formal and informal plane than I had seen of the priests in Ireland. The American priests were likeable. The Irish priests of my day were distant figures whom a child just did not get to know, even an altar boy.

I was taught how to be an altar boy the way

Mickey Rice, a neighbor and no relative, told me he trained his hunting dogs. "The auld dog trains the young dog." No urban spit and polish. We charged around the altar and shouted our Latin responses. Tommy Rice, again no relation, just slightly older, but much bigger, was the "auld dog" bullying us and even threatening to make the younger lads go to confession to him. Being an altar boy in America was a more genteel experience.

The regimentation of a large American parochial school was another thing that took getting used to, since my Irish school had been more informal, although quite effective. I was familiar with Macbeth and other classics because the Master taught them to the upper form and did it magnificently, scattering insight and relishing the poetry while I listened instead of doing whatever I was supposed to do. Study, I think.

I have to say another word about the sisters. They were great women, and while they had to be severe, no injustice rankles me and I have no horror stories. I feel so bad about the old nuns who are living out their days in a certain insecurity, while many authors boost sales by taking cheap shots at the way they used to teach and discipline. Unsung and uncomplaining heroines they, to quote Yeats, "weighed so lightly what they gave."

There was a bit of Puritanism, however, but it was not unhealthy. Most of us were made very strong Catholics. The fear of hell and mortal sin was instilled later on by priests, givers of missions, and retreat masters in the seminary.

We were taught Pius X-type Catholicism with which I was comfortable at the time. In high

> **"I was taught how to be an altar boy the way Mickey Rice, a neighbor and no relative, told me he trained his hunting dogs. 'The auld dog trains the young dog.'"**

school we got The Catechism of Perseverance by De Herb, a translation from the French with strictures against modernism and a bad word about so many good Frenchmen like Voltaire and Rousseau. That took a while to shake off.

All in all, my years at St. Mary of the Mount strengthened me in every way. I am glad that I had been part of the hurrah just before the last hurrah of a system and a way of life that well served God, country and people.

On a less solemn note, I had to get glasses for my myopia, which was bad and progressive, but that brought its own woes. Spectacles were expensive and fragile. Real tortoise shell, which a lively kid like me often broke to the disgust of my rather tolerant father who had to pay. Probably because the things were so expensive, not many kids wore them. One who did was a sport and was often referred to as "four eyes," as in "you four-eyed so-and-so." The language of the rougher parochial school children could be quite undenominational. Strong glasses were an affliction because you were nearly blind when you took them off and you had trouble with sports and fighting. Particularly in the early days, you had to remove your glasses for most violent activities and you were helpless and hopeless without them. Swimming was fine, but not diving.

I had another affliction. I was skinny, and my ears stuck out, oddly enough they no longer do. Some large tougher kids were unkind enough to speak of bird-kite ears and note a resemblance to a taxi cab coming down the street with both rear doors open.

Scrawny kids have special problems if they insist on winning verbal arguments, especially if they are afflicted with myopia and a combative disposition. At least I did. For some reason or other, I am reminded of Billy Conn, the great light heavyweight who almost beat Joe Louis. Rich men occasionally would pay Billy to teach their kids how to fight, something that some kids cannot learn. When he would tell a father

that nobody could teach his kid how to fight, the father would say, "Then what will I do?" Billy's classic response was, "Teach him how to apologize." I wasn't all that good at either.

"Irish and Catholic in the 1920s"
THE CRITIC
Spring 1987

The Biddley Byes (1979)

While the daring escape of Mrs. Soffel and the Biddle Boys took place in 1902, the story was already a legend among Pittsburgh Irish in the 1920s. The murder they were accused of committing took place in a small grocery about four blocks from the Rice home.

"Biddley Byes?" Who they? inquire my younger readers, those under 45 that is. So, I shall a tale unfold.

Edward and John Biddle, French-Canadian desperadoes, cut a swath of robbery, rape and murder on their way down from Canada. Before they were run to earth in Pittsburgh they had, right here, killed a grocer, and in a shootout, a policeman, actually a detective, which last killing was their big mistake.

They were lodged in our handsome County Jail, which was new and considered impregnable. The year was 1901.

In that day ladies of "good family" used to visit jails singing gospel hymns for all and reading the Bible to those who wanted it, or at least did not mind it terribly. The authorities encouraged this sort of thing; who cared what the cons wanted? In that day there were mostly Catholics and very many of them Irish to boot.

The Bible punching of that date resembled that of today, but phraseology differed. Not so much emphasis on being born again, but great searching for the Lord. Have you found the Lord? they would demand. The irreverent might respond, I didn't know he was lost.

One thing was the same. The special meaning of the word "Christian." This was the heyday of those organizations with Christian in their names, which did not consider Catholics to be quite Christians.

A member of an old political family, the Soffels, was the warden at the County Jail. His wife was a Bible reader, and the other "good families" thought it darling that she seemed to have touched the hearts of those bad Biddle Boys. She would sit by their cell for hours as she read the Good Book to them and talked of the Lord. The Boys were Catholics of a sort and it was thought to be marvelous that they were getting some real Christianity.

The Biddles may, or may not, have found the Lord, but they certainly found Mrs. Soffel and, as she read and read, they sawed and sawed on the bars, beautifully concealed by her voluminous dress. The reading nicely muffled the sound of the saw. On January 30, 1902 they emulated the old Monk from Siberia (if you ask I shall tell of him also) and leaped out of their cell with Mrs. Soffel in tow. They commandeered a horse and wagon and headed North toward Butler County, quite possibly aiming for Canada and their homes and hiding places.

Enter Charles E. "Buck" McGovern, once of Teddy Roosevelt's Rough Riders and Cuba, but by now, chief of detectives. Buck too used horses as he and a small posse chased the Boys. It was only a couple of months before, that Pittsburgh had gotten around to having its first automobile accident. So it was horses all the way; autos were for fun, horses for business.

Buck surprised the Biddles and killed them both without ceremony. The result was a backlash and that is not surprising since, although the Boys were bad actors, they were dashing and handsome devils. The tender sex sighed over their fate. Controversy persisted for decades.

Men as well as women were troubled. Was McGovern acting the avenger rather than the law man? Were the brothers given a chance to surrender? Contrary to what you might expect, Americans in that day were concerned about legalities even toward criminals.

Sympathy for the dead men increased with the indication that they well might have saved their own skins and made it to Canada, if they had simply ditched Mrs. Soffel, once she had served her purpose.

McGovern had no doubts and went on to a career in reform politics as a Republican. I came to know him, when he was rather old and I was rather young, but I did not broach the subject of his famous man hunt.

The Biddle Boys became part of the local folk lore and I was amazed to discover that now they are forgotten. But back in St. Agnes Rectory their memory was alive 36 years later, and we all knew what Mary meant when she uttered the immortal words: "It's been b'ilin' since the Biddley Byes was kilt," and proceeded in that context to bite the dust herself.

"Who Were the 'Biddley Byes'?"
PITTSBURGH CATHOLIC
March 30, 1979

An Argumentative Youngster (1977)

. . . . Young people do not wear masks until they begin to mature. When I was in college and we were engaging in political struggles over the student senate and the like, I remember how several times I was disarmed by my opponents being pleasant. I did not notice the mask, and I was slaughtered in the next bit of infighting.

When I was younger still I used to get into trouble because I would argue fiercely with my contemporaries on serious matters. They had the attitudes of their parents and neighbors although they might not be able to articulate

Charles with neighbor boy in 1923

them. In my family the children were in on all discussions, and learned how to express themselves. We were liberal while the rest of the area was incredibly conservative — this was the Twenties. All appeared to be going very well in society and no one liked boat rocking or boat rockers. Arguing fiercely was dangerous, especially if you were a skinny kid and were able to win most verbal arguments. That I was not banged around more was due to the fact that very few kids, including me, knew how to fight or even throw a punch.

Civilized is to be able to argue strongly and hold no grudges. Christianity is to hold no grudges at all, even inside oneself and that is hard indeed. . . . Politicians on the lower level are direct and straight forward. An enemy is an enemy. So it is with the labor chaps. You don't drink with a bum who is out to get you. In some circles this is carried to the ultimate. There was the sweet old Irish lady who used to say, as others praised those who had passed to a heavenly award: "If they were no good livin', they're no good dead."

"Attitudes Towards Enemies Vary"
PITTSBURGH CATHOLIC
February 25, 1977

My Uncle Joe (1973)

My last uncle has died: at one time I had nine of them and three aunts; the youngest, he lived the longest, and his death closed a book. We buried him from St. Mary's of the Mount on Monday.

Joseph F. Rice (the F was something he used now and then but was not christened with — did not stand for Francis or anything) was born in Ireland in 1887, twenty-one years before I was to see the light of day in New York City. He had a life in Ireland before he came here in his mid-twenties, and he had two distinct careers in the U.S., three if you count his active retirement.

Since he was prone to nostalgia I could study the past from him. As a writer I should have taken more notes because he was constantly dropping interesting bits of color and detail.

His father, Patrick Rice, was one of those diligent and enterprising farmers who managed to get a sustenance for a large family out of relatively little soil. The farm was on Dundalk Bay and so the diet was supplemented by fish, shellfish and game, and the soil itself was replenished by judicious use of sea weed, wrack we called it. His mother, Ellen, managed her end well and there was "comfort" in the house even in bad days; there were some of those when the

weather was contrary or prices collapsed; American dumping more than once shattered the market for Irish cattle.

Uncle Joe did not suffer from the bad times because, by the time he was growing up, the older brothers were established as school teachers and neither nature nor the market could wipe them out.

An attempt was made to get him into teaching or the civil service and he went to school (College Prep) in Dublin but he hated it and came back to the farm where he tried to be the same type of farmer as his father. I found an old letter from that grandfather of mine written to my father and telling what a great farmer and help was the youngest boy, Joe.

But that was not to be. An older brother returned from America unexpectedly and, since in that family there was never any land grabbing or wrangling over material things, Joe the youngest bowed out. By then the father had died.

Another factor pushed him out and to America. Let me set the stage. It was before WWI and 1916 so Ireland was still under complete British rule, a stifling rule because England was always a bit edgy about Ireland. The police were a para-military outfit under direct British command and magistrates and judges were appointed by the crown.

Joe Rice was a local leader. It was before the IRA and he was not a revolutionary but he was close, and he was into more than ordinary politics; while guns were not used, there was some severe political fighting, one successful skirmish had him and his friends arrested. Openly anti-British and anti-establishment, he was marked as a trouble maker so he almost had to leave. We often used to speculate as to what might have happened if he had remained in Ireland through the troubles of 1916–22.

When I was growing up in Ireland, although he was gone, he remained a legend of leadership, light heartedness, wild escapades and jokes, and fierce partisan quarrels. In Bellurgan's Hibernian Hall there hung a great drum and many a man pointed to it and said, "Your Uncle Joe used to lade us batin' that drum and there is not a man around today to equal him."

In New York he followed my father into the employment of a pious, mean-spirited and enormously wealthy Irishman who was a chain food store pioneer. As they used to say, James Butler hired them off the boat.

Revolutionary or not, Joe Rice had the puritan work ethic and did well, moving into supervision almost at once. Some people are naturally organized and can organize others — they can get work done. There are also people who are not anxious for great wealth but live by principle. Uncle Joe was in both categories. Pride in personal dignity, a fierce temper and a critical attitude toward the abuse of authority are not the best prescription for getting ahead. It is a tribute to his efficiency that he got as far as he did.

When he moved over to the ranks of labor and became a CIO organizer in 1930, it was the same thing. Efficiency helped him but his refusal to curry the favor with authority or to compromise the welfare of the workers for any reason was not an asset. The great Alan Haywood once shook his head and noted: "that is the most independent man I ever met." Alan, an Englishman, admired spunk and ordered that Joe Rice be let alone to do his work.

After the CIO merged with the AFL and the death of Haywood, the older organizers were treated shabbily. Uncle Joe did not improve

> **"S**ome people are naturally organized and can organize others — they can get work done. There are also people who are not anxious for great wealth but live by principle. Uncle Joe was in both categories."

his popularity by trying to start an organizers union but he survived until he was pensioned.

Among the labor leaders, he despised Walter Reuther (whom I liked) because Walter opposed the organizing of organizers and thus was a hypocrite to Joe. The reverse for Meany, who was decent about the organizers' union and was considered fundamentally honest. I. W. Abel's recent no-strike pact had my uncle shaking his head in disgust.

The Miners (UMW) were his favorite union because of the decency of the rank-and-file and the purity of their trade union spirit; the leaders he understood and condemned almost without exception. In the brief scrap in West Virginia that followed the Lewis-Murray split, Uncle Joe was taken for a ride by some UMW thugs from Kentucky but he outwitted them and got away. From then on he packed a gun.

Joe Rudiak, a retired organizer but much younger, worked with my uncle and he marvels that the two of them are living; they had rough experiences in hostile anti-union territory down toward the South and occasionally closer to home.

I used to draw my uncle out on what it was like before the unions and before mechanization. Firing was brutal and workers had no protection at all, he had horror stories about men being killed or crippled with no thought of compensation to them or their families. No overtime and long long hours. Nobody was free and if you were any sort of boss you were expected to show up even on Christmas Day.

Once he told me something fascinating about the effect of new found freedom on human beings. In the depression, men who were fortunate enough to get or hold jobs were often despicably underpaid and driven. With the sudden coming of a strong union (in this instance the Teamsters), for a brief period some of them would not work at all. These were white American workers but their reaction to sudden liberty makes one understand the early reaction to liberation.

My uncle disagreed with me on the war; he was strong for the IRA; he disliked McGovern but voted for him because he had the same opinion of the Republican Party as he had of the British Empire. Needless to say President Nixon was not one of his heroes and it made him sick to see labor leaders fawning over the man. He died happy over Watergate but fearful for the country.

There will always be people like that dead uncle of mine and when they get into positions of influence, as they do occasionally, it advances the cause of freedom and decency.

"My Uncle Joe"
PITTSBURGH CATHOLIC
July 27, 1973

An Influential Neighbor (1987)

A salesman for Red Seal Lye, Ed Volk by name, "called" on my father, the buyer. We were also neighbors. The Rices lived on Bailey Ave., a reasonably posh address — the house cost $10,000 in 1920. Papa probably paid too much, at least he bought at the top of the market. The house, still standing, is worth more now. Volk lived behind us on Kambach St., not so posh. We overlooked the city from a height and were the first Irish Catholics on our block.

Our immediate Protestant neighbors at first were not overjoyed at the arrival of us Irish Catholics, but we got along. They were not Kluxers, although my mother would mutter the word after an argument over religion. Volk was no ordinary neighbor, being a Marxist and an all-around intellectual rebel. On the Russian Revolution he looked kindly and that had some influence on me over the years, here and there. Ed was an atheist, sort of. There must have been a tacit understanding between him and Papa because he never dropped any atheistic propaganda on me or Pat, my brother.

From Volk I got an admiration for Clarence Darrow and H. L. Mencken, accepting their version of the Scopes trial as I do to this day. That was an exciting trial. The verdict was not important, but the trial itself was, as Darrow sparred with William Jennings Bryan, who, as you know, had been a Democratic candidate for President more than once, and was a flat-out, corn-fed fundamentalist. Catholic Democrats were always a bit uneasy with Bryan. Darrow whipped him, but the Tennessee jury favored Bryan and voted that Scopes was guilty. The climax was the sudden death of Bryan who had grown enormously fat. If Darrow had died suddenly, the fundamentalists would have taken that as a sign from the Lord. Volk and our whole family followed the thing as if it were an athletic contest. Can you imagine what TV would have done with that?

We Rices were caught up in the Irish struggle for independence and Volk agreed with us. Natural Democrats, we were uncomfortable with Woodrow Wilson and his Puritan outlook, but what caused the family to vote for the Republican Party in 1920 was Wilson's hardnosed stand against Irish freedom. In his Fourteen Points, he demanded freedom for small nations, but excepted Ireland. In 1924, Papa voted for Robert Marion La Folette, the Progressive Senator from Wisconsin, but 1928 found us back in the Democratic fold because of Al Smith. Could we have been a bit bigoted ourselves?

Ed Volk was an early radio buff and provided us with a crystal set, cat whiskers and all. We had a long aerial reaching from our backyard fence to the third floor. Later we got hold of a loose coupler. I am not sure whether or not that thing was battery-operated. If it was, we used a dry cell which was rather bulky. Then we assembled a radio with vacuum tubes and a regular storage battery. It was a while before they worked out how to operate a radio from house current. However it was on one of our primitive radios that we listened to the Dempsey-Firpo fight. Graham MacNamee's announcing of that fight is still a vivid memory. You could actually see Dempsey being knocked out of the ring and coming back in to wallop the big Argentinian. Jack Dempsey was a Mormon, but to us he was an Irishman. Our neighbors did not like him, claiming that he was a slacker in WWI, but in our impartial Irish way, we ignored that. Dempsey was very unpopular in that day, believe it or not, as he blasted all before him. He did not join the Services during the War, being too busy in the ring, but a picture was published of him in overalls working in a shipyard. Unfortunately, a pair of expensive patent leather shoes peeped out from beneath the overalls. How different from the noble Ronald Reagan, who acquired no opprobrium from putting on a military uniform so that he could make war movies, causing him sometimes to fantasize publicly that he saw action.

Volk was also a photographer and had me taking and developing my own pictures. Fortunately I turned out to have an allergy to the developing fluids, or I might have wasted tons of time on that activity.

"Irish And Catholic in the 1920s"
THE CRITIC
Spring 1987

Editing the Duquesne Duke (1979)

Young Charlie Rice was scrawny but scrappy. As an undergraduate at Duquesne University, he acquired a taste for journalism that would become a lifelong avocation. He also discovered that the pen could make ferocious enemies.

Due to the strike of our daily newspapers we have received only a sketchy account of the tempest that buffeted the Duquesne Duke as that college weekly ventured on the choppy sea of lampoon. How scabrous or scatological was its material is something that was not conveyed by the electronic media, which have the news field to themselves these days and, as usual, are making the least of their opportunity. . . .

It was of more than passing interest to this columnist because in days long gone, he had been editor of the illustrious Duke and, although he could say with Longfellow that never had he "blotted a line that could bring the blush of shame to the brow of modesty," he managed to outrage authority and disturb the peace. His crime was a far fouler one than mere pornography, he criticized the football team, its members, and, a less heinous act that was not even a high misdemeanor, he criticized the administration.

That sort of thing was not done in college papers in those days, but I did it. How well I remember that tempest and remember myself bravely whimpering "the pen is mightier than the fist," as a football player proved that it wasn't. I was even supposed to be fired from the post but, unknown to mine enemies, the old president of the school, Fr. Martin Hehir, C.S.Sp., was born in the same county in Ireland, County Clare, as my mother and I, of course, used that to unfair advantage, and survived.

So much for my initiation into journalism, which was so propitious that it is a wonder I did not totally become one of the ink-stained

Duquesne University graduation photo, 1930

wretches of the Fourth Estate instead of combining journalism with my main vocation, and let me add, enjoying both.

"Catholic Press Then and Now"
PITTSBURGH CATHOLIC
March 30, 1979

St. Vincent's Seminary (1992)

Charles Rice followed the path of his older brother into the priesthood, from Duquesne to St. Vincent's in Latrobe, Pennsylvania. St. Vincent's was a refuge from the deepening economic depression that was gripping Pittsburgh. The New Deal swept into western Pennsylvania and ended seventy years of Republican political domination. Rice began writing book reviews and completed a thesis on the Anglo-Irish literary revival.

Recently, I taught a class at St. Vincent Seminary, where I had studied theology 60 years ago, and afterward, over lunch, reminisced with students about how different it had been in my day. One difference was the food, which is now fine, but had been execrable.

Cardinal Mundelein attended the seminary a century ago. At his 1915 installation in Chicago, an anti-clerical crank threw something in the soup that made everyone sick, except the cardinal, who said "after my time at St. Vincent's, no food can poison me."

The present-day Benedictines enjoy that story, and they also relish the fact that the good cardinal was expelled by them. Not every seminary can boast that it had expelled a future Prince of the Church.

In the course of the reminiscing, an incident came up that I shall relate without embellishment.

The date was 1932, Father John T. Flaherty, now retired, was a year ahead of me in school. One afternoon "Monk," as he was known, came in from a stroll bearing a fallen branch, which he had picked up and was using as a walking stick. I had a good clasp knife and offered to trim the scruffy but sturdy thing.

We were in a new building which had been erected in the late '20s. Solid as ever, it now is part of the college. The materials used were first-class, nothing shoddy. The floors were and are of a substance that wears like iron and is fireproof.

As I whittled on the branch, which had dried somewhat, shavings accumulated. I worked sitting cross-legged on the floor, and when I finished, it was obvious there was a disposal problem. Neither dust pan nor brush was easily available, and I did not want this debris in my room permanently.

What seemed a sensible idea at the time was a small fire in the middle of the floor, vigilantly watched and carefully controlled. The weather was mild and the windows might be opened fully.

As I already mentioned, the floor was fireproof. There was no danger from other combustible material since I normally piled everything on the bed, which was pushed into a corner. I would make the bed once a week when clean sheets were provided. The authorities, who insisted on order and neatness, had given up on me and did not inspect my room — probably preferred not to see it. Apart from this, I was not a disciplinary problem and did well in my studies, so it was live and let live in that sensible place.

All was going smoothly. I sat cross-legged and at peace as I fed the tiny fire small slivers from the branch, until a fellow seminarian popped in. We conversed with the door open for just a short while, but alas smoke from my little blaze went all through the building. Incidentally, the seminarian, whose name I forget, did not comment on my activity or seem to think it remarkable.

However, the smoke alerted the prefect, a

sober Benedictine professor, who went looking for its source. I remember vividly that he opened the door, saw me sitting on the floor calmly tending my small fire, burst into a giggle and left abruptly. He said nothing, seemed to be overcome. It began to dawn on me that my enterprise might appear a bit irregular.

Fr. Nepomucen, the rector, was a stickler for order but no martinet. Stern of mien and unflappable, he must have been secretly amused. When I was hauled before him the next day, he did not explode when I respectfully noted that I had not broken any of the rules in our manual. No punishment, and no black mark; not even a major chewing out, just a pointed discussion.

Old pre-Vatican II St. Vincent's — tough and tolerant! You were expected to learn; you had to toe the line, but you were treated as an adult, and were on your own just so long as you were not defiant or given to outrageous conduct.

"Latrobe Seminary 'Tough and Tolerant' "
PITTSBURGH CATHOLIC
April 17, 1992

Fr. James Cox (1989)

Father James Cox was a famous Pittsburgh labor priest. In his commitment to the unemployed and use of the radio to broadcast his message, he was an influence on Charles Rice, the young seminarian.
Father James Renshaw Cox was a Pittsburgh priest a generation older than I. During a particularly violent taxi strike he burst on the scene with his support of the drivers. This was in the mid to early '20s and was without precedent.

It happened that, when he was made pastor he inherited a dead parish but also a radio program. Mass was broadcast from Old St. Patrick's at noon every day over WJAS and Fr.

Cox gave the homily. What homilies!

WJAS was owned then by an Irish Catholic named Brennan who was his own man and intensely loyal to his radio priest. Radio was just finding itself and daytime radio did not amount to much.

Jimmy Cox, as we priests affectionately called him, was made for radio with his pleasant, flexible voice and his ease. No scripts for him, he ad-libbed and could go on indefinitely, or within strict time limits, to fit the occasion.

His advocacy of the taxi strikers during his broadcast homilies was a veritable bombshell. The strikers did not prevail quickly; there were no cabs on our streets for years, but when they reappeared they were union.

In no time Fr. Cox with his radio program was an institution. This was before Roosevelt and the area was antiseptically clean of Democrats, so Fr. Cox was a reform Republican. There were few voices for social justice but his was one. I can't recall what he did in the Al Smith campaign, and there is no one around to ask and no records.

But when Hoover got in and the Depression hit I know what he did. Using cab strikers he set up a soup kitchen and a shanty town alongside his parish, and he collected food and clothing. Because of the similarity of names, people will get one of his dramatic actions confused with Jacob Coxey's of Ohio who is in the history books for his Populist March on Washington in the last century.

What Fr. Cox did was even more dramatic. In 1930 he organized a caravan of trucks and jalopies which he led from Pittsburgh over the Alleghenies to the White House on behalf of the unemployed and for the Soldier's Bonus. The new Coxeys Army they called it.

Plans were made for him to run for President in 1932 but he ended supporting Roosevelt though he remained a Republican. At home, using radio homilies he defeated and elected congressmen.

Fr. James Cox's unemployed army leaving Pittsburgh for Washington, D.C.

He also got jobs for the strike leaders who were blackballed. His homilies were wide-ranging but when he gave a purely religious sermon it was a good one. He promoted devotion to Our Lady of Lourdes and led pilgrimages. He also staged Passion Plays and ran raffles.

He cooled on Roosevelt, did not care for the CIO and was a staunch opponent of bigotry in all forms, especially anti-Semitism, not hesitating to criticize the other famed radio priest, Fr. Coughlin.

Why is he not remembered? He did not leave a paper trail. Even his newspaper record is sparse. In those days the papers were jealous of radio and covered radio personalities only when there was trouble or a mistake.

"Remembering Fr. James R. Cox"
PITTSBURGH CATHOLIC
December 15, 1989

Fr. Charles Owen Rice was ordained a priest of the Catholic Diocese of Pittsburgh on June 17, 1934. In 1937, he burst upon the Pittsburgh scene, first showing up on a picket line at the H. J. Heinz plant and then becoming an aggressive and vocal defender of the Congress of Industrial Organizations, the CIO. Over the years he supported many causes and engaged in many political battles. For forty years as a radio commentator and nearly sixty years as a writer for the Pittsburgh Catholic, *he helped to shape and interpret Pittsburgh's history.*

John L. Lewis and Rice at first CIO convention, Nov. 14, 1938

CHRONOLOGY

☎ **1937**
February 11, General Motors and the United Auto Workers sign an agreement recognizing the union and ending the sitdown strikes at Flint and other locations.

☎ March 2, the Steel Workers Organizing Committee and United States Steel announce an agreement recognizing the union.
☎ March and April, Fathers Rice, Hensler, and O'Toole begin a series of Catholic Forum meetings that will lead to the formation of the Catholic Radical Alliance.

☎ May 30, the "Memorial Day Massacre" at Republic Steel in South Chicago kills ten workers and slows the union organizing drive in steel.
☎ June 3, Rice joins the picket line at the H. J. Heinz plant.

☎ September 29, St. Joseph's House of Hospitality opens on Wylie Avenue. Moved to larger building on Tannehill St. on March 31, 1938. Rice becomes resident director on February 8, 1940.

☎ **1938**
November 14, Rice prayer opens founding convention of the Congress of Industrial Organizations (CIO) in Pittsburgh.

☎ **1939**
August 23, Nazi-Soviet pact signed. On September 1, Germany invades Poland. Later that month Russia occupies Eastern Poland and then moves against the Baltic states.

Picket Line 1937–1941

2

◭ America's Darkest Decade (1987)

Rice's career as a Catholic priest began in the depths of the Great Depression. As a young curate in a city parish, he wrote book reviews for the Pittsburgh Catholic *and commentary on national issues for* Commonweal. *As workers began to organize into industrial unions, the young priest threw himself into the struggle for industrial unionism with an intensity and dedication that set him apart.*

Capitalism's bubble had burst and the Great Depression had settled all over the world. I remember going in to the teeming class rooms at St. Agnes school and reflecting sadly that one-fourth to a third of those kids would spend their lives on relief. And well they might have but for the energizing effect of World War II and the preparations for it. With one exception, these were white kids. . . .

Although I was raised middle class, it was almost inevitable that I would jump into the ferment of the 30s and remain an activist. My family background helped to make me a bit of a rebel. The Rices in Ireland, who raised me, were a devout Catholic family who produced four priests in two generations, but did not hesitate to disagree with priests and bishops on secular matters. The family respected priests but did not think that they knew everything. . . .

As I look back, I remember that the priests we most respected were the ones who took a stand, particularly if it was an unpopular stand and on the side of the people. My father's

brother, Peter Rice, of the Superior, Wisconsin diocese, was that sort of priest. His flamboyance and love of controversy kept him stuck in rather small parishes for a while. Who cared? From the day I finally made up my mind to become a priest, I was determined to be the activist type and not only speak my mind, but support causes and charge rather than hold back. In the mid-30s, there were plenty of causes, very good ones, and there was a need for the Catholic clergy to speak out and act.

Hence, the Catholic Radical Alliance. The name was peculiar to Pittsburgh. Peter Maurin, Dorothy Day's guru, had wanted to call their paper The Catholic Radical, but she insisted on The Catholic Worker.

When she and her disciples first appeared on May Day in 1933 in New York's Union Square peddling the paper for a penny a copy, they were greeted with: "Why the Ketlik Woikeh? Ain't we all Woikehs?"

Dorothy was an inspiration to me. Her lucid articles in the Commonweal, beginning

23

around 1930, and then her own paper really grabbed me.

There were many other influences—the two social papal encyclicals, particularly "On Reconstructing the Social Order" in 1931. There was a flood of social writing, much of it Catholic. Other influential persons were Msgr. John A. Ryan of towering fame and Father Virgil A. Michel, the Benedictine from Collegeville, and his magazine, Orate Fratres. Poor Virgil died very early. I must have been already rather well known because he came to see me in 1938 or 1939 (while I was still at St. Agnes) on his way home from Louvain; little did either of us realize that the strep throat that was bothering him would kill him shortly. Among the few pertinent works that I studied intensely was his set of pamphlets on the encyclicals, which was later made into a book, the title of which escapes me. I grieved for him as for an old friend.

Peter, Dorothy and Virgil all stressed that we should feed the poor, spread the social gospel, and be engaged. My cup of tea, exactly. You needed action, not just talk. Feeding the poor was action, but you had to go beyond that. Dorothy, an ex-Communist, sort of, was fervently pro-union.

America entered the black decade with all its mass industries open shop and with only a scattering of unions elsewhere.

Franklin Delano Roosevelt's New Deal was a spur to unionizing and heartened all of us. Yet when he was elected in 1932, although I had voted for him, I really hadn't much hope that he would be all that great.

His first fabulous ninety days convinced me otherwise, as it did the rest of the country. FDR was my hero, and I could see no flaws in him.

In 1935 some excellent pieces were written in the *Pittsburgh Catholic* by Father Carl Hensler, and I got in touch with him, and through him with Msgr. George Barry O'Toole. For my part, there was a discussion

group I had organized at St. Agnes, tapping former members of my Junior Newman Club (which had been axed), and when the Catholic Radical Alliance was launched, we had troops.

Preliminary to the organization of the Alliance, we had articles in the Pittsburgh Catholic and we had discussion sessions. Some were in parish halls, and there was "The Catholic Forum" which a group of rather progressive Catholic women maintained with a modest headquarters and hall in the center city. Beginning in late 1935, we had meetings and discussions there. But before we got to the Catholic Radical Alliance, we were almost sidetracked.

I have to confess that in that period we used to soften up the opposition within the church by saying that if we didn't serve the workers and champion their cause, the Communists would take over. That sounds ridiculous now, but the Communists did seem to be on the march supporting all the right things and making all the right noises domestically.

The Spanish Civil War was a disturbing element. It seemed to indicate that Communists and other anti-Catholic elements were powerfully attractive. I know better now, but that was then.

Somehow or other, a priests' group got started with the okay of the bishop, I think, and its purpose was to investigate the Communist menace in various parishes. We were to go out and interview pastors, which we did. None of them had experienced the Communist menace firsthand. . . .

I didn't like this whole business, because it was not my thought to have a purely negative anti-Communist Catholic association with me in it. We had a public meeting with priests and laity, and I was supposed to be the chairman. Deliberately I came late, and Father James Delaney (the man whom I succeeded at St. Agnes and diocesan director of the Holy

*Rice, Fr. Carl Hensler and Msgr. George Barry O'Toole at rally of Canning
and Pickle Workers at H. J. Heinz plant, June 1937*

Name Society), who was no intellectual and
did not understand the situation, took over
the chair. That was his modus operandi, as I
knew. The story is too long for this short article, but Jim and I had a row on the floor, and
that ended this ill-conceived, totally negative
venture, and cleared the way for what Hensler

and I wanted, a sensible organization which
would be composed of, and run by, priests and
laity of a progressive disposition.

A touch Machiavellian, I confess, but
Machiavelli was a good Catholic.

The name, Catholic Radical Alliance, was
cooked up by us three priests. The brilliant

conservative, Msgr. George Barry O'Toole, was the one who suggested the name Radical because, he said, Catholic social doctrine is truly radical doctrine; radical means, of the roots, from the Latin radix, root. . . .

Through the pages of the Pittsburgh Catholic and various statements that we made, some of which appeared in the daily papers, the name Catholic Radical Alliance attracted attention and began to stand for something. It was really a great name. Perhaps as some critics have pointed out recently, we were not entitled to the noble name Radical, but we acted as if we were, and we had a small, young, bright, enthusiastic following. We had a few older enthusiasts also.

May and June of 1937 were hectic and crucial months for labor. Various organizing drives were sputtering because of stiffened management resistance and the inventory of "depression."

Steel and other manufacturers had begun to come out of the Depression doldrums stimulated by the threat of war and by orders from overseas by those who were preparing for war or who feared it. To counter the effect of a possible strike, the steel corporations and others had piled up massive inventories, and so there were layoffs. Layoffs dampened spirits.

U.S. Steel and some others had signed a contract, but Bethlehem, Republic, and Youngstown Sheet and Tube refused and were struck. The "Little Steel Strike" was in the process of being lost. There was violence, and workers were killed in Chicago and northeastern Ohio. Roosevelt had uttered his "plague on both your houses." John L. Lewis had roared back, but some momentum was lost.

The New Deal itself was a bit on the defensive, after all, Roosevelt was in his second term and suffering the second-term blahs.

In Pittsburgh there was a strike at the H. J. Heinz Co., the huge food factory, and that, too, was not going well—an AFL union was involved.

As we entered the Depression, the AFL, American Federation of Labor, was labor. Unfortunately, it was dominated by craft unions and their ancient leaders who were convinced that the only trade unionism that could endure was craft. Fifty years previously, the Knights of Labor had disintegrated and the IWW, another noncraft union of only a decade before, had come to naught.

In the meantime, while they dithered during Roosevelt's first term, opportunities were being lost in not only steel, but also oil, electric and automobile. Then, John L. Lewis of the United Mineworkers stepped for-

> **"John L. had a famous fight on the floor of the 1935 AFL convention in which he socked big Bill Hutchinson of the Carpenters after Bill had called him a coal-cracking sonofabitch (lovely rhetoric)."**

ward as a champion of the industrial mode of organizing, that is, everyone in the plant in the same union and no more aristocrats of labor with their benefits trickling down. John L. had a famous fight on the floor of the 1935 AFL convention in which he socked big Bill Hutchinson of the Carpenters after Bill had called him a coal-cracking sonofabitch (lovely rhetoric). Lewis was flamboyant in word and deed and caught the imagination of the press, of the workers, and of most intellectuals.

John L. pulled together a Committee for Industrial Organization, the CIO (which quickly became a magic word) and was expelled by the AFL for dual unionism. So he started his own Federation, the Congress of Industrial Organizations, still the CIO, with a half-million dollars of the Miners' money. The CIO started organizing everything everywhere; this woke up the AFL, which then went into the same sort of organizing and prospered at it.

In 1937, the CIO and its component, the Steel Workers Organization Committee (SWOC) were groggy. Few of the new CIO unions were really healthy. Union shops and dues checkoffs (automatic dues collection) had not yet been negotiated in most of them.

This was the time for action and our CRA following was ready. So I rallied a contingent of them, including some nice looking young women, and the two other priests, and with our Catholic Radical Alliance signs simply went down and joined the pickets at Heinz. Some of the pickets were a bit timid and didn't like our use of the word Radical, but we held firm and kept the signs. I saw to it that the newspapers covered our foray. There was an uproar. Priests had not picketed before anywhere, to my knowledge. We were denounced from pulpits and in the papers by a few of the clergy. Heinz was a paternalistic company, and had helped neighboring parishes.

Father James R. Cox, a great radio priest, had supported labor in the darkest days of the 20s and early 30s, but he was a Republican, albeit a stormy and rebellious one, and was AFL-minded. For him, the CIO was a bunch of Communists. Heinz had helped him feed his large Shantytown and its soup kitchen in desperate times, and he was frankly grateful. We were denounced by him. He said there were Communists involved in organizing Heinz. Indeed there were, although I wasn't sure of it at the time, and stoutly denied the allegation. Even if I had known, I, and I am sure the other priests, would have supported the strikers anyway since their cause was just, and we were not about to abandon them to the Communists or to fate. We addressed many meetings, and I was very vocal and rhetorical. (The owner of Heinz, grandfather of the present Senator told a confi-

dant later on that I had made the difference. I hope that was true.)

This action even made the pages of *Time*. On the strength of it, the Steelworkers asked me to help in Youngstown, and I got the other two priests in my little Chevy and we hit the picket line there. We all spoke, but mine was a riproaring, no-holds-barred denunciation of the steel magnates and the infamy of great wealth.

The memory of talking at Stop Five in the dark in front of a huge mill with search lights trained on us and an engine and some cars shuttling back and forth to drown us out is fresh in my mind. There is a picture of me speaking in the rain under an umbrella. The umbrella was held by a Communist, Shorty Steuben, who later disappeared somewhere in China.

The local clergy denounced us, of course, especially some Dominicans. I believe they were the ones who entered the mill to say mass for the scabs. I made a number of trips back to that area and drove Father Hensler up to Johnstown, Pennsylvania, another steel strike center.

The Little Steel companies were huge and powerful; they eventually broke that violent and bloody strike. All the blood shed was workers' blood. . . .

Back home in Pittsburgh, I became involved in every labor struggle and strike. There were many of them. A recital of them would just be a boring list. Sometimes I had one of the other two with me, but often I ventured alone. Msgr. O'Toole shortly went off to Catholic University. Father Hensler remained until 1940, I think. He was a scholar and very well informed on the issues and had mastered the literature, but I was the rabble-rouser. Quite radical things said by him would not get people excited or too angry because of his scholarly mien. Not so with yours truly. Among my fellow priests in Pittsburgh, reaction was mixed. Some said I was merely a publicity hound, but a surprising number gave me credit for good works.

Never did I avoid my fellow priests and always enjoyed and sought their company—at Forty Hours, dinners, at Confirmations, on retreats, at priests' funerals, etc. Baiting me face to face was not done too often because I had a ready tongue and would argue fiercely. Because of all this, I enjoyed my priesthood and enjoyed my fellows, whether they agreed with me or not. I never felt any bitterness, thank God.

Of course, in all this, I had an ace in the hole. Bishop Hugh C. Boyle approved of me in general and actually enjoyed the stir that I was making. The bishop was inclined to be reclusive. Priests stayed away from him, but I went to see him frequently and was told, go ahead and do what you feel you should do, but don't allege me.

The bishop was pastor in Homestead at the time of the 1919 strike. In that strike the corporations rallied the communities and their organizations, including most churches, against the strike, which was un-American. Father Hughey Boyle, as he was then, went to the picket line and expressed sympathy.

Also, interestingly enough, his brother was sheriff of Cambria County where Bethlehem's Johnstown Mill was engaged in breaking the 1937 strike. Mike Boyle supported and assisted the strikers.

So the bishop, in the background, was all for us. He would chuckle at my actions and sharp ripostes as he read about them. He was never one to praise, but once, while relaxing after a Confirmation, when my name came up he said, "he has made no major mistakes." Hensler and O'Toole were also respected and the association with them helped.

Here is a partial list of the unions I helped in strikes or organizing drives by industry:

Steel, electrical manufacturing, chemical, aluminum, laundry, bakery, retail clerks, butchers, packing house workers, newspaper guild, newspaper distributors, restaurants, clothing workers, police, Westinghouse salaried, commu-

nications, teachers, musicians, operating engineers, plant guards, postal employees, hospital, insurance salesmen, government workers, auto workers, utility workers, textile and paper workers, and some others that I forget.

An unsung hero of the times was John Collins, lay editor of the Pittsburgh Catholic. The paper, privately owned, is the oldest west of the Alleghenies, or something of the sort. John, truly erudite, was in Catholic journalism for the love of it. His high standards and strong principles hurt him. His belief in social justice was as strong as ours, and his support unwavering, although he lost subscriptions and ads.

While Bishop Boyle rather enjoyed me, it was another story with other bishops whose territory I either invaded or planned to invade. Our bishop was not a fearful man, but he respected protocol. Besides, he was quite popular among the other bishops, just as he had been popular among the other priests when he was young. I invaded other dioceses with some impunity until complaints started to come in about the wild young radical priest who so vituperated capitalism and some of its more successful practitioners. Championship of unions was not popular. Many of the older bishops believed that the CIO was really a hotbed of Communism and had their doubts about the wisdom of the Catholic proletariat being stirred up by its own clergy for any purpose. Cardinal O'Connell of Boston thundered by telegraph: Keep that young man out of my Diocese and where he belongs. I think he added something about bishops minding their own business. Daugherty, the sour cardinal of Philadelphia, was, if possible, less gracious; and the old bishop in Ogdensburg went into a very hysteria of rage at the possibility of me entering his sacred satrapy. I think this was Bishop Conroy, who died shortly thereafter, perhaps as a result of getting himself worked up over my request. There were other lesser contretemps, but I wandered many dioceses more or less freely and was welcomed in places like Erie, Indianapolis, Louisville, Baltimore, Cleveland, Albany, Buffalo, Chicago, and Detroit.

In due time, I penetrated Boston and Philadelphia, but never did get to Ogdensburg.

As the years went on, and I stayed the course, most of my fellow priests came to respect me.

There were exceptions, of course. One very crusty and conservative older Irish priest, a Corkman, was in the habit of having a cocktail before dinner with his curates, and there was a long stretch during which he opened nearly every one of these social occasions with the words, "That goddamned Charlie Rice, did you hear what he did today?"

THE CRITIC
Winter, 1987

 # Catholic and Radical (1937)

The inspiration for Rice's activism were the social teachings of the Church as filtered through the American experience. An admirer of Dorothy Day and the Catholic Worker movement, he was a founder of Pittsburgh's House of Hospitality which fed the poor and provided temporary shelter to the homeless. He quickly focused on the growing industrial union movement as a force that could reform and improve society. In the Pittsburgh Catholic, *in articles under the* Catholic Radical Alliance *byline, he reported on his activities with the group.*

I still think it's the best name. Father Tom Lappan, white-haired youngish director of the St. Vincent de Paul conference, was quite emphatic. I thought it was the best name too but—what of all the people who would not understand? The word radical is a perfectly good one in its true sense. Monsignor O'Toole can tell you that. You want a label that will both attract attention and tell what your outfit is up to. Catholic Radical Alliance as a title isn't just good—man it's perfect.

OK! Catholic Radical Alliance it is. I wonder what the Bishop will say. So we wrote out the title. Looked at it a number of times in pride and some trepidation, and turned to other matters.

We had been holding open forums for some time on the social questions. Learned talks had been given by Monsignor O'Toole and Father Carl Hensler and some not-so-learned by myself. At the question period each night people were always jumping up demanding to know what we were going to do about

things. Later I found out some of them were egged on by Father Lappan, who wanted action.

We had roundly condemned the present social order, had made the point that the Church had marvelous remedies to offer. That some type of definite action was necessary, etc. That, however, was as far as we got.

Now we are going to do something. A definite program was to be submitted at the next meeting of the Forum. An organization with a nice name and everything was to be proposed. I, the proposer, was doing a neat spate of worrying and working.

The grand social encyclicals were our ultimate guide of course; and our immediate inspiration and example was the "Catholic" worker crowd of New York. The program, as submitted to the Forum and approved, called for long range action through education toward cooperatives, farming communes and the distributive ideal in general for the immediate here and now. We had plans for action among the poor, the workers, the intelligentsia. Classes in principles with the object of molding a fully indoctrinated, enthusiastic body of supporters were started immediately. But that wasn't enough. . . .

UNPUBLISHED MANUSCRIPT
Probably written in May 1937

How the CRA Started (1938)

The Catholic Radical Alliance was not started to be merely just another study club or lecture circuit. It was intended to be nothing less than an agency to reform and remold society. The alliance set itself to procure a long range reform and a spiritual change in society. So early in the game it realized that its reaching for these objectives could be gained chiefly by means of propaganda.

However, the CRA, in company with its parent group, the Catholic Workers in New York, recognizes certain immediate things which it can do. These are mostly in the way of helping along palliatives for society's ills: in simple language, helping those who are giving medicine to society.

Among groups which are administering good and badly needed medicine to a sick society are labor unions. Unions, moreover, are more than merely a medicine to relieve immediate distress; they are first steps on the road to a permanent cure.

The CRA has aided both CIO and AFL unions, trying to keep out of the inter union wrangle. The type of aid given has consisted for the most part of supporting morale through speeches and picketing, educating workers and others as to the benefits of unionism, by speaking and distributing literature, and, when at all possible, feeding needy strikers, giving advice, etc.

The next activity was when the alliance helped the AFL Canning and Pickle Workers local in its strike at the Heinz plant. Full page advertisements had appeared in the newspapers of this city denouncing the strikers and lauding the company. The next day Father Rice and Father Hensler appeared at the plant. Four lay members of the alliance carried picket signs and walked in the picket line in front of the plant.

Both parties agreed to a labor board supervised election. On the eve of the election Father Hensler, Monsignor O'Toole and Father Rice personally urged the workers to vote for the union. The union won the election by a proportion of 5–4, and it is conceded that the alliance turned the tide in the union's favor.

A very vicious attack was launched against the priest members, particularly Father Rice, for their part in this matter. One local priest—in a charitable, priestly fashion took issue with the Alliance action. He was answered. Another cleric denounced the union, bringing in bewhiskered charges of Communism and racketeerism that are hurled at every union. He was answered by Father Rice in the public press. . . .

The next venture of the CRA priest leaders again brought them into conflict with fellow priests. At the invitation of the SWOC heads, Father Rice, Msgr. O'Toole and Father Hensler went to Youngstown, Ohio to address the strikers during the disastrous strike in

> **"The Catholic Radical Alliance was not started to be merely just another study club or lecture circuit. It was intended to be nothing less than an agency to reform and remold society. "**

Little Steel. The permission of Bishop Schrembs of Cleveland had been obtained in advance. The priests spoke at two meetings that day in a driving rain.

The Youngstown papers published no account of the event, but a friend of the union, Geoffrey Burke, in a paid advertisement in the "Vindicator" gave an account of the talks and the event. Mr. Burke did not report the words of the priests entirely accurately, though he did give the spirit of their addresses, by and large. A local clergyman publicly deplored the CRA activity—he had been active on the side of the company. He quoted the Bishop as having deplored the speeches. Bishop Schrembs later denied that in this matter he had been quoted accurately. . . .

In the local field, in the meantime, the CRA became active in the Loose-Wiles Bakery strike (CIO). Father Thomas Lappan, CRA member, through the Society of St. Vincent de Paul fed 200 needy strikers for two weeks. This prevented the strikers from being starved out, and the strike was won.

Up to the first of the year, the alliance helped in three other strikes: the Heppenstall strike (CIO), three local box factories (AFL), and Penn Salt, Natrona (CIO). Before the Heppenstall strike, at the request of union officials, Father Rice on one occasion helped postpone the strike by urging the men to listen to their officials and wait. This strike was settled without a clear victory on either side. The box factory strike was settled with something of a victory for the union in each factory.

In several cases—Heinz, Heppenstall, box factories—an alliance member took part in the negotiations between the management and worker in making for a settlement.

(A review of the CRA's first year written by Rice)

PITTSBURGH CATHOLIC
February 10 and 17, 1938

The Dynamite of the Encyclicals (1937)

Last month some of the good Catholic people of Pittsburgh were startled to hear that a group of priests had been interested in organizing, of all things, a Catholic Radical Alliance. There was a general lifting of the eyebrows all along the line at the idea of Catholic Radicals. The newspapers were a bit afraid of touching the thing and friends of the station KDKA blinked when they saw the combination. As for those individuals with Communistic—dread name—leanings they have been scandalized, not a little, at the idea of a Catholic claiming to be anything so worthwhile as a radical.

The question is asked of us, are we really radicals? And the only answer we can honestly make is: Yes, we certainly are. A radical is one who goes to the root of matters, and we count on doing just that. We are dissatisfied with the present social and economic set-up; we want to see it drastically changed. We, however, are not in favor of making the changes by the use of violence. We don't want to beat up or shoot people. We intend to work for change the hard way, by the method of love, not hate; and that, in this day of dictators and bullets and bloodshed, is radical in itself.

Before we go further it might be well to find out how we get that way. It might be reasonable to inquire, whom are we following? What prominent Catholics are radicals in this sense? Well, off hand, the first name that comes to my mind is that of Pope Pius XI, Bishop of Rome, Vicar of Christ, visible head of the Church. This program, by the way, is commemorating a radical document that he issued six years ago this very day; and it is commemorating another radical document that was issued forty years before that again: The Encyclical "On the Condition of Labor" by Leo XIII. . . .

Rice watches furniture loading on House of Hospitality truck, March 1939

The Popes issued these documents to the entire world, one of them forty-six years ago, and the other six years ago; but it is an annoying fact that the principles in them have not gotten around. Outside her fold the Church has the reputation, unfortunately, among all too many of being reactionary—the friend of the rich rather than the poor; the friend of the bosses rather than the masses. And yet, if the plain facts of Christian principles and practice were known, it is just the opposite. The Church is the Church of the poor and must be. She is the friend of the oppressed against the oppressor. . . .

To be brutally frank, there are Catholics, many by no means obscure, who act not like followers of Christ, but like followers of the devil in their dealing with and attitude toward the problems of social justice; that is, toward the workers and the poor.

There are many other Catholics who impede the advance of the truth by their blundering. Notorious examples of these are to be found among our prominent American "Red-Baiters." Most of these misguided people are being duped. They rant and rave against the menace of Communism, against its Godlessness; with never a word about the menace and Godlessness of Finance-Capitalism. They let the hatred of Communism, which is proper, blind them into breaking Christ's law forbidding hatred of persons, and they hate and would like to wipe out Communists. Worst of all, they are led around by the nose by reactionaries. They yell Communistic at decent reforms which are obviously for the common good. The result of this is that the Church is marked down as reactionary; and the ordinary person is beginning to think Communism must be pretty good stuff, since so many good things are labelled Communistic.

Many well-meant tirades against Communism are in the same class. They lead people to believe that all we can do against Communism is deliver long-winded orations, and that there is no positive program. We Catholic radicals have run into that difficulty. People will insist on labelling us anti-Reds, or anti-Communists. We don't want that. We are against not only Communism but every form of social injustice.

The Pope clearly states that it won't be enough to change the system, we must also change men's ways of looking at the system. The best system in the world will go on the rocks if individualism and materialism are the ruling ideas. Individualism is simply the doctrine of every man for himself. Materialism is the doctrine that we are just animals, that there is no other life but this one, no other values but those we find on the earth. These ideas have been in the saddle in modern life and they are what have made such a mess of civilization. Under them the point is: look out for number one, get what you can while the getting is good, you are going to be dead a long time. They rule the present system; they rule business today, and they will rule in the Communist or Fascist super-state, and don't fool yourself. . . .

Right at the start, we must note that the Catholic attitude on the distribution of property marks it off most sharply from both Communism and the concentration of today. Today ownership of real wealth, productive property, is in the hands of the few. The masses just don't own any real property, and the middle class is really but little better off. Under Communism that would be carried still further and the masses would continue to own nothing, but would be joined by everyone else; while the ownership and control of real property would be piled up in the hands of whatever gang of politicians happened to be running the state. The Church, on the contrary, advocated the distribution of real property as widely as possible. She wants all people to own something, because only when a man controls his tools and his work is he free and secure. Today what worker is secure? His fate is in the hands of the boss. Under Communism it would be in the hands of the politicians. . . .

PITTSBURGH CATHOLIC
May 20, 1937

House of Hospitality (1937)

Visitors are always welcome to the House of Hospitality and there is always work to be done if anyone should desire to give some time to

At the House of Hospitality. To Rice's right is Alan Kistler who became Director of Human Resources Development Institute, AFL/CIO, 1939.

active, personal practice of the works of mercy. We can't stress too much that we are not a formal, organized charity. Don't expect too much of us when you come to visit us. All we have is one small store room, where we feed nearly three hundred a day and where anywhere from five up sleep at night. The room is kept clean enough and it is warm but it is not particularly nice looking—certainly not beautiful. The type of person you see around there mostly is not a very engaging type. Most of our visitors are derelicts, "the undeserving poor" some say, but they are Christ's poor and we are trying to help them in Christ's way.

You will find a lot to criticize when you visit. We are not particularly efficient. The few good, regular workers are terribly overworked. There is any amount of things we should be doing which we don't do.

You will find that you can make many suggestions to improve our methods. But what we would really like would be if you would do something to put those suggestions into practice.

Of course, the work is not romantic, or particularly dramatic. You don't get your picture in the paper for doing it and there is very little earthly glory about it. Perhaps that is why there is so much more work than workers. But it is the part of the whole scheme that really matters. The picketing, the speaking and the sensationalism are of some value but the active, personal practice of Christ's charity toward Christ's poor is what really counts.

The woman who came down alone Christmas day, leaving a comfortable festive home, and personally waited on the ragged, disease-ridden, cold and hungry crowd—some of them half drunk, the poor fellows—she had the spirit. God send us some more like her.

PITTSBURGH CATHOLIC
December 30, 1937

Speech to Little Steel Strikers in Youngstown (1937)

Nineteen thirty-seven was the turning point for organized labor. In February, Autoworkers broke through company resistance to union organizing with the Flint, Michigan, sit-down victory. In March, Pittsburgh was rocked by the news that U.S. Steel had signed an agreement without a fight with the Steel Workers Organizing Committee. However, the momentum of the CIO organizing drive was slowed by a defeat in the Little Steel Strike, which was marked by violence and determined company resistance. Rice wholeheartedly entered the fray in the weeks following the "Memorial Day Massacre" at the Republic steel mill in South Chicago.

If you men organize and stay organized in a strong and just union, this will be good not only for yourselves, but for the country at large and for your employers themselves, though at the moment they can't see it. The principle of union and cooperation is a good one and we can only regret that it is so lacking in American life today. You men, organized and loyal to each other, to your country and your God, have a chance to bring that principle of unity and cooperation into our life; and I hope, and know, that you will not let that chance slip by.

Because I have come here at this moment I shall be accused of injecting religion into the labor issue, and I reply: It is about time that religion was introduced into that issue. The reason we have labor strife today, the reason we have had it for generations, the reason six men lost their lives in Illinois last week is that religion and religious principles have been kept out of the labor question. Because religion was forgotten, no not forgotten but deliberately thrown aside, too many industrialists have conducted their affairs as if Christ had never lived and died, as if there were no just God in heaven, and have tried to rule like the absolute Pagan Emperors of old, forgetting that they were dealing with human beings, endowed with human rights by the God who made them.

If Christianity were injected into the labor issue, and if the Charity of Christ reigned there rather than the naked greed of Hell, laborers would long since have been treated as partners and cooperators, to be helped and loved, not as wage slaves to be exploited and kept down; all employers would have given decent wages, decent working conditions, security of employment and common human liberty to their workers. But the Charity of Christ has been absent from the hearts of the great mass of these rulers of industry and trade, and the result has been the class war, rather than class cooperation. Sad to relate, many of the malefactors, who in practice were flouting the straight doctrine of Christ, have brazenly masqueraded as Christians of the holiest kind.

There are those who today view the march of labor with alarm. Some do this because they have been fooled by false cries of Communism, directed at labor leaders, others do it out of sheer white collar snobbery and others still because they fear the laborer whom they have exploited and can exploit no longer. Let them put their fears to rest, the laboring man in this country does not demand a Godless soviet system, the SWOC does not demand it; but they do demand and we all demand that the Godless features of our own system cease and give place to an order that recognizes God and human

rights and duties and justice for all. Such an order, a true Christian one, will never be realized until stubborn, selfish, lawless employers see, or are induced to see, that they must extend the hand of fellowship to their workers, who are men, not chattels, that they have no right to rule the liberties and lives of these men, but have the bounden duty, under heaven, of giving justice and decent treatment to them.

Labor does not want to strike, nor do I or any other sane, Christian man. I hate strikes and you do too. But there are times when strikes are necessary and legitimate, and this is certainly one of them. I pray for a speedy, peaceful ending of this one, an ending that will mark the beginning of cooperation and the abolishing of exploitation and brutal control. I pray God that never again will this country be horrified to witness the shocking slaughter of workers that it witnessed in Illinois a short time ago.

There is no more fitting way for me to end this address than to pay tribute to those men whose lives were snuffed out on the labor front. I pray that their wives and little ones will never be permitted by your union or yourselves to suffer want. Let me ask of you the difficult request that you keep Christianity's hardest commandment, that you bear no hatred in your hearts for this or anything else, but that you forgive your enemies and give them and the world a Christian example. Only when the methods of hate are discarded can there be any hope of labor peace and justice. The methods of love are hard but they win out in the long run.

Standing on this public platform I beg you forgive your enemies, use not violence. Pray for your enemies. Pray for the souls of those who died in Illinois, may their souls rest in peace.

UNPUBLISHED SPEECH, YOUNGSTOWN, OHIO
June 6, 1937

Rice addresses Little Steel Strike rally at Youngstown Sheet and Tube plant, June 6, 1937.

A Private Letter to a Bishop (1937)

Most Rev. Bishop:

I am really sorry that the Youngstown thing turned out as it did. . . . We go to Youngstown. We talk mildly for the strikers. The local paper ignores our visit. A poor well meaning fellow. . . . pays for an ad, and puts in what he thinks we said, which really is just what he thinks himself. What happens then? White collar men, straw bosses, etc. rush to Fr. Gainor, he in turn rushes to the bishop, an official denial of authorization appears as to Burke's words, all of which are true even if we did not speak them. No official denial of authorization appears as to the words of Fr. Gahn, who ripped the SWOC with calumnies, gathered by the steel men, from the altar. The result is that the people who had begun to hope that the Church was with them, sigh and feel that it was a dream too good to be true, and that is the end of that.

Most Rev. Bishop, I am a young man and as such I had no business writing the implied censure above, but it is written, and I let it stand with humble apologies. Father of the Poor, the wolves are leading your children astray; wolves both within and without. Fr. Gainor with his nice regard for the feelings of the white collar men and bosses is a very mild type of wolf. Fr. Gahn and the Catholic bosses are the virulent type. The wolves from without are the Reds who seize with glee on speeches like that of Gahn's, on actions like that of Gainor and in their powerful, well circulated press they pass the good word around. When we spoke in Youngstown they said to the people: "That's all right, let them talk, but in a few days you'll see; they will be repudiated. Nobody repudiates Gahn but this crowd will be cracked down on." The people did not believe them. They crowded around us, they shook our hands, they said: "God bless you Father for being with the worker," many had tears in their eyes, but the Reds just held back, they knew that when reaction came they could lead the sheep back into camp. One of these individuals said to me: "You are just talking through your hat, the Church is not for labor. You men are here unofficially, you are outsiders, you may not even be priests! . . . Then I flattened him, I showed him your telegram and that took the starch out of him. I felt great. The Catholics around felt great, but we were the ones who got flattened. . . .

A nasty thing I have noted is that there is a movement of cleavage in Catholic ranks. Many of the comfortable, white collar people are shying very hard away from the worker. They who are the proletariat themselves, they who own not a stick of real property distrust labor. The fools, let them unite and strike for social justice. Strike, as I always insist, not with violence and hate but with the charity of Christ and we will see peace and justice reign.

I have bored you, Your Excellency, and I have written execrably; but I have written as it came to me and send you the effusion as it stands. You are a fighter, you are an artist, Bishop, you have not the soul of a shop keeper or I would not have dared to set my heart and soul on paper and submit it to your eyes. Don't take me for a fanatical fool, don't take Hensler for one, we are hard headed young men who would be making great strides toward successful careers in our "profession" if the Charity of Christ, the meaning of Christianity had not got us and made madmen out of us.

Sincerely in Christ,
Rev. Charles Owen Rice

UNPUBLISHED LETTER WRITTEN TO JOSEPH SCHREMBS, ARCHBISHOP OF CLEVELAND
June 11, 1937

Speech to Canton, Ohio, Strikers (1937)

In this present struggle I appeal for peace and urge all within the sound of my voice to work for peace and to shun violence and bloodshed. I make this appeal to both sides impartially. At the same time I frankly say that my sympathies are with the worker, and I don't want my words understood to mean that I am asking the worker to cease striving for his rights with every just, legitimate means within his power. Keep on: it is for your own good that you win this thing, and more than that for the good of the community in general.

The real issues in the struggle have been concealed by camouflage and misunderstanding. Even without the propaganda of recent manufacture, there already existed misunderstanding concerning the fundamental issues. Our profit-mad, business-worshipping civilization has forgotten certain things. It has forgotten that human rights are above property rights; that there is a certain fundamental dignity in labor that must be respected; that money and profit are not the ends of industry. The material goods of this world were created by Almighty God not just for a few, not for the sake of business and trade, not that they be the monopoly of one class but that they serve the people as a whole. Our materialistic system has ignored that, and the lives of men have been warped, twisted and destroyed that they might serve the ends of the false gods of trade and profit.

The twin evils of Fascism and Communism have grown up across the water and they have been brought into being and nourished by the injustices of the social and economic setup. These horrors have been worse than the disease they set out to cure and we in America want none of them. We have it in us, I believe, to avoid these excesses, but if we are to avoid them and keep intact our country and our traditions we must overcome the things that breed Communism and its reaction. Here is where labor unionism comes in. The labor union is a middle of the road attempt to cure certain of the more flagrant abuses in current history. . . . The labor union, the CIO, in particular, has been called everything from Communist to Fascist, but it is none of these things. It is a normal American, Christian attempt to right certain unbearable wrongs and in my mind it may well serve as the first step toward the building of a new, just, Christian, United States of America.

I appeal to the rulers of industry to recognize this plain fact. Some of them in all truth have already done so. I appeal to the white collar worker man to rid himself of his snobbish distrust and fear of labor. If this recognition and trust be not forthcoming we in America will see class war. I don't want that, labor doesn't want it, nobody wants it, but we are rushing blindly toward it. Let us in the name of God apply Christian principles to the thing. Let us recognize the primacy of human rights, let us strive to understand, to cooperate with, to love one another. Let us have give and take and

> "**O**ur profit-mad, business-worshipping civilization has forgotten certain things. It has forgotten that human rights are above property rights; that there is a certain fundamental dignity in labor that must be respected; that money and profit are not the ends of industry."

then we will have class cooperation instead of class warfare.

UNPUBLISHED SPEECH
August 20, 1937

Heppenstall Strike Speech (1937)

. . . The Heppenstall Strike has presented us with a typical steel strike in miniature. The people of Pittsburgh can learn from this strike in their own back yard how such things start and who is responsible for them. The usual procedure is this: the workers are organized into a union. They are goaded by company tactics until they strike. Once they strike, violence is provoked by misguided company tactics.

The Heppenstall strike has followed this model exactly. I know for a fact that the union leaders did not want this strike. Several months ago, at the request of some of them, I addressed a group of Heppenstall workers who had a grievance and who wanted to strike. I and their leaders advised them not to strike but to wait until every possible, peaceful means of settlement was exhausted. This strike threat was averted, several other similar threats were likewise averted. Then came the inevitable hour when the tempers of the men boiled over and they came out on strike.

Now the SWOC, which we have heard damned as irresponsible, postponed that strike as long as was humanly possible, giving the people of Pittsburgh a concrete example of how unions want not strikes but peace, not conflict but cooperation.

After the strike started, a whole series of unfortunate, ill advised incidents began to happen. Calm discussion and clear thinking would have avoided them all. There was riot in front of this plant on Monday, that was unnecessary. Luckily it turned out better than many another

riot and there was no one killed or given serious injury, thank God for that. But that riot could easily have ended fatally.

That fuss is over with and I hope and pray that it will not be repeated. Let us hope that instead of clubs and bricks all the parties in this dispute will have recourse to the council from now on. I don't want to paint the Heppenstall people as irreformable villains, or anything of the sort. But they have been thoughtless and unreasonable, and that sort of thing must stop. . . .

I hope that management will agree to sit down with the representatives of labor and iron the thing out before hate and misunderstanding grows so deeply into the hearts of all concerned that they will remain there and fester and never be removed.

Finally, I appeal to you workers to remove hard feelings from your hearts. Stick up for your rights by all means, hold fast to principle, but don't get to hating Bill Heppenstall and the other young hotheads. There is still hope that the thing will reach peaceful settlement in a Christian manner. . . .

UNPUBLISHED SPEECH
July 29, 1937

Memories of a Union Strike (1981)

In 1937 the labor movement was resurgent under the aegis of the New Deal. John L. Lewis's CIO was organizing basic industry, which had been open shop. Phil Murray was in charge of steel, and Big Steel, that is U.S. Steel, came into the fold. The Little Steel Companies, Bethlehem, Republic, et al., were enormous corporations employing nearly 200,000. They decided to fight rather than sign and the strike was on.

A bitter, violent strike it was, a sort of Last

Hurrah for the union busters; the old tactics were trotted out: lies, spies, guns, red baiting—the whole bit. Temporarily it was successful. The union lost the battle, but eventually won the war.

[My] speech. . . . had been delivered in Youngstown to which city Father (now Msgr.) Carl Hensler, Msgr. George Barry O'Toole, and I journeyed at the invitation of the Steel Workers. They wanted us because the whole local establishment had been mobilized against them: politicians, police, newspapers, businessmen, professional men, and clergy, including a couple of highly vocal Catholic priests. Even the local AFL craft leaders had a bit of the anti CIO hysteria.

After the strike was over the LaFollette Senate committee established the sordid details of the anti-union campaign and ended that nasty business for a long while.

We made our contribution during the worst of it, June 6. Only a few days previously, Memorial Day, May 30, there had been a massacre of union supporters and strikers in Chicago at the Republic Steel plant. Chicago city police fired on an unarmed crowd and killed ten, wounding scores. In the Youngstown area, before the strike was over, eight were killed. No policeman, non-striker or company official was hurt.

Our visit did not win the strike but it definitely helped to win the minds and hearts of workers to the union side. The anti-union clergy had been getting away with murder until we challenged them, quoting the Pope's encyclicals as proclaiming the worth of trade unions and the dignity of labor.

Fr. Hensler and Msgr. O'Toole were recognized scholars of high repute in the hierarchy, both being distinguished graduates of North American College, Rome. Me, I drove the car and was the most rhetorical. Those two marvelous priests were great cover, let me add. . . .

Our foray did more than influence the work-

ers, it was a factor in changing the Church and its reputation from anti-labor to pro-labor. Priests all over the country began sounding off on the union side and supporting the CIO, but ours was the most dramatic and effective action—it got national attention. I was a fledgling priest, three years ordained, I've been flying since.

Those local priests, who were loudly pro-company and anti-union, were furious and counterattacked, but we creamed them. Bishop Dearden had been stationed in that area and when he came to Pittsburgh years later, he is said to have carried a not-too-favorable impression of your humble correspondent who had dared to make fiery speeches in a time of turmoil.

PITTSBURGH CATHOLIC
September 4, 1981

A Talk with Two Labor Leaders (1938)

Rice began doing local and national radio broadcasts boosting the CIO in 1937. Support from Catholics was critical to the survival and growth of the new labor federation. The choice of Rice to give the opening prayer at the first CIO convention held in Pittsburgh was a recognition of his pivotal role in defending and promoting worker organization.

Sitting between John L. Lewis and Sidney Hillman on the stage at Islam Grotto while waiting for the first national convention of the CIO to start last Monday morning, I spoke to Lewis about an article I had received in the mail recently: an elaborate reprint from "Mill and Factory" concerning labor in Mexico and prominently discussing Lewis' much argued-over trip to the International Labor Congress in Mexico City.

Lewis spoke of certain misrepresentations in the article. He smiled wryly over the insinuations concerning the palatial quarters he occupied. On the matters of red flags and Communist salutes he was earnestly explanatory. The red flags displayed were not Communist emblems, he pointed out, but the insignia of Toledano's labor union. Said Lewis: "There was one fellow from Europe giving the clenched fist all the time." He was referring to Edo Fimmen, Holland's labor leader.

Lewis mentioned that he thought the religious situation in Mexico is in better shape than it had been for years. Most Catholic observers agree with him here. He knew of the increased cooperation between hierarchy and government as evidenced by the stand of certain Bishops on the expropriations questions. He was surprised to hear that Josephus Daniels, U.S. Ambassador to Mexico, was in bad odor with Catholics in general. Obviously he had relied on information given him by Daniels. Any imprudence that marked the entire Mexican venture might be charged off to Lewis' acceptance of the statements of diplomatic officials.

Lewis said that his trip to Mexico was in line with the trend among American officials and businessmen to establish "good neighbor" relations with Latin America. Thinking in terms of markets for American industry, which increased standards of living in Latin America would bring, motivated his excursion.

Lewis spoke very earnestly of his friendship and respect for Msgr. Haas and Msgr. Ryan whose contribution to the advance of American labor, he says, cannot be praised enough.

Even casual conversation with Sidney Hillman impresses one with the truth of the estimations which credit him with a trigger quick mind. No non-Catholic labor man, and few Catholics, have his grasp of the intricacies of labor union tactics as regards Catholics and Catholicity. For instance, he gets letters of introduction from priests of his acquaintance, Msgr. Haas and others, for his organizers, who

are instructed to present these credentials to operate. Furthermore, his organizers are instructed to leave the Spanish question severely alone. They do not always follow their orders. It was in connection with one such violation that the matter came up.

PITTSBURGH CATHOLIC
November 17, 1938

Prayer at First CIO Convention (1938)

Our Lord and Savior, Jesus Christ, You were once a worker yourself. We beseech You to bless and prosper those assembled in this convention. May they, leaders of the working men, be given the strength to carry on a struggle of overwhelming odds. Give to the ideals that sway this group a successful carrying out. Grant to American labor enlightenment, strength and unity. Especially we pray for unity that the great labor movement of this country may march forward as one to victory. Grant it victory, we pray, for labor's cause is Your cause, its victory Your victory. May it prosper and carry on its valiant struggle to gain its ends which are the ends of justice, Americanism and Christianity. In the name of the Father, and of the Son, and of the Holy Ghost, Amen.

Pittsburgh
November 17, 1938

John L., the Man (1969)

John L. Lewis was at the height of his power and popularity when he came to Pittsburgh on Labor Day 1937 to speak at the County Fair Grounds. I sat beside him and was awed by the great man. It was the apogee of his career: his friend was in the White House, to which he had easy access; he was all over the media and his

41

every word was news; his new labor federation, the CIO, was marching ahead; he was the social lion of the nation's capital; and he was the idol of the workers and the intellectuals.

Lewis' enemies were apoplectic; they spewed hatred of him in letters to the editor, in interviews, at debates and open forums, and that added to his glamour. He was glamorous, dramatic and colorful.

He was shorter than I expected but he was burly. His oratory on that occasion was a disappointment; no spell binder with arms waving, he rumbled. However, before an audience of miners or CIO delegates it was very different; such an audience hung on every word and followed the subtleties of this orator who depended on content and language rather than pure forensics.

Vapid feature writers still wonder that Lewis was a cultured man with a full vocabulary and the ability to quote English classics although he had not finished his formal schooling; as if a normal American elementary or secondary, or even, college education ever made a cultured person out of anyone. Lewis was reasonably cultured because that was his bent and determination.

In recent years, as I contemplated his career and the inside stories, not always favorable, that I received from intimates, I came to appreciate John Lewis more and more. For years I opposed him because of his split with Philip Murray and President Roosevelt; my veneration for the two other great men and my devotion to the New Deal controlled my judgment.

I have talked to Lewis' friends and admirers but also to his true enemies, men whom he had broken and made again, and men whom he had tried to break and failed; if anyone knows the other side of John L., I do, and I say he was a truly great man. This is not a tribute to the recent dead but a change in my estimation of a man caused by a change in my evaluation of

very many persons, movements and events.

Lewis was on the scene at the right historical moments and he did what desperately needed doing and what others could not do: organize the unorganized in the factories, mills and shops. The United States went into the great depression "open shop," that is, no unions or tiny, weak unions in all the basic industries— auto, steel, electric, oil, rubber, aluminum, iron mining, and even coal. The great coal miner's union had been virtually destroyed during the prosperity that preceded the crash. With Roosevelt and the New Deal the United Mine Workers came back fast, 500,000 strong with several million dollars in the treasury.

There was fighting in the labor movement over who would be allowed to organize what; each craft wanted a piece of the industrial masses. Lewis waited as long as he could and then went ahead on his own; his new federation, the CIO, picked up most of the basic industries and stimulated the old AFL to stop bickering and to work so that virtually all the organizable were organized.

John L. recruited his CIO organizers where he could: old miner opponents such as John Brophy and Allen Haywood whom he had run over and crushed, idealists such as Clinton Golden, malcontents and homegrown radicals, old Wobblies, Socialists by the bushel, wide-eyed college chaps, Communists, too; and, as I look back, I see that he was right in grabbing them all and turning them loose.

It worked and the timing was perfect. Lewis' disdain for critics and his hauteur were good medicine for the rather downtrodden workers who needed a tough and sassy leader with the grand manner. Lewis rubbed the conservative squares and the right-wingers about the same way as some of more magnificent Black militants do today.

Lewis fell out with Roosevelt and Phil Murray; I had a front row seat for some of it and thought that Lewis was scandalously wrong, but I see it differently now. Lewis opposed American involvement with, and preparation for, World War II. He stood virtually alone and, although his coal miners stayed with him as their union leader, they deserted him in national politics.

Phil Murray and the rest went with the establishment for conventional liberal and patriotic reasons: Lewis dared to dissent. He saw more clearly than anyone else the danger of unions becoming satellites of the Democratic Party and the tame seals that they are today.

During and after the war John L. Lewis had brief moments of glory as he refused to be bound by wage freezes and guidelines while the corporations were making hay; but automation wrecked his once great coal union. Not that he opposed automation; he once said mining was such a hazardous occupation that he looked forward to the day that no men at all would go down into the earth. His cherished dreams on miners' hospitals and clinics were victims of changed economics, and he must have had sad thoughts toward the end.

He shunned the limelight in his last decade and he rarely if ever engaged in controversy; then he, who had done so much else dramatically, died peacefully.

John L. Lewis had his share of human faults; he could be cruel and arrogant as well as charming and kind; on the one hand he would encourage young rebels and on the other silence internal criticism; but, "Take him for all in all. We shall not look upon his like again." He had insight, timing, and courage and he earned his place in history.

PITTSBURGH CATHOLIC
June 20, 1969

Workers Wise Up! (1937)

While Rice vigorously defended the CIO against charges that it was Communist dominated, he simultaneously attacked the Communist Party's policies and activities. He bitterly criticized liberal Democratic support for the republic in Spain and their flirtation with the Communist's Popular Front. He fervently believed that an alliance of organized labor with the Communists would lead to the destruction of the unions. He publicly picketed various "popular front" activities sponsored by local Communists.

Workers are sincere lovers of liberty! It is about time that a certain element among you begins to show some common sense. Do you people realize there is a strong Fascist sentiment in this country, that there is danger of a swing to some sort of Naziish dictatorship in the United States? Do you realize and remember that Fascism came in Italy and Germany as a reaction against the growth of Communism?

The Popular Front in the United States is a Communist device. It started up after the "Reds" got the life scared out of them by the way things turned out in Germany. They switched overnight from an active contempt of the labor movement and all things not ultra-Orthodox, Communistically speaking, to a sudden love for the labor movement and labor leaders. Like silly fools, droves of "liberals" have fallen for this act. In their respect for the noble Russian experiment they have lost their heads.

Fascist Danger

That sort of thing has brought a vaguely

Very Important

OPEN MEETING

For all Pressed Steel Car Company Employees and their Families

at St. Michael's Hall
310 Catherine St. (Bottoms)

WED., JAN. 24, AT 7 P. M.

Hear discussions on the coming Labor
Board Election and what it means to YOU

--- SPEAKERS ---

CLINTON S. GOLDEN
Director North East Region Steel Workers Organizing Committee

FATHER CHARLES OWEN RICE
Director, St. Joseph House of Hospitality

Vote Thursday, January 25th

AT UKRAINIAN HALL
Munson and Ella St., McKees Rocks (Bottoms)

VOTE SWOC

Strike Meeting

Under the auspices of Lodge No. 1601 of the Steel Workers Organizing Committee of the C. I. O. of Heppenstall Employees will be held to answer the unprovoked attack of Bill Heppenstall upon a peaceful strike picket.

TIME: **SATURDAY EVENING, JULY 24, 7 P. M.**
PLACE: **ARSENAL HIGH SCHOOL GROUNDS**

There Will Be Band Music

The Speakers will consist of:

Rev. Father Rice of Saint Agnes Parish
Robert Jahn of the S. W. O. C.
William Hart, President of Blawnox Lodge No. 1243
Rose M. Stien, Pittsburgh Authoress
Guy Hall of Heppenstall Lodge
John Danko of Phoenix Lodge No. 1147

...rge the Public to Attend. Express Your Solidarity
...ith the Strikers.

...Will Be a Parade
...and Butler Streets at 6:00 P. M. and

Mass Meeting

Of All Steel Workers in Carnegie, McKees Rocks and Coraopolis District
Will Be Held On
SUNDAY, FEBRUARY 20TH, 2 P. M.
CARNEGIE LIBRARY HALL, CARNEGIE
If You Wish to Hear Something of Vital Importance, and Why the Recession of Work, Be Sure to Come to This Meeting.
The Following Speakers Will Talk On the Need of a Real Union, and What
It Can Do For You

SPEAKERS

DAVID J. McDONALD
Secretary-Treasurer SWOC
DR. ELMER MAGEE
Burgess of Carnegie
HAROLD RUTTENBERG
SWOC Research Director
JUDGE M. A. MUSMANNO
Allegheny County Court
REV. O. C. RICE
Catholic Radical Alliance
LOUIS LEONARD
Secretary-Treasurer, Amalgamated Association of Iron, Steel &
Tin Workers
SAM PERRY
Canonsburg, Pa.
JOS. A. MATLAK
President, Carnegie Lodge, 171, Pa.
JOS. O'HARA, SWOC

THE MEETING WILL START AT 2 P. M. SHARP
COME ONE, COME ALL—EVERYBODY INVITED
AUSPICES CIO AND SWOC
JOHN TAFELSKI, Sub-Regional Director, SWOC
905 Island Avenue, McKees Rocks, Pa.

Flyers advertising Father Rice as a speaker, 1937–38

Fascist reaction already. Don't you people see that you are endangering every progressive movement, that you are risking the work of the generations of sincere workers for liberty and social justice? The closer "liberalism" unites with Communism (and the stronger Communism, therefore, becomes) the stronger Fascism grows.

There is a strong, normal, American progressive trend which has enlisted the support of religious men of every creed. This is in danger. You don't need to be a "Red" to fight for justice. You can do much better elsewhere. The Catholic Radical Alliance represents a Catholic movement, for instance, which is world wide, which has the support of the highest authorities and greatest intellects in Christendom and which is compatible with the American way.

As for Spain

The Spanish situation is so involved and the truth so hard to get that we of the Catholic Radical Alliance avoid discussion of it where possible. We must note on this occasion that a steady campaign of propaganda has been conducted in this country with the connivance of the capitalistic press to misrepresent the issues, to paint one side in heroic colors and the other in the blackest available. We warn labor unionists who fall for this campaign, a feature of which is vilification of Spanish Catholicism, that they will alienate the 20 million Catholics of this country if they are not careful.

Europe is in danger of being plunged into war over the thing. Communist and Fascist dictators are making unhappy Spain a bloody testing ground. For God's sake let us not pull America into it. Let us not start a civil war of our own here. We accuse those who support this meeting tonight of being either instigators or the dupes of a Communistic tactic. It is ridiculous to say that the Madrid junta represents democracy, just as it is ridiculous to say that the other junta has simon pure religious motives. There is a deliberate effort being made by left wing elements in this country to drag the United States into another European war. The same lying slogans are being used that were used before.

"Over There" Baloney

Once again we are called upon to rally around Democracy, to make the world safe for Democracy. The labor issue is being dragged in. Haven't we had enough labor faking in local issues? Tonight you will hear the same old clap-trap that pushed the U.S. into the last World War. War mongering about "returned heroes," "comrades in arms," "cigarettes for boys in the trenches." The same old baloney, but this time our "peace loving" brethren of the Popular Front are behind it. . . .

HANDBILL
September 20, 1937

On the Spanish War (1937)

. . . A deliberate and very successful attempt has been made . . . within the past year and a half to instill a very spirit of war hysteria and hatred in the professedly peaceful breast of the liberal, progressive, peace crowd in the United States. This amazingly sheep-like group has been taken in just as thoroughly by this war mongering as by the United Front game which preceded it and still goes on.

When about four years ago the Communist Party line changed from studied contempt of parlor pinks and assorted liberals to extreme love and desire for cooperation with them, the ease with which the lambs were taken in shocked many observers, including myself. This showed us once more how bankrupt the well-meaning liberalism and progressivism is as it wanders vaguely with tropish, if I may coin a word, yearning for nice, peaceful, happy stuff, having cast away religious and ethical principles and standards. It showed us, moreover, the tremendous driving force and vigor of Marxian Communism.

So it is that we were prepared for the turn of events which saw the attitude taken by liberals on the Spanish Civil War molded by the exigencies of the Party line. We were, however, taken aback to see the success of this tactic: how it spread until it became the accepted viewpoint of the tragic Spanish incident.

By following the Communist lead in this matter American Liberalism has made a tragic error. It has sown seeds which will be reaped as a whirlwind that will split the move for progressive reform in the United States. It meant an about face on every liberal tenet: impartiality, weighing of evidence, hearing of both sides, et al., have gone by the board. Liberals and weepers for peace have gone in for war mongering, have substituted atrocity stories for arguments, have taken out and dusted off all the old hoary calumnies about the Catholic Church, have accepted and circulated the propaganda handouts of the Madrid junta without question and are descending to name calling: you don't argue with an opponent, you call him a Fascist; at the same time you yell bloody murder if he calls you a Communist.

Where do I stand in the matter? I am a Catholic radical who stands for true social and economic reform. I want justice, equity and charity for all. I am no authority on Spain, but I do read the papers, the magazines and an occasional book—and I read both sides. The loyalists, in my opinion, are Bolshevik-controlled and dominated. There are but a few Communists in official positions you say; yes, but don't you know that one Red is worth a thousand liberals? Franco is not a Fascist, though he probably intends to remain a dictator. His government appears to be a popular one because there has been no popular revolt against him and no rumor of one. There have been mutinies among the troops due to jeal-

ousy of the Italians but no popular uprisings. When this war started I was of the opinion that Franco was pretty awful, but right now I am not so sure.

What I am sure of is this; I don't want to see my country dragged into another war. I don't want to see her duped into going out to save democracy either in Europe or in China. I want a moratorium on atrocity stories. I deplore the studied attempt to get America all excited about foreign scraps, the ins and outs of which we do not and cannot know. I deplore the feeding to the American public of the selfsame horror stories that got us into the last war, a war that, by the way, was to make the world safe for democracy.

SPEECH TO THE PITTSBURGH COUNCIL ON
PROGRESSIVE SOCIAL ACTION
PITTSBURGH CATHOLIC
December 16, 1937

Letter to Len De Caux
November 17, 1937

Thank you very kindly for sending me a copy of the C.I.O. pamphlet. I think it is a very good presentation. I remember meeting you at the Ship Builders Convention in Camden; enjoyed your talk that night very much. It is not often that newspaper men are such good talkers.

I would like to make a slight beef about one issue of your C.I.O. news sheet, which I get. I note that you have a little plug in there for the peace convention the American League Against War and Fascism is having in Pittsburgh in a few weeks. It is difficult to say this but you know that I am heart and soul for the work you are doing for the C.I.O., for social reform, etc. I don't like the American League Against War and Fascism, probably you do like them. It strikes me that the C.I.O. getting actively in with them is a bad thing for the C.I.O. because it gives our enemies, whose name is legion, another chance to yell Communists in the movement. Of course these people have done splendid service for the C.I.O. and you feel that it is but right to give such loyal friends a hand when possible. I appreciate that viewpoint but to tie the C.I.O., in however small a measure, in with that group will hurt the C.I.O. eventually.

I am afraid the end will be some sort of Fascism. This is still a very conservative country. The reactionary groups may seem impotent now but remember that Germany had one of the strongest Socialist, Communist, Liberal Catholic, and all-around liberal setups in the Western World, and look what Hitler did to that outfit.

Thank you again for sending me the pamphlet and knowing that you will take my beefing in the right spirit.

Sincerly, Rev. C.O. Rice

Can a Catholic Accept the Outstretched Hand of the Communist?

Rice was very active in public debates with Communist Party representatives who during the Popular Front period were anxious to make broad alliances with all forces that they viewed as "progressive." Rice was viewed as a particularly difficult antagonist because of his credibility in labor circles. The debates were spirited and well attended as Rice proved to be an articulate and forceful spokesman.

(Rev. Charles Owen Rice in the negative)

We cannot accept the outstretched hand of Communism because in doctrine and tactics we are diametrically opposed. We believe in, we

love, we try to serve Almighty God. We see in our fellow man the image of God and for that reason we affirm our respect for human personality. We affirm for the human person certain rights that can be violated by no power under heaven for any reason whatsoever. The state was made to serve man, not man the state.

We abhor class hatred and would conquer the world by love. We see that the present social system is a rotten mess and must be reformed. We do not lose our heads, but we say that this reform must come by just and equitable means.

We stand for progressive legislation, co-operative action, the right, nay, duty, of working men to organize in unions of their own choice.

We hold no brief for "malefactors of great wealth" nor for the type of Christian who gives lip service to Christ's doctrine, who is planted in the front pew on Sunday, and can hardly wait for Monday morning to take the axe to his fellow man.

(Clarence Hathaway for the affirmative)

Communists are working side by side with Catholics and with all other groups for the improvement of the economic and social well being of our country.

Why has this increasing cooperation come about? Certainly not because the Catholics in the progressive movement are ready to accept Communism. They are still opposing Communism. This cooperation is proceeding today because it is an urgent and unavoidable necessity. The forces of reaction and Fascism are threatening us alike on a world scale. When our trade unions are subjected to the activities of the employers, when wages are cut, when hours are lengthened; all workers regardless of their religion or lack of religion suffer alike. All workers feel the threat to their economic well being. These most common interests bring them together in their factories. It forces them to cooperate, one with the other. Common efforts to maintain and improve their living standards. Their actions are stronger than any forces that can be laid down by any political body. Workers naturally intend to unite and do unite. They are uniting on a national scale. . . .

The fact that many Catholic spokesmen ignore is that the world today is divided into two camps, Fascism on one hand and the forces of progressives on the other hand. They still insist that the issue is Communism vs. Catholicism. The communist movement is relatively small. Its adherents are not too numerous. They should not frighten anyone. We are making no threat to substitute Communism for the present social system. Such fundamental changes can only be made by the majority of American people and we Communists are not even approaching such a majority. Though the Communist Party has grown, we number today only some hundred thousand while the Catholic Church boasts 20 million in the Faith. Certainly our number compared to the number in the Church should not frighten any Catholic of the Communists. But the Church in American and on a world scale is justified in being frightened by the attacks of Fascism. In every country, where Fascism has achieved power, it not only crushes the communist, socialist, and the unions of the workers but also crushes the Church. The Catholics cannot ignore the persecution threat they have been subjected to in Germany and Italy. . . .

The communists are interested in the preservation of democracy. As long as the capitalist system must exist, we favor the democratic capitalist system. We urge the unity of all forces that are subject to Fascist destruction. ***Debate held on October 10, 1938***

▨ The Machine and Society (1939)

With the economy improving as industry gears up for the war that looms on the horizon, Rice writes a prescient article about technology and employment that prefigures his preoccupation with plant closings and worker dislocation nearly fifty years later.

It is typical of our muddleheaded society today that the New York World's Fair, having for its theme "The World of Tomorrow," has proceeded to ignore the problems that must be solved today if we are to have any tomorrow. The fair features mechanical and automatic marvels, advances of science. These are some of the cancer cells that have made our body politic vomit up its twelve million "normally" unemployed. There is nothing unusual or startling any more about these industrial "advances." What would be unusual would be an attempt at sensible control. I notice that attendance at the fair is far below expecta-tions. The people have sense. They want to see something new, and mechanical "doodads" that eliminate jobs and payrolls are decidedly "old hat.". . . .

Some startling statistics have been compiled by Harold Ruttenberg, research expert of the Steel Workers Organizing Committee, concerning the continuous hot and cold strip steel mill. This monstrosity might well be termed the machine to end all machines. As social-wrecker it can find no equal.

In 1926 the first continuous strip mill was put into operation; today there are 27. Not all of these are in operation as yet, nor are all the

Rice and Clarence Hathaway, editor of the Daily Worker, *after debate before more than 2,000 people, October 10, 1938*

old style hand mills eliminated. But is only a matter of a year or two until the changeover is complete. Some hand mills will be kept in operation to take care of small and special orders, but the bulk of them will be swept away.

Under normal conditions, 125,000 men were employed in the hand mills, the annual maximum capacity of which was 15,500,000 tons annually. The capacity of the 27 new continuous mills will be 14,000,000 tons annually. They are manned by 15,000. That is, 15,000 men will be able to do the work of 125,000.

Strip steel is being made considerably cheaper in terms of payroll costs. The effect this has on consuming power is quite obvious. The report of a record heat at the new Irvin mill shows that six men on an eight-hour shift turned out 447 tons of tin plate. Add seven men to shear to these six men and you get a payroll of about 110 dollars—110 consumption dollars as a result of this 447 tons. On a hand mill it would take 74 crews, 9 to a crew, and 50 shearmen and 100 openers, making 816 men to do in an eight-hour shift what 13 did at Irvin. The payroll for the old type would be 10,740 dollars, as against the new type's 110 dollars. Quite a difference in consuming power!

Founding convention of the Congress of Industrial Organizations (CIO) in Pittsburgh, November 14, 1938. On the stage: Cornelious D. Scully, mayor of Pittsburgh; John L. Lewis, president of United Mine Workers, and the CIO; Sidney Hillman, president of Amalgamated Textile Workers; and Rice

What is the justification that is given for this tremendous and wholesale sociological revolution? What are the reasons that induced the steel industry to mechanize? They are the same reasons that have caused machines to displace men in our industries. The primary one is the profit motive. The continuous mills have replaced the hand mills because it seems that more profit would thus accrue to the stockholders. With industry being conducted as it is today, it did not occur to anyone to consult the interests of the workers. Profits, as a matter of course, were sought first; the welfare of the workers and the communities in which steel mills are located were consulted secondarily, if at all.

After the fact, certain justifications are being offered. The old Liberal explanation that advances in mechanization reduce prices and thus make for a wider market is trotted out. This and certain kindred arguments that are given add up, in my opinion, to wishful thinking. The only reality in the situation is profits; the process that will make for the most profits is used. It is then hoped that the matter will adjust itself—the workers will find other jobs—and so on.

When we were an expanding economy that may have been so. But now we are a mature economy. People who are supposed to be hard-headed are waiting hopefully for new industries and new inventions to solve the problem. The automobile and electrical advances helped us out of a few bad holes in the past. It is being vaguely hoped that something else will turn up: that the masterminds of industry, or perhaps the automatic processes of trade, will pull a rabbit out of the hat.

The new labor-saving steel making devices have abolished occupations—they have put men on the street. They have not reduced prices substantially; they have not made new jobs. Their use has brought nothing that I know of except grave sociological and moral harm.

The Steel Workers Organizing Committee came on the field too late. When this union was organized the damage was already done. During its brief life it had devoted more intelligent study to the problem of mechanization than the steel management has for generations. But it does not go far enough. Even Harold Ruttenberg, in his writings, hesitates to come right out and say we must control the machine. So do most of the other writers on the subject. I don't imagine many of these writers would shrink at the danger of being called "Red" or "radical," but they quail at the epithet "moss back," "medievalist," etc.

Well, I don't quail at either epithet. I say, "Let us reverse the process." Rather let us put first things first. The important thing is not the making of profits. It is not the turning out of more cheaper and better products. No, it is the proper sociological and moral use of the instruments of industry. The machine must serve the common good. When it is being debated whether or not to install new machinery the decision should hinge on the welfare of the workers and the community as a whole. There are no inevitable laws of economics left —the depression has repealed them all.

What a topsy-turvy world we live in! The psychological attitudes of the day see nothing fearful in the interference with the laws of God and nature, for instance, in the matters of birth control, euthanasia, sterilization, etc. But we are in thrall to the machine. People who would curb populations by putting into effect untried, unproven and unscientific Malthusian theories hesitate to interfere with the machine. They shrink from any suggestion that we curb the machine or that we interfere with inventions and inventive trends.

We have solved the crude problem of making machines. The infinitely harder problem of fitting machinery into our lives has hardly been approached. Those poor "light-weights" in New York who are exulting over gadgets and machinery are cheering a race that is over. The real contest is on another track.

My final word. Let us stop for a moment and think. Then with courage let us do the logical thing. The machine must be controlled.

PITTSBURGH CATHOLIC
June 22, 1939

Against Prejudice

The Catholic Radical Alliance targeted work on behalf of the Negro from its inception. Support for the African-American community would be a consistent theme of Rice's writings. He also attacked Father Coughlin, America's most famous radio priest, for anti-Semitism and spoke out against anti-Jewish acts in Pittsburgh before and during World War Two.

Catholic Contempt of the Negro Must End (1938)

A writer . . . remarked that the attitude of the average Catholic toward the Negro is one of indifference. He is wrong. The attitude of the average Catholic toward the Negro is one of a hostility which is often so pronounced that it is hatred. . . .

Where in God's name is the Christian charity of the Catholic who mouths in rage concerning what should be done to the Colored man who approaches a dance floor? Who heartily and vocally approves of the barbarous restrictions placed on the Negro in the uncivilized South?

There are over ten million Negroes in the United States. About one-fortieth of them are Catholic. This race needs Catholicity. And the Church in America needs this race. But Catholicity can never be carried to the Negro until our people change their abominable attitude. . . .

Every individual Catholic in the United States is responsible for the Negro's conversion or lack of it. Every Catholic, who harbors hate of the Negro in his savage heart, sins against God and man. He helps drive away the souls thirsting for the blood of the Redeemer. He is doing his bit as the devil's helper in obscuring the truth from eager seekers. . . .

It is safe to say that a majority of the Catholics in the United States is of Irish descent. Irish Catholics have tasted the bitterest dregs of persecution. They have battled through the horror of the penal days. They of all people should be friends of the underdog. But they are not. They have borrowed the race prejudice of the Anglo-Saxon and made it their own. The contemptuous dislike in the Irish-American hearts, the Godless expression of hatred on Irish-American lips must cause Erin's saints and martyrs to hide their faces for very shame in the high court of heaven.

Let us end this disgrace. Before we Irish Catholics say "Back to the gutter, you black _____" let us in all humility recollect that once in New York and Boston there were signs "No Irish need apply."

Before any Catholic says "The Negro must keep his place," let him find out what right he or any other lump of the slime of the earth has to assign any race to an inferior place. Christ has something to say about those who pick the highest place for themselves and leave the lower places for others. They end up in the lowest place. In God's providence, we shall see black faces shining high above us in Heaven, if we haters of men manage to get there.

PITTSBURGH CATHOLIC
August 1, 1938

Catholics and Anti-Semitism

We live in an unusual country . . . in a great country. It is not our great wealth, nor is it our power that makes us so uniquely great. No! The quality that makes us great and which will make historians remember us is our great freedom and toleration.

Rice with two altar boys, Dukie Pratt and Willie Hyatt, at the House of Hospitality, ca. 1941

Now bear in mind that I am not claiming that the spectre of intolerance has never raised its head in our fair land. It has. There has been both racial, national and religious discrimination. In each case, thank God, it has blown over in time. . . . Take the KKK excitement for instance. We Catholics took the brunt of that. We were angry and upset over it, at the time. Looking back at it, now that it is over, we see it as a spasmodic upheaval that cleared the air and wasn't so bad after all. A wonderful thing about it was the way in which many Protestants went right down the line for their Catholic and Jewish brethren on this issue. Even in the deep South men risked their public careers to oppose the mob and proclaim their belief in the American Way.

This causes me to reflect on the fact that the American Way of tolerance and freedom has made our nation a place where my beloved Catholic Church has been able to flourish and grow. It makes me love America more and more to realize that this nation founded in the main by Protestants, has been true to the principles of tolerance that under God, its makers subscribed to.

Today another wave of intolerance is rising. I hope it will just be another of those spasmodic upheavals due to recede of itself. However there are indications that it will be more than that if permitted to get out of control. There is a menacing parallel with what has happened in other countries.

The victims in this case are the members of the Jewish race. It is particularly sad that they are being harassed here when their brothers in race and religion are being hounded and harried in so many other parts of the world.

As a Catholic I regret to note that among Catholics, whom I know, anti-Semitism, as it is called, is quite strong. I am more than sorry that some of my fellow religionists see fit to vent hatred on the blood brothers of Our Lord and Savior Jesus Christ.

I ask you for a moment to analyze your feelings toward the Jew. If as a result of propaganda, you are against him, reflect! Is there anything of hatred in your attitude? If there is, you are committing a mortal sin, whether you realize it or not. You can't hate a group any more than you can hate a person. All men are our brothers. God made them all. He destined them all for salvation. . . .

Let us be frank and get down to cases. In many instances, dislike of the Jew is founded on traits possessed by the Jews which grate on other nationalities. All right—so the Jew has traits that we may not like. Every race and nationality have traits that irritate other ethnic groups. Admitting that other nationalities and races irritate us, we can't hate them. It is the American way that we accept every race, overlooking their faults, trusting them to overlook ours, and knowing that all our national and racial irritations will be purified in the crucible of American life.

The Jew is intensely active mentally and physically—and financially. Some people resent that. Isn't much of this resentment just sublimated jealousy? We know people who tell us how some Jew got the better of them in a deal? Maybe they were trying to beat the Jew. "You can't cheat an honest man," you know.

The Jew's intellectual activity has got him into more than one tough spot. Many people who have gone to Red or Pinkish meetings have reported that an unusually high proportion of the audience was Jewish. Well, they would have to say the same if they went to the symphony concerts, the good plays, etc.

Communism is a great stick to beat the Jews. I know from my own experience in labor that the strongest fighters against Communism are Jews. Yet these valiant fighters for Americanism are themselves accused of being Communists because they have Jewish names. It is very stupid and laughable but very dangerous and harmful.

I could go from specific complaint to specific complaint, but I think it best to lay down the simple rule that governs them all. It is the Christian and American rule of love and tolerance. You violate that rule when you assume that any one race is evil. For a Catholic to hold this is for him to commit grave sin. The Jews are not an evil race. It is not good theology to fasten a curse on them. Christ's blood fell not on the race, but on the group responsible for the death and the surge of intolerance that brought it about.

It is poppy-cock to prate of the Jews killing Christ. We killed Christ; our sins did it. The Jew has no monopoly on sin and has no monopoly on the guilt for Christ's death. Of all the sins that tortured Christ on the cross be it noted, among the most excruciating were the sins of hatred and intolerance perpetrated upon His people in His name.

Jews are our brothers. We Catholics love the Blessed Virgin Mary more than we love any other created person. With some of us, our love for her is so real and personal that it is greater than the love we bear for any living persons. She was a little Jewish girl when God made her his mother in the obscure Jewish village of Nazareth.

In previous broadcasts I stressed that charity works both ways. It helps him who receives, but most of all it helps him who gives. Hatred and uncharity works the same way in reverse. Hatred may harm the one to whom it is directed. Most of all it harms the one who hates.

Do not deprive yourself and your Church of spiritual strength by harboring hatred against anyone under whatever guise, or whatever noble, impassioned, empurpled phraseology.

Radio address on station WWSW,
August 7, 1939
PITTSBURGH CATHOLIC
August 17, 1939

Why Aid England?

As Rice became more fully aware of the horrors committed by the Nazi regime against Jews, and totally disgusted by the Hitler-Stalin pact, he began to move away from an antiwar position toward support for England's struggle for survival. As a well-known Irish Catholic spokesperson, he quickly became an important voice speaking out against isolationism.

. . . Let me inform you frankly at the outset of my talk that I advocate every possible and necessary aid for England in the present war. I submit that I cannot be, in justice, called either a warmonger, a capitalistic imperialist or a lover of England. I, who advise aid to Britain, am a lover of peace, a friend of the worker and the poor, an enemy of the abuses of capitalism, a life-long critic of the British Empire and supporter of Ireland in her fight against that Empire.

Let me develop the last item first. From earliest boyhood I have been instilled with a deep-felt anger and disgust at England's treatment of Ireland over the centuries. Myself and my relatives have consistently taken part, in our humble way, in the struggle of Ireland for absolute independence. A few illustrations:

Some twelve years ago Eamon de Valera, now head of the Irish government, visited

Pittsburgh. I chauffeured him around in the family car. When, about five years ago, Sean Russell, head of the outlawed Irish Republican Army, visited here, he was my guest—he had few other supporters in this country. Several articles from my halting pen in defense of Ireland's position have appeared in the past in national magazines.

Why have I taken pains to establish my love and contact with Ireland? I'll tell you. It's because there are those who malign any supporter of England in this war as an Anglophile, a dupe and a tool of the British interests. Let me say, calmly and mildly, that I defy any one so to charge me.

The fair-minded American of Irish birth or descent, or any other birth or descent for that matter, must admit the following:

This war is not between England and Ireland. Factually, the sympathies of most Irishmen now living in Ireland lie with England in this struggle. And the best interests of Ireland lie with England, also. Ireland has come close to complete freedom, in a German-dominated Europe she would be just another vassal state. . . .

Of course, England does not come into the war with an entirely clean record. But bungling, heartless, cruel and brutal as she has been toward Ireland and others in the past, in recent decades she has tempered her attitude, and has been reasonably humane–although still stupid enough as regards Ireland. At any rate Ireland and India and the others were getting somewhere in the direction of freedom and justice—it would be tragedy for the small nations and the subject peoples of the earth to have to come to grips with a new, fresh, incredibly ruthless and efficient tyranny.

England for all her faults, and they are many, has stood for democracy and freedom in the main, albeit she has often been inconsistent and hypocritical. And under her, freedom has progressed. Don't let us forget that there have not been lacking Englishmen in every generation who have loved Ireland and fought for her and for other victims of injustice.

As for the Nazis—from my reading, from the writings of top-flight Nazis themselves, from personal contact with those who have seen and suffered at firsthand, from scanning the anguished protests of two Popes and many Cardinals and Bishops, I am deeply and firmly convinced that Naziism constitutes the most coldly efficient, heartless and brutal enemy that democracy, freedom, decency and Christianity have ever known. Just as with marvelous efficiency and success the Nazis undermined the will and courage, and defeated the armies of the continent of Europe, so they have proceeded and are proceeding to destroy religion and stamp out the image of God in the hearts of men under their sway.

As Americans and Christians we must resist with all our strength of heart, soul and body the propaganda and the armed might of the scourge of the world.

Bishop Hurley, Catholic Bishop of St. Augustine, Florida, is one who speaks from a firsthand knowledge. Until recently he was attached to the Department of State of the

> **"I am deeply and firmly convinced that Naziism constitutes the most coldly efficient, heartless and brutal enemy that democracy, freedom, decency and Christianity have ever known."**

Vatican, in Rome. He says: "Today, the first enemy of our humanity—the killers of our priests, the despoilers of our temples, the foe of all we love both as Americans and Catholics—is the Nazi."

We, of whatever racial origin, must face this problem as Americans. Our question is, what is best for America and for human freedom, religious freedom and political freedom and ideals that are part and parcel of our way of life? Who can hesitate to say that what is best and necessary for all these is defeat of Nazi Germany and victory for her foes?

War-monger you say? Listen! Until nearly two years ago I was a loud shouter for appeasement and peace at nearly any price. I was against those who wanted to rearm the United States and I yelled about war profiteers. I was a consistent and bitter opponent of the League of Nations and the World Court, an isolationist from heel to toe. I was the local promoter of the Catholic League for International Peace, and three years ago helped stage a large Catholic peace rally in this city.

There were countless like me then, living in the past and enjoying an orgy of wishful thinking. Hitler's deliberate breach of his promises at Munich started to wise us up. The Soviet-Nazi pact completed the process and we got really alarmed, almost too late, when the fat was in the fire. Many of us who supported President Roosevelt in virtually everything else had been strong against his foreign policy up to then. We came to our senses barely in time. There are all too many who, for one reason or another, still cannot see the realities of the situation. They regard propaganda as truth and truth as propaganda. There are some who let ancient hates, and outmoded habits of debunking govern their thoughts on the war. . . .

*Radio address on
station WWSW, Pittsburgh, 1940*

Poland's Mighty Role (1942)

As the strength and skill of the Russian army continues to stand up against the hitherto irresistible Nazi war machine, giving the United States and England time they otherwise would not have to build up their fighting array, it becomes apparent that when Hitler is finally overcome a great share of the credit will have to be given to the Soviets. Will Communism thus acquire a position that will make it a dominant force in the world? There would be grave reason for believing so, were it not for the fact that it is not Communism that is waging war against the Nazis, but the Russian people, with their devotion to their land and their national traditions. And the position of Poland offers further reassurance that while Russia will emerge powerful and respected from the terrible test it is now undergoing, it will not be the Russia of the Comintern and the "Internationale" but a Russia with roots deep in Christian soil.

There is something mysterious, one might say holy, about Poland's role in this conflict. When there was an earlier assault on Christian civilization Poland bore the brunt of it, was nearly wiped out, but saved the west from the pagan hordes. That same country suffered the first assault of the present savagery, and now lies prostrate; yet its relations with Russia have brought that country into the war on the right side, there is now the closest cooperation between the Polish leaders and those of Russia, and there are definite indications that the relationship has already mitigated the anti-religious spirit which Communism brought to the Soviets. "Watch Poland," will be a wise admonition to follow, as the great drama of this war unfolds. Her role bids fair to again be that of civilization's savior.

PITTSBURGH CATHOLIC
July 9, 1942

*Anti-Communist Riot at Carnegie Hall
North Side, Pittsburgh, April 2, 1949*

CHRONOLOGY

☎ 1941
June 22, Nazi Germany invades Soviet Russia. December 7, the Japanese launch a surprise attack on Pearl Harbor. United States responds with a declaration of war.

☎ 1942
August 3, Rice is appointed rent control director for the city of Pittsburgh.

☎ 1946
September 24, the 27- day Duquesne Power strike begins.

☎ 1947
June 26, Rice begins his series of columns, "The Condition of Labor," in the *Pittsburgh Catholic*.

☎ 1949
April 2, an anti-Communist riot erupts at the Carnegie Hall in Pittsburgh's North Side.

☎ 1949
In autumn, the United Electrical Workers Union (UE) withdraws, and then is expelled from the CIO over the issue of communism. A rival union, the International Union of Electrical Workers (IUE) is chartered at the national CIO convention.

☎ 1950
February 7, Joseph McCarthy, an obscure junior senator from Wisconsin, addresses a Lincoln Day gathering of Republican women in Wheeling, West Virginia. He claims to be holding a list of 205 Communists working in the U.S. State Department. The speech opens a politically and socially divisive campaign now known as "McCarthyism."

☎ 1952
In December, after the arrival of Bishop John Dearden, Rice is exiled upriver to the town of Natrona. Two years later, when the diocese for the first time assumes direct control of the *Pittsburgh Catholic*, Rice's column, is discontinued.

Reds and Workers 1941–1959

3

☰ Lewis, Murray, and the CIO (1960)

By the time Philip Murray became the president of the CIO in 1940, he and Rice had developed a relationship of friendship and mutual respect. Murray's home was in the south Pittsburgh neighborhood of Brookline, and when he was in town the two would meet for lunch. Both men were intensely Catholic and were united in their loyalty to Roosevelt. It took some time, however, before Murray came around to sharing Rice's deep concern about the dangers of Communist influence in union affairs.

When Philip Murray was elected president of the Congress of Industrial Organizations in December, 1940, the big news story was not that he had stepped up, but that John L. Lewis had stepped down. Lewis had cut a great figure, rivalling even the towering Franklin D. Roosevelt in public stature, and while his fame was now beginning to diminish, it was still great. Murray, on the other hand, was known mostly as a lieutenant of Lewis, a warm and friendly man of integrity, but no giant. Observers, even the informed ones, could be pardoned for not realizing that they were witnesses of a profound change of roles and a significant and lasting transfer of powers.

Murray was destined to assume immediate and firm command of the CIO and so to conduct its affairs and himself, as to dominate the entire labor scene for more than a decade in a fashion that even the formidable Lewis had not equalled; while Lewis, in these same years, an embittered man, would recede in importance, appearing on stage infrequently, expressing in national affairs merely a special minority point of view and, in labor, representing only a segment. . . .

In that prewar winter of 1940 when Lewis handed the scepter to Murray, the men had not become enemies but they were no longer at complete ease with each other; a wariness had crept into their friendship. Here was a strange transfer. Lewis was giving up the presidency of the CIO ostensibly because he had said he would do so if the workers did not follow him to vote against Roosevelt in the national election. There is evidence that he actually no longer wanted to be head of the CIO, which had lost momentum and was in difficulties, but he apparently did not want to give up all control. Murray accepted the transfer only after the most solemn assurances that he was to be his own man and could be this while retaining Lewis's friendship. Lewis apparently had no idea of what would happen when Murray took over and he evidently no longer knew Murray, because the younger man had changed, and was a stronger and bigger man than the one Lewis thought he knew so well. . . .

In many ways this transfer of power was most fitting and useful. In the very earliest CIO days (only five years before) Lewis's roaring dash and dramatic confrontations were needed and sufficient. The workers had to have an arrogant and swashbuckling champion if they were to throw off their fears and hesitancies and rush into the new industrial unions. There was a timidity in the hearts of many of those millions, who had not known the confidence that comes from union membership; but they forgot their timidity and followed this latter day Danton as he stormed the barricades with unquenchable audacity. In that fight against the entrenched corporations, finesse and responsibility were not too important—daring and action were.

Unfortunately Lewis, the audacious, had little knack or stomach for the arts of conciliating and nursing along; and the CIO's millions came to need someone who would hold them together, knit their leaders closer, allay suspicion and charm away factionalism. The earlier days of organizing the unorganized were simpler and easier. A more complex, more patient and more constructive leader was the requirement, and happily for the CIO, Philip Murray met the requirement to the full.

Lewis had reached an impasse. His great

> **"One might say that [Lewis] and Roosevelt were demi-gods, and [Lewis] had, for reasons of his own, turned on the other demi-god [Roosevelt] , had with temerity met him on his own grounds, national politics, and been soundly defeated."**

CIO triumphs had come as he rode the wave of the New Deal. One might say that he and Roosevelt were demi-gods, and he had, for reasons of his own, turned on the other demi-god, had with temerity met him on his own grounds, national politics, and been soundly defeated. At the moment he was more interested in vendettas than crusades and the CIO could ill afford his adventures. Murray on the other hand refused to make the quarrel with Roosevelt his own and, in fact, remained passionately committed both to the New Deal and Roosevelt. He did not want to stand still and wanted to prod the waning New Deal into additional services to organized labor; but as a realist he knew that his fortunes and those of the CIO lay with FDR. Four years later he put it bluntly, as to a cheering pre-election rally he proclaimed "all our eggs are in this one basket."

There was more involved than the domestic fortunes of the industrial labor unions, because, as the days of social turmoil were ending, international affairs were crowding everything else off the stage. This was a new situation presenting a new set of dangers and opportunities; calling for a complete change in strategy. Here Lewis stumbled as he took a stand against Roosevelt and international commitment. Whether it was peevish reaction or whether it stemmed from an atavistic turning to old fashioned mid-western isolationism is immaterial, because it was deep seated and all consuming. It was aggravated by the fact that the strong Communist machine inside the CIO was temporarily in loud and energetic support of Lewis's isolationism and was damning Roosevelt's concern for the threatened world.

***Franklin D. Roosevelt opens Terrace Village housing project in Pittsburgh, October 11, 1940.
Rice looks on in upper left.***

Had Lewis remained in command of the CIO, he would almost certainly have shattered it as he attacked without restraint, first, the internationalist drift, and then war mobilization. One can only judge from what he did with the Mine Workers, whose control he retained. As war threatened, he was rabidly and continuously isolationist in his speeches. During the war, he conducted a series of stormy negotiations with the mine operators

61

Pat Fagan, Rice, and Eleanor Roosevelt in 1940

and the government. He would not accept war-time restrictions on wage increases and other benefits. With superb, but ill-timed, brinkmanship he came to the verge of strike several times and once he actually struck. In peace this would have been taken as just normal hard-boiled labor relations but in war it was extremely dangerous. Since Lewis controlled only a segment of the movement, his intransigence could be passed over; had he controlled the entire CIO and had he managed to push its constituent unions into uninhibited and aggressive industrial conflict, it could have meant destruction of the unions and serious interference with the war effort.

On the other hand, Murray's patriotism and good sense led him to a sound new strategy and his reaction to the crises helped both the war effort and the unions. He merged his two loyalties; union and nation. He and his followers put the nation first and labor disputes were almost non-existent. As a reward the CIO unions were handed concessions by the government that it would have taken them years of haggling and striking to get from industry. The CIO emerged from the war period high in prestige and firm in structure—with different handling it could have been damaged beyond repair.

There is every reason to believe that John L. Lewis did not comprehend the change in the times, nor mark the close of an era. With the end of the thirties and the half realized promise of the New Deal, social reform had lost its dynamic and ceased to light the eyes and lift the hopes of the young and the earnest. Even without the war the New Deal would have waned, but the onrush of global conflict made for a sudden stop and called for the most abrupt of transitions.

Murray knew the minds of the ruling American powers and he was party to their inner councils. He was in tune with the overwhelming majority of the country's intellectuals and thoughtful leaders of business and politics. He also knew the temper of the workers; as always, his reasoning was in harmony with theirs.

Poor John L. could be forgiven for wanting to live a little longer in the glorious and simple days of the middle thirties, those days when he exercised command in exciting and decisive fashion. When other labor leaders were asleep, he was wide awake, while they hesitated and bickered, he dashed ahead. He was largely responsible for planting labor unions in the forbidding industrial citadels that had grown up non-union and open shop and had crushed every previous attempt at organization of their workers. At that time he had sensed the mood of the people and seized the chance to smash through with a commitment of all resources. His strategy was brilliant, as he massed everything that he had, or could muster, and roared ahead. In one year's time he formed the Committee for Industrial Organization (CIO) of the AFL, and got viable unions in being in six major industries.

His stature in those glorious days justifiably grew to gigantic proportions. He was a power in politics, the greatest single figure in labor, a social lion in Washington, his name was dropped by the leading droppers: a legend in his own lifetime. And, at the moment we are considering, he was in process of throwing nearly all of this away.

Lewis had earned his title of hero and the name of his CIO became magic. In the darkness of depression, and after decades of company domination, there was a new breath of freedom. In that day the CIO was not just an organization, it was a living idea. It spoke of hope and victory. Here was the embodiment of the dignity of the common man. How it fired the imaginations of millions of workers and gave them their first delicious taste of industrial liberty! Every worker in an industry regardless of his skill, or lack of it, regardless of his race or nationality, was welcomed into the CIO, was given full equality and participation, and was drawn into a crusade that had clear objectives and equally clear opponents. The members of this crusade were enriched with a fine supply of villains and heroes. Franklin Delano Roosevelt and John L. Lewis stood about equal in the pantheon of heroes. Phil Murray was a lesser hero; but a well known one. The villains were bankers and industrialists, company controlled sheriffs and police, all the malefactors of great wealth and entrenched privilege, and their miserable lackeys.

Oh! It was simple and wonderful, one of those rare times when the world was full of good things to be done and bad things to be undone, and with the marvelous possibility of a final breakthrough to a sort of earthly paradise.

The reality was not quite so glorious as the dream, but the reality was, nevertheless, solid enough. Justice for all was the aim, the honest aim—justice in an orderly and decent society. Progress in that direction was discernible, since victories, material and of the spirit, had already been won. That the workers had lost their fear and gained confidence in sincere and reliable champions who could cure the social and economic sickness of the nation, was an imposing spiritual victory by itself. The existence of unions where none had been, and the steady improvement of wages and conditions of employment were practical manifestations of the victories of the spirit. . . .

EXCERPTS FROM "PHIL MURRAY,"
AN UNPUBLISHED MANUSCRIPT,
JUNE 2, 1960

East Pittsburgh (1941)

Beginning in 1941, Rice launched a brief but intense foray into union politics over the communist issue. Rooted in pre-existing union factional struggles and fueled by Communist party shifts in policy toward the European conflict, the episode would prefigure the epic struggle of the post World War II period.

New Communist Line (1941)

Members of the Communist Party in America for the past two years have been violently anti-war. In the American trade union movement they have hampered the defense effort and have been a big factor in the wildcat defense strikes that have slowed down our re-armament effort. They have shown themselves to be utterly disloyal to the United States and loyal only to Communism and Soviet Russia.

Germany is now fighting Russia. We may expect the Communists to execute another brazen about-face. They will be super-patriots. They will become avid partisans of the aid-Britain and speed re-armament movement. They will set out to fool the loyal workers of the nation into thinking that they have democracy's best interests at heart.

As chaplain of Pittsburgh's Association of Catholic Trade Unionists, as a proven foe of Communism and a friend of Labor, I solemnly warn the workers of the Pittsburgh district to have nothing to do with the Communists or their stooges. They are going to resurrect the Popular Front. We must for the good of America and the trade union movement, absolutely refuse to co-operate with them or their stooge organizations. Stooge patriotic groups, Communist controlled, will spring up like mushrooms.

The battle against Communists in the labor movement, locally and nationally, must go on. As far as I and my organization are concerned it will go on, until Communism becomes the negligible factor it deserves to be. In East Pittsburgh, New Kensington and other danger spots we will not relax our efforts.

*PITTSBURGH CATHOLIC, ACTU
(ASSOCIATION OF CATHOLIC TRADE
UNIONISTS) COLUMN*
June 26, 1941

Westinghouse and Reds Again (1941)

The giant Westinghouse Local 601 of the United Electrical, Radio and Machine Workers of America, held a significant meeting last Sunday. Communism is very much the issue in this local, and in an election for delegates to the union's national convention, eight out of ten members endorsed by the "Reds" were elected. Only two men of the opposition slate made the grade. This is tragic, because it is well known, in labor circles, that the "Red" element of the Electrical Workers' Union, is out to "get Carey" at the national convention.

James B. Carey, youthful international president of the union, is a practicing Catholic and an anti-Red. Local 610 in Wilmerding, under the aegis of Albert Smith, has already declared against Carey. If 601 moves against Carey it may tip the balance against him, and place the entire international under complete domination of the "boys of Moscow."

Not all the men on what is called the "RED" slate are Communists or Communist-dominated. At least one is a good Catholic, a popular natural leader, whom the Communists are playing up to.

Rice on picket line. West Penn Hospital strike, ca. 1941.

Straight Shooting (1941)

If 601 and eventually the whole international union are to be rescued from the Stalinites, it will be done via plain speaking and straight shooting. The issue will have to be clearly drawn between the Americans and the friends of the Soviet Union. That there is definite hope for 601, is to be found in the fact that the American Youth Congress was rejected by a fairly substantial majority at the same meet-

ing which saw the "Red" slate successful.

This indicates that 601 is still full of good Americans, who do the right thing when they "see it plain."

PITTSBURGH CATHOLIC, ACTU
July 17, 1941

Brazenness (1941)

The best word that can describe the actions of some of our Communist friends is "brazen," for brazen they are. A neat little example of this brazenness was shown at a meeting of District No. 6 of the UERMWA (United Electrical, Radio and Machine Workers of America or UE). The Communistically inclined people in labor had sniped assiduously at Philip Murray and at his policies until Soviet Russia and Germany began to fight and the "Reds" in this country began to like America again, because America was helping Russia.

Philip Murray has supported the President's program from the start. The "Bolos" have not liked this up till recently. They like it now, and, consequently we find Charles Newell of Local No. 601, proposing that District No. 6 go on record as endorsing Murray's Industrial Council plan. This plan has been kicking around a long while and Mr. Newell just discovered its merits the other day. A coincidence no doubt.

PITTSBURGH CATHOLIC, ACTU
August 28, 1941

Carey (1941)

Nationally, about the most significant union news of the past several days has been the defeat of James B. Carey as international president of the United Electrical, Radio and Machine Workers' Union. Carey backed an anti-Communist resolution and also backed an interpretation of the union's constitution holding that local unions had the power to exclude Communists from office. Both Carey and his proposition were defeated. This puts a group, frankly friendly to Communism, into the strongest position of any such group in the United States.

Control of the destinies of 232,000 workers is really something. Time will show us how this control is exercised.

PITTSBURGH CATHOLIC, ACTU
September 11, 1941

Stormy Weather (1941)

Local 601 of the electrical workers is still having its stormy moments. A very important general election is being held, by mail. The first ballots were mailed about ten days ago, and the last ones must be mailed by tomorrow. Two strong slates of candidates are in the field. There has been some neat pamphleteering on both sides.

One slate, headed by William Simpson and Charles Kelly, charges that the other slate, headed by Charles Newell and Margaret Darin, is Communistically controlled and dominated. In turn Darin and Newell assert that Simpson and Kelly are dominated and controlled by (of all things) the ACTU, and that furthermore the ACTU is directing their campaign.

Joseph Goney issued an unhedging denial that the ACTU had anything to do with the fight. He said the ACTU was keeping out of it specifically because of certainty that any ACTU participation would be the signal for Communistic elements to start stirring up religious bitterness. Goney also pointed out that he had seen no evidence linking the ACTU chaplain with the fight.

Your chaplain has been somewhat flattered by the attention he has received in this elec-

tion. He has been bracketed in importance with Joe Stalin. One side says "Stalin is running our opponents." The other side says: "Father Rice is running our opponents, which is much worse."

PITTSBURGH CATHOLIC, ACTU
December 11, 1941

More Victories (1942)

This week, in the Westinghouse Local 601 of the United Electrical Workers, a sort of mop-up victory was scored by the forces of right order.

Michael Fitzpatrick, who was seeking re-election as chairman of the Stewards' Council, has in the past, unfortunately associated himself too closely with Communistic elements in the union. At times he has been their mouth piece. He used his chairmanship of the Stewards' Council to "sound off" on matters of general union policy which should have been touched only by the president of the local. But Fitzpatrick and his entire ticket were defeated on Tuesday at the re-organization meeting of the Stewards' Council by a little better than three to two vote. Around 200 of the 300 stewards in Local 601 voted.

Communism can be defeated in American unions no matter how strongly it has entrenched itself and even when Communists are riding a wave of quasi-popularity. All that is needed is a straight-forward and well organized campaign, without mud slinging and invective.

The leaders of the loyal American workers in Westinghouse deserve to be congratulated. They have done a fine job of eliminating outside influence from their mammoth local.

PITTSBURGH CATHOLIC, ACTU
January 8, 1942

Communists and the CIO

Rice would direct a broad-based campaign against Communists in the CIO. While his major impact would be on the electrical workers' union, he lobbied behind the scenes with union leaders and was deeply involved in the struggle on the national as well as the local level.

Who Put Them In? (1942)

. . . Until June 22, 1941, the Communists could count on John L. [Lewis] to back them in a pinch. He and his daughter never failed them. Most of the CIO strength that the Reds have today came because John planned it that way.

Rice as union spokesman in 1946 Steel Strike

A Catholic Priest Speaks Out FOR THE Steelworkers

Philip Murray, on the contrary, always opposed the Communists. It is significant that in the Steel Workers Union the few Communist organizers were quickly ferreted out and quietly dropped. Shortly after Murray became the big factor in Automobiles, the Commies began to take a shellacking. If the war didn't happen to be on, the Communists would be almost wiped out in the CIO. That is, they would either go or behave. As Communists they couldn't behave.

Since Pearl Harbor, there are more important things than leading a crusade against Red elements in the CIO, that is, as far as the top drawer is concerned. Such a crusade by the higherups might really impede war production. Since Hitler's invasion of Russia this time last year, the Reds have behaved, because now the Soviet policy is to have the United States in the war and as efficient as possible. They are fooling nobody, least of all Phil Murray. But Murray is a wise, patriotic citizen with a sense of timing that surpasses that possessed even by most very wise men. He makes no false moves and wastes no motions. . . .

Up until the invasion of Russia, the Reds were John Lewis' chief cohorts, sniping at Murray, sneering at his support of the Defense effort, and organizing opposition to him all down the line. Lewis' District 50 was full of them. They were hired by his closest friends and relatives. After the invasion, the Reds waited impatiently for a while for John L. to swing into line. They waited just so long and then they opened up on him. They lined up behind Murray and his wholehearted support of Roosevelt — not for the sake of Murray, Roosevelt or the United States, but for the sake of Josef Stalin and the Soviet Union.

PITTSBURGH CATHOLIC
June 25, 1942

Letters to a Friend (1946)

OCTOBER 30, 1946
Rev. Benjamin L. Masse, S.J.
Executive Editor
The Catholic Mind
329 West 108th Street
New York City (25) N.Y.

Dear Ben:

I saw Phil [Murray] the other day and had quite a talk. We did not go deeply into the Communistic Issue. It seems to me as if he is coming around.

When we talked some months ago we went into every phase and angle. At the time I did not think I did much good, but I believe what I had to say sank in. Even though he parried my every argument, I believe it was effective. Vin Sweeney is a great battler against Communism. His influence is very effective.

The eradication of Communism is not a simple matter. If it were, the A.F. of L. would stamp out Communism in its sore spots, namely: New York City and the C.S.U. in Hollywood. We will have to string along with Phil and hope that his campaign to cut them down, gradually, will bear fruit.

The most we can hope for, at the moment, is a steady concentrated campaign within the Unions against the Communist influence. The terrific campaign being waged by the miners and the A.F. of L. to destroy the CIO will force Murray to go cautiously. He has to move with caution and I think it would be a harmful thing for the country if the CIO were destroyed, even with its Communist drawbacks the CIO is a very necessary part of the American Labor movement. If the CIO were to go down, a lot of freshness, honesty and good Liberalism will go out of the Labor movement and out of American life. The Labor gangster would be strengthened.

Phil, God help him, has to figure all these angles and balance one thing against another. He has no easy task as we both recognize.
Sincerely Yours,
COR

NOVEMBER 11, 1946
Dear Ben:

I, too, have had the feeling that Phil regarded Communism as a sort of lunatic fringe of Liberalism, etc. However, Sweeney has worked hard on him and I think he has seen the Light.

All indications are now that he has set his face against The Brethren.
COR
Archives of Industrial Society,
University of Pittsburgh

An Exchange with Harry Bridges (1948)

The following correspondence between Harry Bridges, president of the International Longshoremen's & Warehousemen's Union, and your humble servant seems too good to keep quiet. The letter to Bridges was mailed last week. So there can be no discourtesy in its unilateral publication at this time:

Reverend Father Charles Owen Rice
Joseph's House of Hospitality
Pittsburgh, Pennsylvania

Dear Father Rice:
I am writing you with respect to your handbook of instructions to members of the A.C.T.U., entitled 'How To Decontrol Your Union Of Communists.'

In this handbook I notice on the back page that you state: 'If your union is one of these listed below — your local union is in the hands of Communists.' Below that statement is a list of unions and the ILWU is included in that list.

I would appreciate a statement from you giving your reasons why you list the ILWU as a Communist controlled union. If you wish, I will make your reply available to our membership.

I hope you will in all fairness comply with this request.

Very truly yours,
Harry Bridges, President

JULY 22, 1948
Mr. Harry Bridges
International Longshoremen's
and Warehousemen's Union
1500 Golden Gate Avenue
San Francisco 2, California

Dear Mr. Bridges:

I have received your letter of July 17. You asked me why I listed the ILWU as a Communist controlled union. My chief reason for listing the ILWU as a Communist controlled union is that you control it.

The record of yourself and your international union has been one of consistent support of the Communist party line.

Let me give you an example or two: I remember talking to you at the 1940 CIO convention in Atlantic City. At that time you were isolationist and anti-war. You supported strikers at North American Aviation and so on. You made no secret of your views, but you shouted them from the house top. It was an imperialist war, you told me that day, and you said it was wrong.

On June 21, 1941, Hitler invaded Russia. That changed the war for you and it became a democratic, a people's war. You were so enthusiastic for the war when it was Russia's war that you cooperated with the bosses. You promoted a no-strike pledge and you even went so far as to suggest that the no-strike pledge be contin-

ued after the war, because at the time you and Browder and Pressman and others believed that Russia would want a decade of peace and amity with the United States.

I also remember that during the war you were so opposed to strikes and so careless of the true interests of the working man that you instructed your people to do the work of the strikers in a Montgomery Ward warehouse — the short ugly word that describes this is the word 'scab.'

With the end of the war when the Communist Party line changed, you changed. You became aggressive again. You forgot the no-strike pledge. You turned on 'our glorious allies' and you discovered once again that there was such a place as Wall Street and you dusted off the old word 'Imperialist.'

You have followed the Communists in their third party adventure. This alone would not make you Communist controlled. None of the things alone would make you a Communist or a Communist fellow-traveler. But taken all together as a pattern—they spell 'Communist controlled.'

The Communist controlled unions of the CIO today are bucking Philip Murray and the vast majority of CIO members in the CIO's policy of no labor-splitting, third party wild goose chase in '48. You and your ideological colleagues are trying to defeat progressives who aspire to the halls of Congress or the Senate if these progressives will not pledge themselves to support pro-Communist foreign policy. You and the others have opposed the Marshall Plan, you have opposed the admittance of displaced persons who seek a haven in this country.

Finally, if I knew of one single instance in which you opposed or even failed to support enthusiastically a Communist party line policy I would hesitate to say that you and your union are Communist controlled. I regret that you are so controlled because if you were not, you could perform a service for the working men and women of America that they badly need. But as matters stand I am afraid that for all your labors, you have done the workers of American more harm than good.

You may make this reply public or you may make it available to your members if you so desire.

Sincerely yours,
Rev. Charles Owen Rice

PITTSBURGH CATHOLIC
July 29, 1948

Rice doing national radio broadcast on ABC two days before nationwide steel strike, ***January 19, 1946***

Pittsburgh's Power Strike

One of the most dramatic labor confrontations in Pittsburgh's history was the electrical utility strike in 1946, which significantly curtailed the life of the city for several weeks. As a knowledgeable radio commentator and potential mediator, Rice closely followed the events of the strike.

A Company Union Finally Succeeds in Standing on Its Own Feet (1946)

In labor's burgeoning days—the late thirties—the Utility Company which served Pittsburgh and surrounding territory set up a neat little company union (the Independent Association of Duquesne Light Employees) as a device to avoid the ugly labor trouble which other companies were having. The Utility Company, which was called Dusquesne Light Company and Associated Companies, was wary of dealing with either CIO or AFL. The CIO Utility Workers were taking neighboring utility companies by storm. The AFL had a monopoly on construction work locally and was also interested in acquiring utility production workers.

It was a very good scheme and it had worked marvelously elsewhere. It worked perfectly here too, because the AFL and CIO never did get a look in. The CIO managed to organize one of four power stations belonging to the company but eventually lost it. The AFL tried to organize two immense construction projects of the Light Company but the company and its independent union made an unbeatable team. They even smashed efforts of the AFL Building Service Workers to organize scrub women, elevator men and janitors in the utility's main office building.

There was one little flaw in the Company's plan; it did not stop labor trouble. The supervisors and foremen who helped the union get started feel rather hurt about that. The workers took seriously the statements of the independent union organizers that here they could have a real union of their own which would do wonders for them, and keep them out of the hands of the bad people running the CIO and AFL.

They got rid of their first president and elected a chap called George L. Mueller. Mueller was a slow-spoken man who had taken advantage of the Company's policy of encouraging and partially paying for higher education for its people. He got himself a college education and a degree in engineering. George appeared for a while to be a run-of-the-mill "independent" union official.

He blasted the CIO as Communistic. He fiercely attacked the AFL as racket ridden, and pointed out that its International Brotherhood of Electrical Workers would give his members only secondary status.

But there came sign of trouble in paradise. The union put out a paper. As early as 1941 it began to say nasty little things about Company officials and began to run fighting articles. Then the lawyer who had organized the union was given his walking papers. Nicholas Unkovic is his name and he turned up, during the strike, working for the firm of lawyers which represents the Company. After this came a sit-down strike in the clerical department. The other officers turned on George and tried to impeach him, but he had them fired by the membership. He emerged stronger than ever. He got rid of another lawyer, Charles Seif, who in the present crisis turned up as urging George's members to join District 50 of John L. Lewis's Mine Workers.

71

And about a year and a half ago there came a brief work stoppage which the court settled by recommending arbitration. The union won the arbiter's decision, but due to a lot of technical hugger-mugger they lost the effect of it.

Then in February 1946, the entire city became conscious of this man Mueller. He announced that there would be a strike. He refused to negotiate any more because the deadline was passed and his members had authorized nothing but strike. The Mayor, David L. Lawrence, blew his top, but the strike came off. It was a strike with the lights on and in 19 hours it was suspended. It was rescheduled but in the meantime the company offered arbitration and the union was pressured into accepting.

Mueller at all times declared that his people did not like arbitration. They had too much of it. When the arbitration was over he said that the members were not satisfied and would never go for it again. But observers put this down to talk and bluster and forgot all about George.

Around the end of June we began to hear from the union again. There was more talk of strike if the Company did not negotiate properly. No one paid much attention. After all the last time it had all fizzled out after a little excitement. Besides the deadline was not until August 31, two months off. All during August the newspapers played up the crisis hard but the citizens were not too interested. Nobody got steamed up. George and his union wanted quite a few things. It seems as if they had gone through all the union contracts in the world and picked out the best clauses from each one. The Company was not disposed to offer much of anything. They said the last award exceeded Wage Stabilization directives and they would pay no more. Whether the contract permitted a strike at this point or not has been a moot question, but it was never tested in court.

The Mayor of Pittsburgh took a strong part in all negotiations. He would force Company and union to negotiate. He generated all the pressure he could to force them to get together. In the battle of statements and hand-outs and radio talks before the strike, Mueller did not do too well. He did not prepare his releases well and did not put over his case as clearly as was necessary. At times he appeared to be contradicting previous statements. Of course, a basic reason for this was that the employees of the Light company have long memories and long, involved grievances. To tell their story they had to start back rather far and they had to explain a lot of history: company policy, company promises and so on.

That brings us to the strike itself. It began one minute after midnight Monday, September 9, 1946. It lasted for forty-five minutes in its first appearance. The City Administration got a temporary restraining order against the strike one minute before the deadline. Forty-five minutes later the union leader bowed to the court order. Thursday of that week he [Mueller] entered into negotiations with Leo T. Crowley, chairman of the board of Standard Gas and Electric, the utility's parent holding company. An arbitration agreement was signed. It was to be presented to the membership Friday, September 20. The injunction was to be withdrawn. Everything seemed to be all settled, everyone was happy and friendly. The Mayor felt wonderful and his brilliant City Solicitor Anne X. Alpern, who had presented the injunction, seemed like something only slightly less than a modern Joan of Arc.

There had been growls and rumblings over the injunction from both houses of organized labor who felt, very properly, that if this could be done to Mueller's union it could be done to anyone. No one paid too much attention to this because it all appeared quite academic. But then there came rumblings from the Independent Association. The members did not

Mayor David L. Lawrence introduces President Harry Truman to Father Rice during campaign whistle stop in 1948. To Rice's right is Arthur Goldberg, steel worker attorney, and steel worker secretary David McDonald. Directly behind Rice is Jock Yablonski.

like the whole business. The president had been talking to lawyers who told him the injunction was illegal as all get out. It was against an anti-injunction act which the Mayor himself had lobbied through the State Legislature.

The day before the membership meeting signs appeared on union bulletin boards telling the members to attend the injunction hearing as defendants and to shut down live equipment to be on the safe side. The meeting voted down arbitration about two to one. Mr. Mueller made his famous statement that the injunction was a "scrap of paper," without legal authority in any shape or form, that the members' souls belonged to God but their bodies did not belong to Duquesne Light Company and Associate Companies.

Tuesday morning over a thousand members of the union stood in front of the City County building where the hearing was going on. They booed and cheered and got a little rowdy but there was no violence. A temporary injunction was granted. The union chief was asked to take back what he had said and call off the strike. He respectfully refused and the addled judiciary poured gasoline on the flames by sentencing him to a year in jail without bail.

That did it. The sporadic wildcat strikes, which had been popping up all over, threatened to become a general strike. Plain citizens who had no contact with unions and no love or understanding of them could see what this was. If Mueller could be put in jail like this anyone could be put in jail.

The only thing to do was to kill the injunction and get Mueller out of jail as quickly and neatly as possible. The city went before the court and asked that the injunction be dissolved. The request was granted. A mass meeting of the members was scheduled for that evening, Wednesday, September 25. Mueller was spirited out to the meeting. First they stood him up in court and he apologized for

whatever he might have done in contempt of court and he promised to take an offer which the company had made and urge his members to accept it. The offer gave a five percent increase among other things. It was presented by Leo T. Crowley himself with the proviso that it was to be withdrawn if not accepted right out.

The members did not accept the proposal. When Mueller returned, they killed the charges against him anyway. He submitted the proposal to another membership meeting. He argued against it and the strike was still on in full force. The street cars and buses, whose operators were AFL members, stopped running. The drivers would not be called scabs. They were definitely on the spot.

Immediately after Mueller refused to push through the offer of Crowley, he and the unions became targets for as neat a campaign of union-busting and maligning as I've ever heard of. All the papers jumped on him. Several radio stations barred him from the airwaves. The belief held by these people was that Mueller was running a one-man show. He wanted glory and personal power. His people wanted peace. They wanted arbitration. The attempt was to undermine the morale of his people and to infuriate the general public against him. I think the results of that attempt are among the most interesting features of the whole unhappy controversy.

The union members held steadfast through nearly a month of concentrated abuse. Their side got very little hearing. Many sins against journalism went into building up the anti-Mueller legend. The general public simply refused to be stampeded. Several citizen committee attempts to promote back-to-work movements or recruit volunteer strikebreakers were miserable failures.

We had everything in this strike. We had an injunction. The jailing of a union leader. Promises extracted under threat of jail. We had combined radio and newspaper pressure. We had several citizens' committee deals. More recently we had a group of unionists attempting to secede from the union on strike. We had them cross over to District 50 of the Mine Workers. We had a quickie NLRB hearing and election. We had a so-called insurgent group holding a meeting at which arbitration was accepted by one-sixth of the members. We had attacks on the union and its leader by other union leaders. We had him attacked by public officials.

He won the NLRB [National Labor Relations Board] election. Not enough voted at the rump meeting to make the vote for arbitration significant. Now a lot of people are beginning to suspect that George L. Mueller was not romancing all along when he said that his people were sick and tired of being pushed around, did not want arbitration and were willing to strike, and keep on striking until they got what they wanted.

Toward the end one newspaper began attempting to give both sides. Several radio stations also steadfastly refused to join the hue and cry against Mueller. One or two public officials have pointed out the Company's guilt. The absentee-owned Utility consistently refused to negotiate. It claimed that it would arbitrate only. . . .

Finally, the union did vote to arbitrate, 1,197, to 797 and brought the strike to a strange and anticlimactic close October 20. During the balloting George Mueller himself made no recommendation to the members either way. Afterwards he told reporters that he had found in Washington "a strong indication" that Wage Stabilization Board restrictions, to which company officials held, would be discontinued by November 1. One of the union's objections to arbitration with the Company was thereby removed. In any case the strike has ended.

During the tie-up the people of Pittsburgh were not panicked. They bore the transportation stoppage until the street cars and buses went back into operation. They bore the lack of heat in office buildings and the occasional brief, localized blackouts. An admirable lack of hysteria.

There are lessons in this for everyone. For industrialists: not to fool around with "independent" unions unless they are prepared for trouble. For municipalities: not to put up with absentee ownership of their utilities. Better erect a public power plant if necessary. For the utility industry: to make up their minds to bargain with their workers through unions of their own choice. Pittsburgh is only the beginning. The one time scared and rabbity employees have hydrophobia. Management may get bitten. For "liberals" and labor people: all is not lost. The American people are inherently in favor of fair play. When the chips are down, they respect unions and they will no longer swallow any "American plan" baloney. For newspapers and radio: if they do not learn to be fair in industrial disputes they may lose the little prestige they have left.

What have we had in Pittsburgh? We have a company union which found itself. We have a union leader who has been very tough and single-minded. He weakened a couple of times but when his people bade him to be strong he stiffened. We have had an absentee-owned utility which wanted a strike and got one. They wanted to strike and get rid of a pesky individual and his union which they themselves created. We have had the unthinkable, a long utility strike. It has not wrecked the town. It has embarrassed a lot of people. It has made the strangest bed-fellows. And, regardless of what happens tomorrow, we shall have no peace in our local utility until the company decides to get along with the union and forget about saving faces and beating people into line.

COMMONWEAL
November 8, 1946

A Postscript (1948)

George Mueller seems to be having some difficulty in inducing his union of Duquesne Light Co. employees to follow him into the CIO. . . . From the outside, I would say that Mueller is probably quite strong, but that the drive of the AFL International Brotherhood of Electrical Workers is causing him more trouble than was expected. The various defections from his ranks need not destroy him, as his personal hold is very strong and he is a militant, successful symbol to his rank-and-file. . . .

The surprising force and tactical success of the IBEW drive is due to the character and ability of its organizer, one Andy Johnson. Johnson is a tremendous worker, a very personable fellow and very, very clever. Johnson's opponents never are blessed with a whole lot of restful nights. The contest between him and Mueller is worth watching. Mueller has the advantage but it is a good fight.

PITTSBURGH CATHOLIC
January 8, 1948

The victory of the International Brotherhood of Electrical Workers (AFL) over the CIO Utility Workers in the Duquesne Light Labor Board election was a shocking surprise to most followers of the labor movement in Pittsburgh. This column indicated some months ago that the IBEW was making a vigorous and intelligent campaign under Andy Johnson, its young resourceful leader; but frankly I hardly expected them to win. . . . All during the last strike, I heard continual murmurings of rank-and-file opposition to Mueller but I discounted most of them. The fellow had been counted out and had come back so often.

PITTSBURGH CATHOLIC
May 27, 1948

The Anti-Communist Union Crusade

After the war, Rice stepped down as Pittsburgh's rent control director and went back to being the full-time director of the St. Joseph's House of Hospitality. As the Iron Curtain came down on Eastern Europe and the Church there experienced increasing persecution, Rice rekindled the anti-Communist fires. He was greatly aided by the Communists themselves, who were being pushed by Stalin to sacrifice domestic issues to an all-out critique of American foreign policy.
A series of articles published in the nationally distributed Our Sunday Visitor *from 1947 to 1949 elicited hundreds of letters largely from rank-and-file correspondents in dozens of unions. Rice sent them updates on the anti-Communist union struggle and furnished them with his pamphlet on how to rid unions of their Red leadership.*

How to De-Control Your Union of Communists (1947)

Your final aim is to remove your top International Communist officers and to stop your union from being used as a Communist tool.

To do this you must clean out your local union and you must join together with anti-Communists in other locals.

You have three immediate objectives: 1, to elect delegates to your international convention and your district council who are anti-Communists and pledged to vote against Communists and Communist measures; 2, to elect local officers who are anti-Communists, and to elect shop stewards who are anti-Communists; 3, to control your local meetings and see that no money or support is voted to Communist causes and that no Communist resolutions are passed. . . .

Caution

An election committee is always selected. Fight to have the Committee elected. No matter how it is picked, fight to get your people on it. Demand a ballot vote on all elections. Watch the counting of the votes. Watch the ballot box at all times. . . .

Issues

Examine your local situation and find out what more the union could do than it is doing. Make up a program around this. You can always kick on wage increases, etc. as not being big enough. You can always embarrass the Communists by yapping about grievances that the workers did not win, etc. Argue for more stream-lined and direct grievance procedures. Better coverage on employment compensation cases, etc.

Walter Reuther slaughtered his Communist opposition because he had a superb pro-union program and platform. You need negative issues too, but never forget the positive ones.

Perhaps your plant needs a job equalization program. Perhaps the time studies are too tight and the company stop-watch brigade is getting away with murder, all grist to your mill and all will not only beat the Reds, but build up the union.

Remember, if you push for something and the union gets it, then you claim credit and claim that you pushed the opposition into going after it. If the union does not get it, yell, "sell out," "double cross," "ineffective," "stumble bum," etc. . . .

Organization

Your first step is to start building an organization. Start small. Get your personal friends together, in your own house, if necessary. Explain the issues to them and ask for support. Then you are on your way.

You will be able to find out what is coming up at the next union meeting. Get your own little group to promise to come to the union meeting and contact you there. Brief them beforehand on the issues that will come up, and on the stand you will take. Pick yourself or one of your group as a floor leader. The others will follow him. This is important. You must follow a leader and carry out the agreed program.

At the first meeting you have hardly any chance to win. But every time out means practice and it is worth while. Try to have every member of the group say something. If they cannot say anything else, they can get up and say, "I agree with what_____ said" or "_____ is always right, he makes sense." There is an endless variety of simple statements for or against.

If you are just starting out this anti-Communist fight you will get recruits by your first stand. However you will be the objects of some fierce attacks. You must brace yourself for the Communist counter attack. . . .

Caucus

After you have been in action for a while, be sure to organize an anti-Communist caucus. Get your groups all together. Before your caucus meets, have your own group well coached as to what you want to do. You want to pick a name for the caucus. Pick one of the following or something similar. "Rank-and-file." This name is used all over the country by anti-Communists. The Communists generally use the name "Progressive." You could use "American Progressive," "Independent," "Save the Union," "Unity," "Pro-CIO." This last name might be effective since the Reds are planning to quit the CIO. . . .

Do Not Depend on Leaflets Alone. You have to do other electioneering. Do not be discouraged if you seem to be the only one working. It always looks like that in every fight. You will find people who will fall down on you, but others will amaze you by their faithfulness. Ring door bells, make phone calls, talk to people in the shop; and check up on your members to see that they are doing the same thing.

If Commies or their friends come into your caucus, just tell them to leave. Do not put a tooth in it. Never beat around the bush with those people. You lose nothing by laying it on the line.

Remember also that a crowd brought to a meeting or an election by leaflets alone, can be swayed the other way.

Meeting Strategy

When your caucus has reached any development at all, you can use more fancy strategy. Place your people carefully in the meeting hall. Try to have a good sized bunch down front. The Reds always pack the first row or two. Get there first or right behind or right with them. Place others on each side and place a nice contingent in the back. This is called the "Diamond," the oldest meeting strategy in the world. It makes it look as if the entire meeting is filled with your people. Very effective.

In your caucus meeting you will explain the issues and how to vote. You will pick speakers on various subjects. One or two for everything if you can. Be alert to jump into the breach if a designated speaker falls down or muffs his cue.

If the Commies boo your speaker, coach your members to yell "Let him talk." This simple strategy is amazingly powerful. If they boo your men, then give them a taste of it when they get up. Train your people to yell "boo, sit down, back to Moscow, etc." You have to tell them what to say and try to pick men who will be sort of cheer leaders. Teach them to yammer at a meeting like a good infield. If Commies talk to them in the meeting, yammer back. You have to do this or you will be cowed. It will take time to get into the swing, but it will be a joy and delight when it is used.

Do not be afraid to use the word Communist when speaking of motions and resolutions. Apply the word Communist and stooge to those who deserve it. This is not being uncharitable, it is being truthful.

Be Pro-Union

I cannot impress upon you too strongly the necessity of being aggressively pro-union. You are for strong action. You want grievances settled. You have no use for the company and its stalling tactics. You want a big raise in wages. You want a better contract. You want more vacations. You want a pension and a company-paid-for health-and-welfare fund.

The Communists' big stock in trade is their aggressiveness for the workers. They like to say that they are the only ones fighting for the worker. Don't be foolish in your aggressiveness, but make a good case for yourself. . . .

General Anti-Communist Arguments and Proof

This fight is hard because it is hard to prove that anyone is a Communist. Communism is a secret conspiracy and the law does not compel them to make themselves known. However you can go by the record.

Communists and their friends when asked point blank will generally refuse to answer, will say Communism is not an issue or will call you names. Ask the question on the floor and then make the above point.

You can safely say that your Commie officers followed the Communist Party line, not only in supporting Wallace and in voting money to Communist fronts but in following Soviet foreign policy. They attacked Roosevelt and called him a war monger from 1939 until June 21, 1941, when Russia was invaded. They were for no strikes and all out production during the war, because it helped Russia. They were for the second front. After VJ day they changed. They wanted to get tough again with the companies. They began to berate American foreign policy, they wanted a weak army. They now fight the Marshall Plan and they plug Henry Wallace. They object to sending American money to help Italy and Greece, but they were willing to send everything we own to help Russia during the war.

EXCERPTS FROM PAMPHLET
1947

On Red-baiting (1947)

See What I Mean?

We have often said that the greatest help to the Communist is the loud, undisciplined, orator against Communism. The orator who, whether through stupidity or malice attaches the label of Communist where it should not be. This man advertises the Communists and mostly he succeeds merely in giving them credit for something good, something or some person for whom they are not responsible.

In the dailies of last Saturday there was a report of one such orator and one such speech. The orator involved appears to be a Catholic priest. Rev. Frank M. O'Reiley spoke

to the realtor's meeting at Bedford. His general talking against Communism was a little on the blood thirsty and scary side, but . . . his labor talk, as quoted, was very bad.

According to the Pittsburgh Press, he said that the Communists were responsible for the plague of strikes since the end of the war. That statement is untrue. The Commie unions scuttled for cover; they were not ready for strikes. The United Electrical workers, for instance, made poor settlements to end strikes and to avoid them. . . .

I suppose Father O'Reiley served Moscow best by calling Joe Curran, of the Maritime Union, a Browderite. The Comrades will love that and will use it to defeat Joe. Poor Joe woke up at long last and began to fight the Reds. He has not been doing so well. Statements such as the Realtors heard will not help him to do better.

The craziest and most unbalancedly vicious statement concerned Walter Reuther. Father O'Reiley called him "Moscow-trained," a lie, and mentioned that he inspired the bloody sit-down strikes in Michigan. Now those strikes took place ten years ago. They were not a Commie tactic but were a legitimate trade union maneuver. Better theologians than Father O'Reiley or myself have stated that all sit-down strikes are not immoral. Congressional action in outlawing them does not change the moral law.

Finally, Walter Reuther is known to every student of the labor movement as the No. 1 enemy of Communism in the labor movement. He has never played ball with the Comrades for one instant. He has his faults, but that is not one of them.

PITTSBURGH CATHOLIC
September 25, 1947

The Battle for the United Electrical Workers

Rice's columns in the Pittsburgh Catholic *between 1947 and 1950 contain far-reaching reports about the battle against Communist influence in and control of the unions. Though he had an impact on events in dozens of unions, the central focus of his efforts was the United Electrical Workers (UE) and especially UE Local 601 at the giant Westinghouse Electric plant in east Pittsburgh.*

The Struggle for UE (1947)

The United Electrical union convention. . . . just concluded in Boston. . . . was given very good coverage in Pittsburgh. The "Press" had its labor reporter, William Jacobs, on hand, and his dispatches gave a thorough picture of just what went on.

A well disciplined majority rode rough shod over its opposition. In any union it is extremely difficult to unseat a machine which is in control. Various unions have been controlled by various machines. Most of this control has been benevolent, but it has been hard to break. . . .

The Communists were driven out of one union. Back in the twenties they attained control of the International Ladies Garment Workers Union. They were somewhat new to the game and they rushed into disastrous strikes. They squandered the union's substance and a counter attack by Dave Dubinsky got them out in short order.

The Communists of today, twenty years later, are not making the mistakes of the earlier crew. They have a smoother approach. They realize that they will have to mark time for a bit while waiting for the "Revolution." Conditions are not ripe.

They use the unions, those they now control, to supply jobs and training for worthy Communists; to dribble amounts of money to various Communist front organizations; to issue endorsements and to pass resolutions favorable to the Party Line and Soviet Russia. This type of misuse of a union does not annoy the ordinary rank-and-file member. This all important citizen is fair game for the Communist propaganda that his particular Communist-controlled union is doing a wonderful job for him and there is nothing to get excited about. That is the anatomy of Communist labor control as I see it today.

At any rate, we have seen the spectacle of a large union of American working men made up of delegates, elected with a reasonable semblance of democracy, endorsing Russian foreign policy at the moment of the most acute crisis between Russia and America; and at the moment when the cleavage between Russia and America has been most clearly established. That is a real Communist victory. The boys have done well and deserve cheers and commendation from their headquarters.

PITTSBURGH CATHOLIC
October 2, 1947

ACTU Flayed (1947)

The Pittsburgh ACTU chapter got its share of verbal buffeting. The chaplain and the president were honored by name. The answer is simply this: ACTU does not interfere in the unions. The Communist Party does. Education and democratic revolt of the rank-and-file will have to do the job of cleaning out the Reds. The action to be successful must come from within. All the ACTU can accomplish is education.

Finally it is no disgrace to be denounced by the people who are flaying the foreign policy of America and its makers, at the most crucial period in recent history; and more than that, upholding the hands of the murderer of the Kremlin and praising and supporting the Russian policy that is continuing chaos and starvation in Europe.

PITTSBURGH CATHOLIC
October 2, 1947

UE Troubles (1947)

General Electric dropped its bonus plan the other day. There was nothing in its contract with the United Electrical union requiring the bonus plan, so the UE rank-and-file members in General Electric are just doing without. The UE is too scared and weak to pick a fight these days, so that will go by the board.

The viciously anti-union Remington-Rand Corporation has moved to de-certify the UE in six of its plants. In one of its plants the Machinist formerly AFL, are certified and they will not be bothered. They may even try a move in which the UE is de-certified. The UE can be decertified under the new labor law [Taft-Hartley] because its top officers have refused to sign the non-Communist affidavits.

The Remington-Rand has a bad labor record. Even though the UE has its Communists I don't wish the corporation any success in its drive against the UE. Communists can be cleaned out through rank-and-file action. That is the way the ACTU likes to see it done.

PITTSBURGH CATHOLIC
November 27, 1947

UE Strike (1948)

The UE should be in a better position that any other large union to strike this year. Its large companies, like Westinghouse, are in the midst of expansion and moving of plants. This makes them vulnerable to a strike. However, the UE leadership has internal difficulties and has lost the confidence of its members.

If the UE leadership will turn its back on the Wallace Third Party adventure, if it will boldly repudiate Communism and it will sign the non-Communist affidavits, which will give it legal status, it will have behind it the united, unbeatable rank-and-file. If it will only soft pedal its non-trade union adventures and campaigns it can do the job. Even with its present disabilities it still could possibly snatch victory with a proper display of courage and daring.

PITTSBURGH CATHOLIC
May 6, 1948

UE Rhubarb (1948)

The tight control, which the United Electrical Workers Union Communist leadership exercises, slipped a little last Thursday. The three top dogs of the UE — Fitzgerald, Matles, and Emspack — came to Pittsburgh. Ostensibly, they were coming to talk wages and hours, but actually they were coming to peddle Communist doctrine on the Marshall plan and Henry Wallace's Third Party. They are making a swing around the country. They gather the shop stewards in each district from every plant and they harangue them. They make a very tortuous attempt to tie in the Marshall Plan and the Third Party with "bread and butter" issues.

It is criminal irresponsibility for them to be engaged in this Communist maneuver now, because they should be devoting all their time and energy to whipping up the fervor of their members to the question of negotiations with the big companies. This Communistic detour is going to cost the members money because it is splitting up the union and dissipating its economic strength.

At any rate, "The Brethren" ran into trouble.

In the face of trouble they did not act like the "supermen" they are alleged to be. They applied Communistic formulae — adjourning, reconvening meetings, etc. — and they did it badly.

James Matles, director of organizations, has been painted as one of the most effective speakers and one of the shrewdest handlers of men and meetings. Under the heckling that he met here he cracked. He lost his head; he yelled and was ineffective. Afraid of their opposition the "Reds" adjourned the meeting and reconvened a rump session. The riot which followed is history.

PITTSBURGH CATHOLIC
February 5, 1948

Sickening (1948)

It is enough to make any good union man's heart sick, and very angry, the way certain unions are breaking up. Unions that under clean leadership could have lasted indefinitely and could have done a splendid job are slipping every day. Some of these Communist controlled unions during the war got into small open shop towns where unions had never existed before. They got in under the magic name of the CIO and now they are breaking up.

Anti-Communists do not want to destroy these unions. They want to reform them. They want to force the Communist officers to sign the Taft-Hartley affidavits so that they can at least get on the ballot and defend themselves. But the members are taking matters into their own hands. Instead of the hard job of cleaning out the Reds, they do the easy job of just dropping out of the union. Anti-labor companies are having a field day. In many cases they just will not deal with the union and it melts away. In some places there is a fight, as in the Univis at Dayton, or a long bitter struggle, as with the Hoover Company in Canton, but the end is the same, unless the union is cleaned up and rescued.

Remington-Rand set the deadly formula, and destroyed the United Electrical Union in its shops. In New Britain, Conn., the American Hardware Corporation and the New Britain Machine Co. applied the Remington-Rand new formula — the UE there is dead. The UAW and the IAM are conducting a contest to see who gets the workers in one out of four plants in New Britain, but whichever wins unionism has been hurt in that town by the betrayal of the workers by the UE leaders.

PITTSBURGH CATHOLIC
August 26, 1948

Probe (1948)

Testifying reluctantly before the House Labor Committee, James B. Carey, former president of the UE and the man who founded it, mentioned two instances in which companies had fired men who were too vociferous in their opposition to the Communist Party line within the UE.

The way this is accomplished is through connivance between the "Red" officers and the company, the company going along for the sake of industrial peace. I know of two cases in Pittsburgh where this happened. One man got his job back, the other didn't. The firing in both cases were ostensibly because of absenteeism during an election campaign.

In the hundreds of letters I have received from various parts of the country, I would judge that countless anti-Communist leaders stand in fear of a back door deal between the company and the Communists that will land them on the street.

Andrew Averey, in his excellent pamphlet

"Communist Power in U.S. Industry" lashes into American business for its collaboration with Communists. When Russia was threatened during the last war, the Communists helped to put in incentive systems and speed-ups in every industry where they controlled the union. The company just loved it because they never, never saw a "Right Wing" union that would do this.

The Communists even signed contracts which allow the companies to review incentive rates any time they want, even where there have not been changes in the job itself. Westinghouse, for instance, has reviewed or is reviewing every rate in the shop.

PITTSBURGH CATHOLIC
September 9, 1948

A Tale of Two Cities (1948)

The smallest, most exclusive club in the world is sitting around waiting for another member. This club consist of just two men. These two are presidents of CIO unions. They once were held in thrall by the Communist Party, which in a sense made them both. They were never members of the Party, but they went along. Their names are Joseph Curran and Michael Quill. They are waiting for a buddy, also an Irish Catholic, also made by the Communists, also faithful to the party line, and now, perhaps, ready to fold.

Albert Fitzgerald, president of the United Electrical Workers, is the prospective new club member, but he will not qualify for membership merely by declaring his independence of the Communists. He cannot join this exclusive little club unless he can take his members with him. That, he is afraid, he cannot do.

But the Communist hatchet men in his union live in fear of the day when Albert Fitzgerald will remember his heritage and will smash his fist into the grey but domineering face of the

Communist Control Apparatus of the UE-CIO. That must be what lies behind that strange convention the UE just concluded in New York City and standing in complete and startling contrast to the strong, arrogant, UE convention that concluded a year ago in Boston. . . .

Albert Fitzgerald as he rapped his gavel last Friday, September 10, and brought his do-nothing, wrangling, inconclusive convention to a close in indecent haste, must have contrasted his union of today, with that same union of a year ago when the Boston convention ended on the up-beat with arrogance and defiance in every gesture, every resolution and every speech. The union was one of the biggest in the world; it had won many victories; it had emerged from the war at a peak of strength and the control apparatus was functioning perfectly. The jubilant, cocky delegates sang in the streets of Boston; taunted the opposition, inside and outside of the Convention Hall; gave Henry Wallace a thundering ovation, and sent the Third Party on its way.

And here is that same union a year later. It has lost thousands of members, while every other union has grown. Perhaps 50 of its local unions have been destroyed and stamped out. Its denunciation of CIO leader Philip Murray and of the foreign policy of the United States, and its wild, extravagant year of following the Communist Party's Third Party irresponsible adventure, have ravaged it. Even the control apparatus is weak, and that generally is the last thing to go.

Well might Fitzgerald hide from his friends and run from his own conscience as he sees his union weak and staggering and his members on the verge of being raided and scattered to the winds. The Wallace Third Party adventure turned out to be a crazy thing from the trade union point of view and must stand as one of the most disastrous moves in the history of American trade unionism.

T. S. Eliot wrote: "This is the way the world

ends, not with a bang but a whimper."

Certainly that is the way the UE convention ended: a sudden adjournment and a run off the stage by the officers as the opposition, which had been gathering strength, rushed the platform to bring up other issues, any one of which might have completely upset the "Red" control.

Will this large union, which has had within it the seeds of greatness, end the same way? Will Albert Fitzgerald perhaps find some courage somewhere and do as Quill and Curran did, or will he continue to bluster and roar and cooperate with the Communists until he and his union fade like the smile of the Cheshire cat?. . .

We know that recent Communist orders have been for Party Line unions and other groups to go down the line for party strategy without deviation and regardless of consequences. At the UE convention, Wallace was not endorsed, the anti-draft resolution was weak and even the foreign policy resolution was a weasel. We know that the Communists control the machinery of the UE. Did the party itself weaken and give orders to slow up?

Or was it that the old reliable wheel horses, at the last minute, could not bring themselves to take the sledgehammer to the beautiful machine they had helped to build? If this last were the case, will the party try to discipline the leaders? Or will the party leadership itself receive a shaking up? There is no way of telling. But we must bear in mind that there is a tremendous resiliency in the Communist party. It is like a snake that does not die until sundown — and sundown is far away.

PITTSBURGH CATHOLIC
September 16, 1943

Atom Bombshell (1948)

David Lilienthal is a recognized liberal. When his Atomic Energy Commission banned the United Electrical Workers from two strategic plants last week it meant that Uncle Sam has decided that he will not fool around. If anyone else but a man of Lilienthal's stature had promulgated this ban, it might be shrugged off; but now it must be faced that this man, after careful study of all the factors, has determined, upon advice of his qualified experts, that the UE is so thoroughly Communist-dominated that it is not to be permitted to enroll Atomic workers in crucial plans.

This ban may not succeed in dislodging the UE Red leaders. These men will destroy the union before they relax their grip. But the ban should make the rank-and-file take notice. It may so inspire them that they will spontaneously rise up and cleanse their union.

The UE was ready for this announcement. In the Red-controlled UE plants shop stewards the next morning rushed from bench to bench with the story that "the UE is being picked on by the reactionaries as part of the campaign to destroy all unions. They are trying out the tactic on the UE, but after destroying this one union they will go after them all."

I suppose a good many workers were fooled. But the realization will sink in and many unwitting Communist supporters will wise up.

PITTSBURGH CATHOLIC
October 7, 1948

Not Weakening (1948)

A talking point of the Communists in their "cornered rat" attempts to survive in our labor unions is that the anti-Communists fight weakens the local unions. That is not so. It may seem strange, but the locals in which there is a vigorous fight are among the best from every point of view.

In the United Electrical Workers union there are many weak locals today. But these are not locals in which there has been the anti-Red battle. The fighting stirs up interest in the local. The stewards function better. The element of competition helps. Ironically enough, in some cases even where the anti-Communist fight has been beaten back all the excitement of battle helps the general morale of the workers for a time.

Morale in controlled UE locals is very poor. Wherever the pro-Red administration officers have things their own way the story is the same. Many people are not interested in the union at all. There are members dropping out, etc.

On the other hand, in locals 613, 638 and 602, the perennially non-Red locals of this UE District (No. 6), morale is high, membership is virtually 100% of the potential and the grievance structure works like a charm. Comparing two real big locals, the controlled GE local in Erie has a poor morale; but out in East Pittsburgh where the giant Local 601 has been brawling and roaring for years, with the Reds on top one day and their opponents there the next, morale is rather high and membership is close to the potential.

In nearly all cases where UE locals have folded in the past year, the locals involved had no active anti-Red opposition and were left-wing controlled unions.

How About It?

David Lilienthal answered the UE protest over its disbarment from strategic atomic plants in deadly fashion. He told the Red leaders that they would get a full chance to prove that they are not Communists; but they will have to answer questions fully and truthfully. No evasion will be countenanced. My guess is that the Red answer will be abuse and not submission to trial.

PITTSBURGH CATHOLIC
October 14, 1948

Effects on Communist Unions (1948)

Strange as it may seem, the complete rout of Messrs. Wallace and Dewey will help the Communist-controlled unions which tried to assist both of the defeated. If the non-Communist affidavit provision is taken away it will be salvation for some of the Red birds. In addition, let it be remembered that Communists in unions, once they have control, thrive in labor's good times. The Communists got their foot-hold during the depression but they really expanded and entrenched during the wartime boom.

What is the conclusion for the sincere anti-Communist? Should the affidavits be retained? No! A solution for Communism in unions, that destroys unions, is no solution at all. For example, I personally would deeply regret the wrecking of the United Electrical Workers union. I want a solution for Communism that will keep the union but get rid of the Reds. Such a solution will take years but it is the only way. The members have to be assisted in doing a democratic job of house cleaning. Slow and hard, but the only worthwhile way.

This type of reasoning is what has kept Philip Murray from issuing a duplicate charter in the CIO to Electrical Workers and opening an all out war on the UE. It would probably at this time mean a vicious fight of uncertain outcome, but with a real risk of destroying hundreds of local unions which are functioning passably at the moment.

PITTSBURGH CATHOLIC
November 11, 1948

A Different Letter

Here is the sort of letter you like to get. It came from a girl [*sic*] worker in a plant of the United Electrical union, just a sincere rank-and-file person with a real union heart, who was frightened and timid but knew she had a responsibility, and then tried to live up to it. "Dear Father Rice:

"I was surprised and felt very shy when I was nominated to the executive board last summer but I attended the meetings very faithfully. The Communist propaganda I heard made me sick. I tried to tell the girls what I thought and a few of us got together, elected a new steward in our department, then started attending the labor classes in the Catholic school. Two of the girls had some of your literature. We read that and passed it around, then started to fight. So far we have elected a new president and one other officer. Made peace with the state CIO and voted down the local edition of the 'Daily Worker'."

I print the excerpt to show what courage and determination can do when aided by some education and a little advice at the proper time. . . .

PITTSBURGH CATHOLIC
February 3, 1949

Soviet System (1949)

The Communists are getting rougher every day in the UE. Their pattern is either to expel anti-Communists from the union or to deprive anti-Communists officers of their duly authorized powers. Mildred Turner of Huntington,

W.Va., has joined Duffy, Falvo and Nolan on the purged list.

The Schenectady General Electric local is an example of the other technique. Five out of seven officers elected a month ago are anti-Communists. However, the Reds took care in that local to have most of the executive board elected by the stewards whom they can control. The Executive Board is therefore quite Red. The board has been stripping the president, treasurer and secretary of their customary powers.

However, that is a technique that can be worked in reverse. Where there is a lone Commie survivor, or interloper, he can be stripped of his powers. . . .

By the Soviet system, members elect delegates, who in turn elect other delegates, who may elect still others. The system permits power to reside in the hands of a few vigorous people. All Communist union machines try to install this system. The perfection of it may be seen in Local 301 Schenectady, where the Soviet type shop stewards council chooses 23 out of 30 executive board members and habitually nullifies the will of 15,000 members.

PITTSBURGH CATHOLIC
February 10, 1949

UE Convention Aftermath (1949)

For some time it has been my belief that the Communists in control of the United Electrical Workers union would try hard to keep it within the CIO; but recent events seem to indicate this is no longer the case. Communist party orders are to get out of the CIO and blast the CIO and Philip Murray, its president. At the moment the Communists are thinking in terms of unleashing the weapon of destruction not only against the right wingers in the UE but against the strategic industries, other unions and the national economy.

The Communist strategists, the top ones, are confident that as soon as they sign the non-Communist affidavits, they will be able to stop, or slow down, raiding by other CIO unions. They realize that they cannot hold the UE together outside of the CIO forever; but they do not need to maintain it as a striking force forever. They need to keep it only until the United States and Russia clash, or come so close to clashing that all Communist fronts will be eliminated and the Party will retain only an underground apparatus.

PITTSBURGH CATHOLIC
September 29, 1949

At Last (1949)

Fed up with disloyal trade union principles, the CIO is now meeting in a convention in Cleveland, and by the time this is written, it seems certain will have divested itself of the Communist unions. The United Electrical Workers charter will have been lifted and a new charter granted to a right-wing CIO-UE.

What of the fate of this new UE? It will be spark-plugged by James B. Carey, original head of the UE, who was ousted by the Communists for opposing their rule. It will get complete CIO support, but will it succeed?

It is my considered opinion that it will succeed. Not only is it the psychological moment for such a move, and not only have the members been long prepared for it, but this union will start with enough locals completely committed to give it a respectable membership, even if it makes no further progress. There are about 380,000 members now in the UE. The new organization will have enrolled more than one-half of them before the year is out. . . .

Communist strategy seems to change from time to time. A year ago, the Communists were

determined to stay in the CIO until the bitter end. Three months ago, they changed and were full of fight. The UE Red leadership pulled the boner of making impossible demands upon the CIO and Philip Murray. Now they wish they hadn't and are beginning to cry. But it is too late.

It will be good to see the Communists get their comeuppance. Too long did they shelter under the strong roof of the CIO. . . . This is a great vindication for James Carey who never relaxed his fight against the Communist uprising of power in his union. May the new union prosper and grow.

PITTSBURGH CATHOLIC
November 3, 1949

UE (1949)

The Reds in charge of the United Electrical Workers are playing a waiting game. They are not following through on the tough course of action outlined in their convention moves. They are not yet cracking down on their internal opposition.

However, they are preparing for stormy going. They have signed the non-Communist affidavits as prescribed by the Taft-Hartley law. They did this at considerable personal risk. Some of them will eventually wind up in the penitentiary on the head of it. However, they signed so as to protect themselves in case of wholesale right wing defections.

They are also going ahead with plans to make the UE a general "refugium peccatorum." All the left wing garbage will be gathered into the one bucket before another twelve months elapse.

Jim Carey is giving very vigorous leadership to the right wing nationally and morale is high. The right wing nationally is well knit today and has several pockets of strength, which guarantee that it will not be crushed, whatever the left wing does. Carey always said that if he had one UE district under right wing control he could make a fight of it. He has at least two now and his forces are on the attack every place where they have strength and the proper issues.

PITTSBURGH CATHOLIC
November 3, 1949

That's All Brother (1949)

It is impossible to sufficiently emphasize the victories that the right wing in the UE scored on Sunday at both Sharon and Fairmont. In both localities the membership at mass meetings voted to leave the Red UE and join the new, clean UE-CIO. This is a terrific and most significant victory for the strategy of James B. Carey, who has maintained that the UE members want the CIO and not the CP [Communist Party].

You may take it from this that the new CIO-UE [*became the International Union of Electrical, Radio and Machine Workers or IUE*] will win even more of the present UE members than previously predicted. Remember that neither Sharon nor Fairmont was on the right side of the ballot at the UE convention.

The fight is not over, but the returns might as well be in. When it gets right down to the final wire, nearly three quarters of all the old UE members will be in Carey's CIO-UE outfit.

CIO Purge

Some of the greatest real life debating took place on the floor of Cleveland's municipal auditorium as last week's CIO convention handled its Communist problem once and for all. Harry Bridges and Ben Gold did the best work for the Comrades. The star for the right wing was Joseph Curran.

For some reason the previous right wing stars, Reuther and Baldanzi, were not up to their old form. But Curran was all anyone could ask for. In a series of off-the-cuff harangues he said it all. He spoke as one who formerly was in the Communist orbit. He spoke as a decent American working stiff who had tried everything in the interests of unity for the working man; and he was fed up, disgusted; and his disgust welled up from him and was visible as finally, in waterfront language, he nailed Harry Bridges.

It was great. Not just as a show, but it was great in its expression of the true loathing your American union man has for the slimy echoes of the Kremlin.

Michael Quill in his one speech was cuttingly effective. Philip Murray in his many references to the Comrades was blunt and chilling and final.

They are gone out of the CIO. To be sure the smaller Red outfits are not finally purged, but they will be in a very short space of time. They fought, they wept, they prayed, they lied, they promised — but it availed them not. They may now proceed to herd together in their own little crowd. As one old trade unionist put it, "Once again the Communists have succeeded in capturing themselves."

The New UE

How fares this new electrical union that bravely steps into simultaneous combat with the corporations and the Communists? It is attempting a new task. Never before in the history of the American labor movement has there been an attempt to create a new union wholesale out of the body of an already existing and functioning union. But a drastic evil called for a drastic cure. Phil Murray and the other cool heads in the CIO did every other possible thing to avoid this final step, but there was no other way to deal with the adventurers and trained professional revolutionaries who had attained control of the UE. Surgery was the only answer. Medication had failed dismally.

PITTSBURGH CATHOLIC
November 3, 1949

SUNDAY zette **7**

of America's Great Newspapers

SUNDAY MORNING, APRIL 3, 1949   Telephone ATlantic 6100   FIFTEEN CENTS

Pickets Rush Reds as Rally Breaks Up In Wild Riot

Police Battle Mob After Communist Rally

Riotous scenes like this marked the end of the Red rally at Northside Carnegie hall.

250 At Meeting Chased, Jostled By Angry Crowd

Police Rescue 5 Fleeing in Cab; Speakers Go Out by Side Door; Five Arrests Made on Northside

A riot broke out around the Northside Carnegie Music Hall Saturday night as a crowd estimated at several thousand closed in on the 250 Communists at the end of their protest rally.

While more than 100 police struggled vainly to control it, the mob battled, jostled and pushed the Communists and their sympathizers as they left the hall by a side door.

The crowd broke completely out of control, jostled police, newspapermen and Communists alike, smashed windows in trolleys and tried to overturn a taxicab.

For more than half an hour the crowd surged out of control but by 11 p. m. police had it well in hand and slowly dispersed it.

700,000 Pray Today Against

Communist meeting at Carnegie Library on the North Side is scene of riot. Rice is called by police to rescue besieged Communists, but is blamed by Daily Worker *for the attack.*

☷ The Eye of the Storm: UE 601

The fulcrum of Rice's campaign to break the Communist Party's influence within the UE was the massive East Pittsburgh Westinghouse plant. There he engaged himself to a degree that with hindsight he came to regret.

A Look Behind the Scene at Local 601 (1947)

On the eastern outskirts of the City of Pittsburgh stands the gigantic plant of the Westinghouse Electric and Manufacturing Company. In the shops of this company a powerful union is in existence. The union is Local 601 of the United Electrical, Radio and Machine Workers Union. Until this union came along a company union had been all that the employees of Westinghouse could look to for protection. Past organizing drives by legitimate unions had resulted in bloody unsuccessful strikes, which had been put down by the oppressive methods common in that day.

Unfortunately the CIO union which successfully organized Westinghouse both in the Electrical Manufacturing division and the Air-Brake Company at neighboring Wilmerding, had more than its share of Communists and Communist sympathizers. Two high-ranking national officers still are suspected of undue friendship for Communism and undue respect for the party line.

Red Organizers

Communist-minded organizers were among those sent into the local field by the international. They were aided and abetted by a small nucleus of Party Members. Logan Burkhart, now in jail over the Communist Election Petitions fraud and father of Alice Burkhart, alias Carolyn Hart, of Laundry Workers' fame, was the outstanding member of the admitted local Communists.

More important and more dangerous than the out and out faction are the supporters and hangers on, men and women who with remarkable fidelity followed the Communist Party Line in its devious involutions of the past five years. . . .

Communist Hold Weakening

There is some evidence that the Communist influence in 601 is dwindling. The evidence is far from conclusive however. The group is still able to put over its program in the old fashion, such as executive board meetings at which various matters are squeezed through; membership meetings ill-attended, at which a mere handful votes on important policy; a union local newspaper, the Generator, heavily slanted in one direction; and an office force under the thumb of the Red sympathizers.

The greatest allies of the Communist element are the inertia of the vast body of decent American, Christian members; the lack of organization, of information and unified plan among the non-Communists in their individual responsibility to eliminate the danger.

Communism Must Go

The Communists and their more notorious supporters must be removed, by election and due process, from all union offices. This is a job that the membership may or may not be aroused to accomplish. If the issues are presented strongly and clearly enough there can be no doubt of the outcome. . . .

ACTU NEWS
June 25, 1947

601 Again (1947)

Life is never simple and never dull in the gigantic local 601 of the United Electrical Workers, CIO. This big sprawling union covers all the local plants of the Westinghouse Electric Corporation. The Communists have lost some battles out there from time to time but for years they have never really been dislodged from power. However, the anti-Communists never give up. They keep scrapping and they can always field a team.

The anti-Communists are always just normal American workers, no brighter or more intense than average. Unfortunately, they have yet to produce brilliant leadership. They need brilliant leadership to win out because they are fighting a brainy, seasoned crew.

The ordinary well-meaning worker does not have much of a chance. Run of the mine working men when elected to office are easily neutralized or taken over by the Reds. It is happening among the present crew of officers elected last year by the anti-Reds.

The small group of true blue anti-Reds would do well to consider backing only a partial slate of men they are absolutely sure of and working with them and them only. In that way, more discipline and hence better results would follow. Anti-Commie fighting where all the cards are in the hands of the Reds is tough and discouraging work, but the antis have to remember they will win, because they must. It will take years, but it can be done.

PITTSBURGH CATHOLIC
September 4, 1947

Defeat? (1948)

The election at local 601 of the UE-CIO in the East Pittsburgh Works of Westinghouse Electric Corporation resulted in a stand-off. The Progressives, a slate which endorsed the international UE administration and was aided by international payrollers, gained half of the six executive board seats for which returns have been counted. The Progressives are, like the international, Communist direct-

ed and controlled. Thomas J. Fitzpatrick, their leading figure, was elected president. The incumbent, Phil Conahan, elected by Rank-and-File last year and repudiated this year, made a surprisingly strong showing without any organization support. He placed second. All the other firsts and seconds were either Rank-and-Filers or Progressives.

The Rank-and-File ticket won three of the six executive board offices. Its most important victory was the election of Charles Copeland as business agent. This is a paid position as is the office of president. The two highest votes were polled by Al Pefferman and Patrick O'Connor, Rank-and-Filers. . . .

PITTSBURGH CATHOLIC
January 1, 1948

Local 601 (1948)

In the final count the Rank-and-File anti-Communist ticket in Westinghouse local 601 of the UE lost the election. The Progressives, who have followed and endorsed the Communist policies of the International UE, won most of the positions on the executive board. However the Rank-and-File retains the position of Business Agent. An aggressive man, Charles Copeland, was elected to this position. The Rank-and-File will probably come back strong next year.

The "Daily Worker" last week ran an analysis of the election, accusing the Catholic Hierarchy of backing the Rank-and-File. No Catholic priest, let alone Bishop, said a word during the election. But facts do not interest the Communists; they are interested in attacking the Church, because they know that as long as the mass of American Catholic workers keep the faith, they will not be slaves to the Communist Party. . . .

PITTSBURGH CATHOLIC
January 15, 1948

At Last? (1948)

The positive campaign to unseat the Communists in the gigantic local 601 of the United Electrical workers in the East Pittsburgh Westinghouse plant won a battle last Sunday. In the very important issue of the signing of the non-Communist affidavits the Communists were beaten. The meeting voted, 147 to 114, to instruct the international officers to sign.

An important and persuasive argument in favor of complying with the law in this matter was given at the meeting. It ran as follows: "The Taft-Hartley law is no good, but we are already complying with part of it; for reasons of expediency our top officers are asking the members to comply with the law by signing check-off cards so that dues can be taken out of our pay; the same expediency dictates that the officers, whether they like it or not, sign the non-Communist affidavits so as to save us members a lot of grief in unnecessary recognition strikes and lost pay."

PITTSBURGH CATHOLIC
March 18, 1948

Local 601 (1948)

When you read this, you will know the results of the election in local 601 of the UE. That enormous Westinghouse local has been balloting for ten days. It would appear that a right wing victory is in the making, but after what happened to other predictors, this writer predicts nothing.

An encouraging sign as the voting proceeds is the fact that the Progressives (the faction friendly to Communism) have been concentrating on saving Thomas Fitzpatrick to the disregard of many other candidates. If he loses the race for president they will probably run him against his brother, Michael, for chief steward.

If the right wing forces win their troubles will

really begin. A victorious coalition in anything, war or politics, has trouble staying together. Victors easily fall out with one another. Also the Communist counterattack will be fierce. The fight will be waged at the membership meetings and in the shop.

The meetings will be in an uproar and it will be hard to conduct business. In the shop the Communists will sponsor mass demonstrations on grievances. Right wing stewards will be given a bad time and right wing officers will be smeared and attacked.

In Local 601 there have been several right wing victories. But no right wing administration has ever served two terms. Will this one be any different? Or, are we indulging in wishful thinking to suppose that the right wing will carry the election?

PITTSBURGH CATHOLIC
December 23, 1948

Victory (1948)

. . . Of recent years the UE has been getting away from the democratic constitution as drawn up originally by Jim Carey and other non-Communist liberals. The tendency has been to take authority from the locals and gradually filter it into the district and international set-ups. That is an old, old story. The Communists find it easier to get control of the more democratic unions; once they have their control, the democracy begins to get tossed out the window.

Need Delegates

Anti-Communists have been winning the elections wherever there is a large vote. In many UE locals, the vote for the local officers is conducted in a manner that makes for a large turnout but the vote for the delegates to international conventions and district conferences is conducted in a manner that makes for a smaller turnout.

Local 601 is a case in point. The local officers and stewards are elected by ballot in the shop.

But the vote for delegates to the district and the international takes place in the summer time at Sunday meetings. To win the delegate vote the Communists need about 500 votes. They find this much easier to get than the 6,000 or 7,000 votes required to be elected to local offices. The position of delegate is actually, in some respects, more important than the position of president, business agent, etc., because to really liberate the UE members from the Communist yoke it is necessary to elect delegates to the national convention who will vote out Matles and Emspak.

Just Skirmishes

We hope the recent spate of victories will not convince people that the battle in UE is over. That battle has hardly been joined. We have been celebrating skirmishes. There can be no real cause for celebration as long as not so much as one district of the UE has been won back from Communist control.

PITTSBURGH CATHOLIC
December 30, 1948

Election (1949)

Probably the most important election ever held in a labor union in the Pittsburgh district takes place next Sunday, August 14. Ten delegates to the United Electrical Workers international convention, with a total of 155 votes, are to be elected. There is a left wing slate called the Progressives; five of its candidates are Communist Party members. There is a right wing slate called the Rank-and-File. There are also assorted independents, who will tend to take votes away from the right wing.

The "Progressives" have been fighting to reduce the voting hours and to have the voting take place in the less accessible union hall. The Rank-and-File has fought to make the hours of voting long and the polling places as accessible as possible.

The natural bent of the members of 601 is

about 5–1 anti-Communist, but the Communists will have their people at the polls and the antis will be lucky to have a fourth of their supporters out.

The Rank-and-File has been in office and the Communists have done a tenacious and workmanlike job of discrediting and disrupting. They stand a fifty-fifty chance of winning the delegates. In their favor is the fact that they have always won all or most of the delegates. . . .

PITTSBURGH CATHOLIC
August 11, 1949

Give Light . . . (1949)

The people of Local 601 turned out in unprecedented numbers to elect for the first time a slate of right wing delegates to the United Electrical Workers national convention and the District 6 Council. The victory means that overturning of the Communists is possible at the September convention.

Spotlighting of the Reds by the Congressional hearings was partly responsible. The people of Local 601 do not want to be represented by men who have to be afraid to say whether or not they are disloyal to their country.

The Reds did everything to win. They even paid stewards from Local 601 so much a car load for people brought in to vote. Some of these people, incidentally, voted Right Wing. Trickery and evasion were to no avail. The American working man can make up his own mind when the chips are down. The day of the Red in American labor is numbered.

Slipping

The hold of the "Progressives" (Communists, that is) on the stewards in local 601 is weakening. It took strong arm tactics and trickery to push through a resolution condemning the un-American Activities Committee. At the afternoon meeting of the Stewards Council a roll call vote was refused. At the evening meeting the voting was postponed until very late at night, when many right wingers had gone home. In addition the chief right wing spokesman, Tommy Sullivan, was assaulted by a Communist bully boy.

PITTSBURGH CATHOLIC
August 18, 1949

Slipshod (1949)

You would not believe the slipshod methods that are used in the elections at Local 601, United Electrical Workers. For instance, there is no actual check up as to who has voted or who has not voted. There is not the slightest doubt that in every 601 election since its inception the Communists have managed to vote from 20 to 200 non-members. This has been worked in many ways. Membership cards can be forged; one of the Communistic office employees can certify a non-member and once he is cleared for voting, there is no way to check back. A member can vote on his badge or check number and then give his union card to some one else to vote on, etc.

When they have control of the election committee, they will not institute efficient voting methods. They want the voters to mill around in disorderly fashion; they want them to go home disgusted. The right wing lost between 100 and 200 votes a week ago in this fashion.

The victory in Local 601, although it was not a complete victory, may tip the scales in favor the right wing at the national convention of the UE in September. The returns are not yet in from sufficient local unions to call the turn. Actually it may not be possible to know who has the votes until the first test roll call at the Convention.

PITTSBURGH CATHOLIC
August 25, 1949

Mayor David Lawrence, Rev. Benjamin Masse, S.J., Phil Murray, and Rice at ACTU communion breakfast, 1952

⬚ Reflections on Anti-Communism

One of the more extraordinary aspects of Rice's career has been his public reevaluation of his anti-Communist activities. In speeches and in writings from the 1970s on, he has criticized himself for over-estimating the Communist threat and not defending the civil and job rights of victims of the purges, especially as Joseph McCarthy and his ilk turned the anti-Communist issue into a witch hunt.

The Tragic Purge of 1948 (1977)

When I was bravely battling Communism in the labor movement a long generation ago, little did I think that when my days were "in the yellow leaf" I would look back on the episode with considerably less than pride. . . .

There were anti-Communists and anti-Communists; we thought that we were the good kind. We made a point of not bothering folks unless they were Communists or followed the Communist party line faithfully, and we distinguished between followers and the real article. The others, the bad anti-Communists, called all kinds of people Communists, including us. There is some truth in the Communist joke about the fellow, caught in a Red baiting campaign, who protested "but I'm an anti-Communist" to the answer: "We don't keer what kinda Communist you are, just git outa here!"

The Communists eased our task by one of their characteristics. There was a Communist line. There was. In domestic affairs you might mistake it but in foreign affairs it was clear-cut. It followed the interest of the Soviet Union. Communists had an orthodoxy with hard edges and were serious about it. That was about all we had to go on, really, and we were not able to upset the rank-and-file with our discreet use of it. Something else turned them off and I shall get to that before I finish.

We made hay out of the Molotov-Ribbentrop Pact, in which Stalin made a deal with Hitler, and the change in the rhetoric

quickly observable in the Communist labor press. We trumpeted loud and long the counter-change which came when Hitler brutally invaded Russia, June 21, 1940.

Communist controlled, or influenced, unions veered then from intransigence to labor-management cooperation. Domestically, their national politics changed with their union politics. John L. Lewis was their darling one moment and their villain the next, while Philip Murray rode the other end of the seesaw. We used to blame one strike on the non-cooperation policy, that at North American Aviation.

I began my anti-Communist activities before World War II. Some of the old-timers at Westinghouse Local 601 drew me into the squabble when the leadership was getting ready to dump Jim Carey from the UE presidency in 1941, and I kept my hand in until the early fifties.

During the war, few would listen to me. The Communist related unions and factions grew strong, along with the rest of labor, but it was a false strength. Since the Soviet Union had a certain war-time popularity, especially with workers of Slav extraction, the domestic Communists gained also, and very many workers who were ideologically unaffected felt strongly that, Communist or not, a man deserved a fair hearing and fair treatment.

Any one time, I reckoned the Communist strength as quite formidable: 1/4 to 1/3 of the C.I.O. with strength here and there in the A.F.L. The U.E., we felt, was under solid control and at one time the Auto Workers were close to being controlled. Farm Equipment was like the U.E. There was some strength in Steel. We felt that they were very strong in the entertainment unions, and they were strong in the Newspaper Guild. They had a base in the government workers and some white collar operations. They had Mike Quill's Transport Workers and Joe Curran's Maritime Union. We, of course, exaggerated their strength, sincerely. We accepted some of the mystique of our enemy, just as we adopted tactics that we talked of as being their sort of thing.

Anti-Communism of the better sort — ours, that is, — was a minor industry and I was a resource. I compiled information and had correspondence with people from many parts of the country and even the Canal Zone. I interfered in the affairs of many a union, always for the best, I thought.

Two or three articles written by me for Our Sunday Visitor brought much correspondence and information on Communists, or their followers far and wide. That Catholic paper had a truly national range. It was horribly conservative and played with the bad sort of anti-Communism more happily, and far more often, than it did with me and mine. God forgive me, I did not mind using it to reach people I would not otherwise have reached.

The Association of Catholic Trade Unionists had significant chapters in the two other cities, New York and Detroit. The Detroit one was almost an appendage of Walter Reuther's caucus. Mine in Pittsburgh was open to the charge of being that for Phil Murray and his Steelworkers. I hope the charge was not totally true. I assure you, that I was pushing Murray to move against the Communist power, rather than the reverse.

The chapter in New York, which was the founding chapter, was a real outfit with a variety of members and resources. It was in the Communist fight but it, also, performed nobly against trade union crooks and mob control.

I fought with Cardinal Spellman over the cemetery strike where he smashed a local affiliated with a Communist connected international. I implied publicly that he was a scab, and I suffered a little. I'm not whimpering; I had it coming for other reasons.

Socialists were big in anti-Communism. Actually, I think they pumped me up. They had long factional memories and they had their own network. Many Socialists were the most bitter against Communists and the followers of the party-line, incredibly bitter. Some local men and women in Pittsburgh could be included in that category and, also, national figures such as Victor Riesel, with whom I was very good friends.

The question naturally arises: if the Communists ran rather good unions, and if their rank-and-file were content, why bother them? They were aggressive, for one thing, and they projected themselves as part of an international movement that was on the march. They were effective and they grew and they had policies which they pushed. They were very visible. Among other things, they rewarded the good and punished the wicked, their good and their wicked. I honestly thought that they had a shot at gaining control of American labor.

I was opposed to Soviet Russia and this was not entirely for religious reasons. The purges bothered me and I knew some of the stories of torture and abuse to be true. I allotted Communists more than their quota of cynicism.

Believe me, I was not a devotee of capitalism, but I was more of an unblinking American-style patriot than I should have been. I could see through American Legion-type rhetoric. But for several decades, I was not only a cold war liberal, but an unforgivably naive one to boot.

Where I was concerned, a great love of the

labor movement played a part. I was one of those who hoped for great things from labor and felt that it was good. One consequently was adamant against elements who might give labor a bad name, and, if one was not careful, one found oneself whapping Reds so that non-Reds would respect you, and your defense of the labor movement would be more effective. . . .

In the last analysis, however, the great Communist Left (I use the adjective "great" deliberately and sincerely) was destroyed by the upsurge of American righteousness and arrogance of which McCarthyism was merely a cheap expression. The United States, the darling, was heeding the call of manifest destiny. . . .

It is tragic that there is not a strong Left in American trade unions today. Was that more the fault of the Communists than of the likes of me? The Communists in the zesty days of the New Deal and the C.I.O. gobbled up the Left and attracted the eager young, so many of whom became disillusioned and abandoned the Left entirely when they abandoned Communism. Others were simply beaten into submission. In those days, the Communists were not models of tolerance themselves, and chewed up their opposition when they could.

Nonetheless, the American trade union movement would be healthier today if Phil Murray had not purged the C.I.O. and if a strong, broad based Communist minority had been able to survive in the trade unions. The split of the U.E. was a loss and so was the transformation of the U.A.W. into a monolith.

What bothers me personally, most of all, is that, in the very bad days of the Cold War, The Day of the Toad, Scoundrel Time, I did not defend all the victims. Of course, I fought McCarthy when he went after people I agreed with, but I did not defend brave people whose careers and lives were destroyed by McCarthyism because of membership, alliance or mere flirtation with Communism.

I was not wrong all the time and in some

good fights I did not hesitate to stand along side of Communists in trade union battles. But I think I wasted a lot of time on a crusade that did more harm than good. Far better had I concentrated exclusively on building strong, honest unions, exposing crooks, organizing the unorganized, and confronting the might of unchecked monopoly and aggrandizement.

*BLUEPRINT FOR THE CHRISTIAN
RESHAPING OF SOCIETY*
Vol. 29, no. 6, February 1977

Cardinal Mindszenty and History (1974)

It was the aftermath of World War II. Russia had taken the Balkans and that meant that country after country was converted to Communism by the sword, and whole Catholic peoples went under the yoke. It was not a happy set of occurrences and we saw it in its ugliest because we did not get the Russian side of the matter. The Russian Communists who had been our noble allies in the War, had very quickly become totally evil enemies.

Josef Cardinal Mindszenty was the Primate of Hungary and even though the Russians had absorbed his country he would not submit and would not be silent. He was a world figure. He opened his mouth and it was on the front pages. . . . He resisted the takeover of Catholic schools and took other brave stands.

The Communist authorities decided on a tough and daring tactic. They would bring this man low and crush him before all the world. He was arrested at the tag end of 1948 and forty days later (were the Communists influenced by biblical numerology?) he was produced in a court room where he confessed to crimes, conspiracies and treason. A broken man, he was tossed into jail, presumably to lie there disgraced and forgotten until he somehow did penance and made final peace with Communist omnipotence. It did not work out that way.

The public trial of Mindszenty was a disastrous Red mistake. It convinced men and women everywhere that the Communists were inhumanly clever and ruthless in that they could break a man of that sort. People believed that mysterious methods of torture and "brain washing" had been discovered and could be effective against anyone, threatening us all. The incident played into the hands of those who wanted a Cold War with Communism.

I could not do anything to help Cardinal Mindszenty in Hungary, but I sure as the dickens could fight with and damage Communists in the United States. To me it was the same fight. I accepted that the Reds were different, that they were dreadfully strong, that they were on the march and were capable of world conquest.

Why I did not realize that Russia was reeling from the effects of the long war and from Stalinism and that peace was possible I cannot tell you. Why I felt that a wipe out of the Communists and their allies from the American labor movement was not only desirable but necessary, again I cannot tell. But I do know this: the Mindszenty trial helped as did the memory of Stalin's many trials and executions of his own comrades. And 1948 was the year that Orwell predicted "1984," the year of final nightmare and totalitarian takeover. . . .

Cardinal Mindszenty lived through the German invasion as well as the Russian: he and his people suffered under both repressions. He was imprisoned by the Nazis but it is my impression that he did not fight them with the vehemence and persistence he showed toward the Communists.

Then there is the added factor of the crime of the century, perhaps the most shocking of history: the attempted complete extermination of the Jews. Hungary had a substantial Jewish population and a large proportion of that population was shipped to the ovens and killed. I have not heard of Cardinal Mindszenty playing a strong role in resisting that crime, although the Pope intervened, and the Hungarian Jews struggled hard in many ways, and did not simply accept their fate.

Did Cardinal Mindszenty know that the Hungarian Jews were being slaughtered? Did he do anything? Could he have done anything? How hard did he try?

PITTSBURGH CATHOLIC
July 5, 1974

Confessions of an Anti-Communist (1989)

Not long ago a young man, a college senior, came to interview me. He was doing a paper on the early days of the steel workers' union. His questions had to do with the role of the Communists in that episode: What threat did they pose? Why were so many of you so worried about them, fearful even?

I had to think, had to scramble mentally, had questions of my own, not for him but for myself. Why would he ask such questions? Were not the answers obvious? Of course they were not to his generation, and at least one earlier generation.

The world has changed. American Communism has lost not only its strength but its aura, its allure. No longer has it a mystique to tempt young idealistic intellectuals; this holds true for Communism in all developed, so called free nations. Marxism has not comparably lost its spiritual clout, but the variety which is called Communism, meaning roughly the Russian model, has.

I shall try as I go along to recreate the atmosphere, to convey the strength, attraction, pervasiveness and apparent durability of

Communism in America before, during and, for a time, after the Depression and then after World War II. Too bad that most scholars writing on the topic and studying it miss this vital point.

The enemy we fought was real, not a phantom. We exaggerated the danger, we went overboard, we were unAmerican and uncharitable, we lost our perspective; but we were, for good or ill, rightly or wrongly fighting real live Communists.

Communism then was much in the air. Tons of red baiting. What is red baiting? When you call some one who is not a Communist a Communist; that to my mind is red baiting. But to the true blue Communist, and his supporters, calling anyone at all a Communist, unless he or she is an open official Communist, even when you are telling the truth, is red baiting.

My connection with this issue began with my involvement with the unions; the birth of the CIO, first the Committee for Industrial Organization, quickly the Congress of Industrial Organizations, 1935–36; the yeasty days of the early New Deal. Henry Wallace said "the common man is on the march." What Wordsworth said of the Enthusiasts of the French Revolution was true of us labor enthusiasts of a half century ago: "Bliss was it in that dawn to be alive, and to be young was very heaven!" True for me at any rate. An old order seemed to be dying and a new one struggling to be born as Yeats once said.

The Communists made a contribution, the real ones with a capital "C," where the building of the CIO was concerned, and the rebuilding of the AFL, for that matter. They provided skilled organizers who were determined and idealistic and almost invariably very hard working. It did not matter that for many, perhaps most, their loyalty was first to the Communist Party and secondarily to the trade union movement. That hidden agenda! Did it hurt the "cause" that much? I thought it did, but, looking back, have to conclude that it did not. This is how I feel and think now. Then, I was more on the doctrinaire side and might have been hesitant to admit that chances were that they, committed Communists as they were, did more good than harm.

> **"Along with many other young people of that generation I held labor to be not just a worthy cause, but virtually a holy one."**

Along with many other young people of that generation I held labor to be not just a worthy cause, but virtually a holy one. Unions were not merely something that would make life better for working people but they could lead to the reform of society. They could energize and transform the working class and the rural proletariat and could actually change people, make them less selfish and so on. Even after I abandoned that rather naive belief I continued to champion unions, still do, and I believe in them today as a necessity for a just society. Stronger unions mean more economic health for most people. Unions should be democratically controlled and have honest leadership, but even less perfect unions are better than none at all.

This extraordinary regard, love would not be too strong a word, for the trade union movement contributed to my intensity in the fight against the Communists. I was sincerely convinced that they had a chance to take over America's entire labor movement or, at least the major portion of it, as they had in France and, after WWII in Italy, and that would have been pure disaster. When I say, I no longer hold that view, I am witness to a tremendous-personal change of attitude and conviction. Their takeover would have been a disaster because of the reaction it would provoke; but there was no chance, absolutely no chance, of that happening.

Their big moment came with the first surge of organizing in the mid-1930s, and a lesser one during World War II when the U.S. and Russia were fighting on the same side. Post war, they thought that opportunities were rife and the times were ripe for their power and influence to swell, and some of us, their opponents, felt the same way. We were both wrong.

A persistent question is, what would have happened if their control of unions had increased, or even been solidified, and if Phil Murray and the CIO had not turned on them? I still believe that the resultant reaction would have been bad, if not disastrous, for labor: more and worse repressive legislation and a hobbling of all unions. The great post-war boom in trade union membership and the consequent economic gains of the American labor force would have been in danger.

I believe that trade union strength and pressure, more than any other factor, were responsible for the good times that rolled. Too much Communism, too visible, would have hurt the cause.

The CP were good organizers technically and in terms of spirit, aggressiveness, and courage. They were, for the most part, on the right side of battles legislative and social.

What was wrong with them and their struggle? For one thing, too sectarian and too merciless in battle. A lot of bodies left on the field. I saw them destroy people who would not go along. They were formidable as well as merciless; they wiped out slobs as well as worthy foes. In my struggle with them, and vice versa, they met a foeman worthy of their steel. I was just as tough as they were, and, God forgive me, as merciless, at least for a while — until I

got religion, so to speak.

Left wing politics was fascinating in those days and I was quite influenced by the blood enemies of the Communists, the Socialists, always retaining a sneaking admiration for the more ruthless, the Communists. The Socialists, I realize now, set out to influence me, and they succeeded. Due to their indoctrination, I was not a routine Red baiter, but an informed one. At least I did not make the mistake of calling an ordinary Socialist, of whatever variety, a Communist and was reasonably precise in my attacks and delations [accusations]. Early I learned to distinguish who was who and what was what among the left, and whacked only the Communists. . . .

Why the hostility of progressives like me? What fed our hostility to them? Many things: they were unwavering in their support of the Soviet Union, including Josef Stalin, and took direction from that quarter; furthermore, they constantly pushed all organizations, unions in particular, which they controlled, or in which they had strength, to follow the same line. They had a Party Line (their term) on everything, it seemed; they advocated the Line powerfully and without gloss.

Control was sought in a surprising variety of societies and enterprises: social, artistic, even charitable. And they would promote their fellow members, their sympathizers or people who were ideologically neutral but cooperative with whomever was running the show. Some few they would try to convert, these would be ones with special potential. No attempt at mass conversions, that might have come later if they had continued to prosper, which was not in the cards.

They were great battlers and gave no quarter, especially in their wars with other Marxist parties, the Trotskyites above all. In addition they had purges within their own ranks. They were scary and were redoubtable adversaries.

However they were not so formidable as

they claimed in their heyday, nor as I continued to think for too long. My regrets about the whole business, on looking back, cluster around my over intensity and my unremitting enmity, almost a blood feud that went on and on until well after they ceased to be a domestic threat along with my complete acceptance of our country's Cold War stance and rhetoric. I should have been fighting the Arms Race and supporting peace then and been an early antiwar agitator.

Johnson's invasion of the Dominican Republic started me thinking properly, and Vietnam completed the process but that is another story. . . .

The Communists were, as I've been indicating, good trade unionists. They were financially honest and dedicated. If in the backs of their minds they were preparing for the revolution, they acted as if they were not. For the most part they served the trade union needs of their members. We will note a possible exception but first let me give you one example of their dedication.

Jim Matles of the UE, one of the three top international officers, worked both himself and his staff mercilessly, and would not take a large salary. Nor did any UE official. They had a rule, still have it, equating their compensation with that of the highest of any working member of their union. When pensions came in and staff pensions were being arranged, Jim said that if they worked as he wanted them to, they would not live to enjoy their pensions. It proved to be true in his case; he died not long after retirement.

Even when I was battling them I realized, after a bit and after looking at American labor history, that often, when they were turned out of a union, less dedicated and sometimes crooked men or women succeeded them. Not that they would not under extreme necessity cut a deal with the baddies for temporary advantage. Expedient, they would be and could be, but not crooked themselves.

The cloud over this bright picture: they were not crooked, but dishonest in another way, their dealings with the Soviet Union. Briefly, they not only accepted, but justified the horrors of the Stalin era: the Gulags, starvation in the Ukraine, the Purges and Show Trials, even the pact with Hitler, but they also insisted, as I noted above, on going on record and making others go on record.

Their brand of trade union politics was rough and marked, when required, with some dishonesty, not stealing money, but telling lies, assassinating characters and stealing votes. They were not the only union politicians to do this sort of thing, but they were a disciplined and clever crew. Other unions, very respectable ones, such as the Steel Workers, were far less scrupulous about ballots and open, honest elections than the Red unions. Retroactively it was hypocritical of me to introduce the subject in connection with the UE, since in that day I did not fuss with my friends in other unions about it. . . .

They were tremendous at stacking a meeting, but also at getting out the vote and selling their point of view. What they wanted was good for the workers; their opponents were stooges for management and for the worst elements of reaction or whatever was evil at the moment. They did it well and certainly

> "**T**hey were tremendous at stacking a meeting, but also at getting out the vote and selling their point of view. What they wanted was good for the workers; their opponents were stooges for management."

applied themselves unstintingly.

What they did was within the limits of acceptable conduct in a democratic society. They were intense and committed; so they were true believers, somewhat annoying for their foes, but not illegal nor unAmerican.

There was a period during which Local 601 of the United Electrical Workers would change hands frequently. When the opposition would gain control, the Left Wing would make the local ungovernable and its meetings anarchic. Once after they had won back the local, I took a leaf from their book and with 20 people or so (I did not dare to be present, but laid out a simple scenario of the sort of disrupting tactics which they employed routinely and expertly) drove them crazy. Tom Fitzpatrick, their splendid, local grass roots leader threw up his hands in despair. I did this just once: hadn't the time nor the inclination to pursue the tactic indefinitely. The moral of this little item? Nothing, other than, in order to beat them you had to have good people who would work hard, and you had to know what you were doing, at least tactically.

Getting good people, good union people, as anti-Communist troops was not easy once the Left Wingers had a local; generally they were the ones who had organized the outfit to begin with. As John M. Duffy used to point out: there is only so much talent in any group of working people, and the first ones on the scene generally pick up that talent and keep its loyalty. They have to be dislodged; I was neither the world's best, nor the world's worst dislodger.

Whether or not I should have been at it, is another question, the answer to which I cannot give. Yours will have to be that verdict.

One can get too close, so close as to impair one's judgment as both observer and participant. In my case I identified with a certain faction of the labor movement; it was a huge faction and I would still judge it to have been mostly right, that is, it supported the right causes and the right people; had the right principles and prejudices; and its social, political and economic dogmas were compassionate and enlightened.

My view of the Communists was colored by what I heard from this faction, which had its clones in Democratic politics, the New Deal bureaucracies, the academic world, social agencies, and within the old American Federation of Labor. You may gather that I was not an innovative thinker, although I might have passed for one at that moment in ordinary clerical circles.

There was a significant complement of learned clergy, all denominations but heavily Catholic, attuned to this same consensus. . . .

John L. Lewis accepted the accolades of the consensus when it was offered but, as in everything else, was his own man for good or ill. Although I admired him immensely and regarded him as a hero, like the others of my frame of mind, I was uneasy over his relationship to the Communists. He had thrown them out of his own Mine Workers well before this, but he welcomed them back, not to the old Miners' fold, but to the new fold of the CIO. Welcomed is too strong a word because it was his way to let bygones be bygones, but to demand absolute loyalty in the future. They understood the game and played it his way, just so long as it suited. Each used the other; they were more wary than he. John L. did not worry about them; but they worried about him.

Individual old Lewis enemies, such as John Brophy and Alan Haywood, received the same pragmatic absolution and were put to work organizing and building.

The Socialists were so upset about Lewis's use and tolerance of the Communists that their paladin, Dave Dubinsky, pulled his union, ILGWU, out of the early CIO and one of his intellectuals wrote a fierce polemic, "The Story of the CIO," that was a long diatribe against John L. and his Red allies. That disturbed me but it did not influence me or most of the consensus. Benjamin Stolberg was the author; he was an early prototype of the ex-Socialist, neo-conservative characters who now dominate Commentary and serve Reaganism.

Once when Lewis was reproached over his alliance with the Communists he said something about the tail not wagging the dog. His foes asked, which is the tail and which the dog? Although we may have had our doubts then, subsequent developments showed that there was never any doubt which was which.

John L. was one of the greats of his time, and he played his part to the hilt with studied flamboyance, more than a touch of magnificence and a sense that he was not as ordinary men; his miners loved it and so did most workers and many who were not workers. The Left Wing flacked for him then and ministered to his celebrity, and vanity.

FDR with his Wagner Act had changed the labor situation, changed it utterly. All unions benefitted. The United Mine Workers with their strong and seasoned leaders staged an amazing recovery; they, who had been reduced to a few thousand in the late 1920s roared back to 500,000 strong by 1935 with Lewis in total control and high esteem. He had the moxie and the clout to invest a half million dollars of miners' money in the founding of the CIO. In '36 he had been a powerful backer of FDR but so had many others. 'Tis said that Lewis expected too much gratitude and a bit of loving from FDR; but here was another magnificent man whose favors were not easily extracted, and who knew instinctively what he had to give and what he could withhold.

To return to the Communists, Murray like Lewis accepted their help, and did not feel like clipping their wings, so long as they behaved; but it was Lewis and not he who had invited them in and they always made Phil a bit uneasy. Not surprisingly, after the "Little Steel" Strike and the violence some of the Communists seem to have had a hand in, Murray quietly got rid of the ones who had key staff positions within the Steel Workers Organizing Committee, his responsibility. They did not fuss but accepted; some of them were very good and were missed, but they acquiesced for the sake of the cause.

Before the Molotov-Ribbentrop Pact, of September 1939, the Left Wing were in their Popular Front phase, with emphasis on anti-Fascism; after the pact they turned decidedly against war and for peace because the only war possible for America was one on the side of the Allies and against Stalin's buddy of the moment. As I remember they did not speak up for Hitler or Mussolini, soft pedaled that topic. They were not comfortable but they dutifully spoke out for American non-intervention.

American Communists had impressive momentum toward the end of the 1930s and that carried them through sticky times. After all, Russia not only made a pact with Nazi Germany, but also took a piece out of Poland while Hitler was invading; and there was her annexation of the Baltic nations. Sustaining the American Communists' momentum was their reservoir of good will among liberals and intellectuals.

One cannot deny that this was earned. There was their tough labor record and their support of fine causes. They were vociferous and eloquent in their anti-lynching and anti-poll tax agitation; withal they were sincere and effective in their striving for racial justice and against discrimination. Their championing of the Loyalist side in the Spanish Civil War displeased some Catholics, including this one unfortunately, but went down well with most Americans. Their support of the CIO and labor in general, and, very importantly, the whole New Deal, helped them in this quarter.

Rice (seated at center) in labor school class for Braddock steel workers. Pat Hammil is the speaker.

Then they had special good causes, which they made their own; free Tom Mooney, the Scotsboro Boys, and other less spectacular ones. All in all they had moral capital and credibility.

Their worst moment in this interlude came when John L. Lewis split with Roosevelt and backed Republican Wendell L. Willkie, who oddly enough was as much an interventionist as the President, in the 1940 election. John L., their imperious friend, tried to get them to follow him, but they evaded him and ran their own slate. They sat out the election and did not pressure the rank and file members of the unions they controlled; and when the election was over they resumed their vociferous support of John L.

In his radio address asking his members and all of Labor to repudiate Roosevelt and vote for Willkie, Lewis had said he would resign if they did not. The CIO National Convention was called to order two weeks later in Atlantic City. As you would expect the sessions were tense and full of exciting and dramatic episodes; also the Convention was a rumor factory. The Communists urged Lewis not to resign and electioneered for him strenuously.

Hard to believe what a good account the Communists gave of themselves at this juncture. Lewis, their champion, at least in their estimation, had gone against Roosevelt, whom the workers really loved, and was sulking because the workers would not choose him over Roosevelt. In addition they were attacking Roosevelt's policies and indirectly the man himself. Their own great leader, Stalin, had done a deal with Hitler and, while they could understand the logic of the deal (I can now, although I do not and could not approve of it now or then); the deal was simply not explicable to the normal American workers. Still the Communists held their ground, and while they were bloodied they survived.

Upon Hitler's invasion of Russia in June of the following year the whole picture changed, the American Communists were off and running and did very well during the War; they were more patriotic than anyone else with a few side bars such as agitating for a Second Front early on. They had turned on a dime.

John L. Lewis, because of his consistent isolationism, was transformed for them into "a hissing and a reproach" and Philip Murray became their hero and the new object of fulsome praise, which was not without its influence on Phil, as I could not help noticing.

During the war anti-Communism was not popular and, you must remember, Uncle Joe Stalin was. Battling his American friends and supporters was no easy task. Less than ever were the Communists pushovers. Actually they were riding high and continued so to ride ad tempus, as we say in Latin.

During, and right after the war, one got a wary reception from the priests for the simple reason that many of their best parishioners were loyal and happy members of the UE or possibly another Red union; then there was the glow of Pan Slavism, pride in the Russians, fellow Slavs, who had behaved so nobly in the war and actually won it. People refuse to remember those days and how it felt, even if they are old enough.

Then, when the cold war got hot, this changed and some of my fellow priests became zealots and things were said from the pulpit that I did not particularly want to have said. The bit was in the teeth and away they went; probably some of it was my fault because I started it.

Eventually Phil Murray moved openly against the Communist controlled unions on trade union grounds; they flouted the decisions of the CIO arrived at in convention assembled. They insisted on backing Henry Wallace in the Presidential election of 1948 and kept on denouncing the Marshall Plan.

The Taft-Hartley Act made it easier to raid the unions whose officers would not sign its infamous affidavits affirming that they were not Communists. There was an exception, of course, and a big one; John L. Lewis and his Miners would not sign and toughed it out; to hell with the Federal Government, its help or its coercion. And no one was foolish enough to try to raid them. But the Communist unions were regarded as fair game and they were raided to pieces. That I did not favor, what I wanted was strong internal opposition, but the labor movement does not work that way.

The CIO is merged with the AFL, something that Murray resisted; both the Steel Workers and the Miners have come upon hard times with the virtual collapse of American manufacturing; neither labor unions nor labor leaders are any longer so important as they were in the glory days about which I have been reminiscing.

No longer do I regard my battle against the Left Wing (Communist) unions as being glorious. It engrossed me then but now I find reflection upon it depressing.

The Communist episode was a sad business: wonderful, idealistic people, deceived and deceiving, crafty but noble — and eventually so often destroyed along with what they had exhausted and broken themselves to build.

LABOR HISTORY
Summer, 1989

The McCarthy Era (1973)

In the aftermath of World War II Joseph McCarthy defeated a great liberal, Bob LaFollette, Jr., to enter the United States Senate. He had stumbled on the tremendous power of anti-Communism as an issue and became the instant folk hero of the right. Up to a point he was attended by great luck but also he was "good," a natural demagogue, one of the best.

Joe scared the stuffin' out of politicians because, when certain distinguished and powerful members of the Senate went after him, he went after them and wiped them out! McCarthy was reckless, fearless, had an instinct for the jugular, and the tide was running with him.

Brave men became rabbits and were afraid to mess with Joe. It turned out that his tactical sense was excellent but, of strategy and long range planning, he had none at all. He went far on what he had, but his downfall was inevitable.

His tactic was simple: shoot at everything that moves and keep shooting. Don't back away or take cover, call the other guy a liar, promise to come up with the proof but don't bother, and always throw the charges, Communist, pinko, supporter of Communism.

He started on the State Department and said he had a list of 250 Communists in there; when he was challenged he waffled for a day or two but as the mail and telegrams started flooding in to support him, he was off and running. He never produced much of anything except charges and new charges but he kept going, the media kept covering him, and he was impervious to the best ammo of the opposition.

Senator McCarthy would apply the dread label, Communist, not only to Communists, their supporters and those who wanted to tolerate them, to liberals, reformers and radicals (even respectables do that to this very day), but also to anyone who opposed or displeased him for any reason whatsoever. He was popping people right in the establishment.

He made the mistake of picking on those who could fight back which is always bad. Too many strong folks felt threatened and the powers went after him. They had all enjoyed him for a while and they used him, but he got too big for his britches. . . .

Joe did many shameful things and he told lies galore but they (the whole establishment, Republican and Democratic, liberal and conservative) chose to check him on a nice specific issue. Did McCarthy, or his staff at his bidding, try to get the U.S. Army to do a favor for a friend of his, or was the Army being nasty to Joe because he wanted to expose Communists within it?

The Senate investigation went far afield and when it was over McCarthy was done. He vanished from the front pages, nobody listened when he barked and in a short while he died; killed by a bad liver rather than a broken heart, incidentally.

Weeks of constant TV exposure as he orated, sneered, insinuated and avoided producing proofs finished him. He, however, has supporters to this day. Our Catholic leadership as it fawned on McCarthy and encouraged him had its unfinest hour. . . .

The powers had set McCarthy up in the hearings. They put him on trial, him not the Army, and they closed ranks against him. The betting was that he could not act with restraint but would knock himself out; he did.

There lay his fault (a happy fault for the sake of decency), no inner censor to tell him when he went too far. You see it was all right for him to smear Democrats, liberal Republicans, the colleges, actors, bureaucrats large and small (others were doing the same and getting by), but President Eisenhower was out of season, so was our grand and glorious military, and so were a variety of respectable men and institutions, which McCarthy did not fear but would have been wise to. . . .

McCarthy destroyed people, most of them little people, and he seemed to enjoy the work.

McCarthyism was an era and a malignancy and it had an effect on liberals of a certain type who became ultra anti-Communist; even some, who had been sensible and tolerant, began proclaiming that their anti-Communism was as strong as anyone's. They would think that they were correct because they were careful to be hostile only to real Communists, or, at most, fellow travellers, but bad laws were passed, some of which were sponsored by liberal legislators, and freedom suffered.

It annoys me that I was one of those bad liberals, my only virtue being that, unlike others, I had not played up to the Communists when they were strong and could help one. I deeply regret that I did not fight to have their rights fully respected. Communism seemed almost irresistible and certainly irreversible; it is only a step from regarding the enemy as super human to regarding him as unhuman.

PITTSBURGH CATHOLIC
August 31, 1973

Murray speaking to CIO Convention during World War II.
"Work. Keep working. Produce. Keep producing."

▣ Phil Murray and Steel

Smug Steel Makers (1948)

If any labor leader ever had a sense of responsibility and a desire to do what is best not only for his members but for the country and the world at large, Philip Murray is that man. Consequently it gave serious students of the labor movement quite a turn when Ben Fairless [chairman of U.S. Steel], with smug and mealy-mouthed pratings about the common good, calmly kicked Murray and the Steelworkers Union.

Murray signed a two year contract with the Steel Corporation last year. At the time it seemed certain that relations were such that if prices continued to rise, the Steel Corporation would grant a "cost of living" increase, without the strike weapon pointed at its throat. It seemed certain that U.S. Steel was pretty anxious for good relations and labor peace over the long haul.

But what happened? The Steel Corporation raised in the course of the year its prices on practically everything it sells. It did it piecemeal. The raise of last February that caused such a hullabaloo was merely the last in a series of raises. Prices were raised so as to bring to Steel over three times its increased wage costs.

After a month of shadow-boxing, the smug Steel makers plainly told the union there would be no wage raise this year and in the phoniest and most obvious of gestures, announced a cut in prices, not quite equal to the increase of last February.

It was sickening to read the praise heaped upon U.S. Steel for its grandstand play, but this is a cheap, momentary victory, that is going to be very costly in the end.

This minor price cut will not stem the tide of inflation. If it had amounted to 70 or 80 million, it could have been effective and the Steelworkers would have objected very little.

A year from now, the members of the Steelworkers union are going to see that prices have continued to rise instead of falling; and no one will ever be able to tell them again that an increase in wages is the factor that raises prices. The Steelworkers will be ready to fight. Their spirit will be better than it was two years ago.

Mr. Fairless and his associates will never again get a nickel's worth of trust from Murray or any other union leader. Relations in steel were on their way to a happy plane of mutual trust and confidence. That is done!

PITTSBURGH CATHOLIC
April 30, 1948

Convention (1948)

The Steelworkers convention . . . was a business session. Its purpose was to make certain constitutional changes, to take a political stand, and to sound off against the steel companies and the Communists. All this was done.

Two years ago Philip Murray, president of the Steelworkers, in spite of his control over the loyalties of his union members, had trouble on two issues, one of which he lost.

It seems to some observers that he stood a chance of losing on several issues this time. It did not seem that there would be much trouble over the increase in officers' salaries but that there might be a row over extension of the terms of officers, increase of dues from $1.50 to $2.00 and reduction of the number of delegates from one per 100 to one per 500. However, the whole thing went smoothly and there was no trouble.

Murray is in a position to strengthen his control by means of muscle or machine tactics. But he operates through persuasion. His directors carry his policy to the members, but their strength alone could not win the day without the force of Murray's personal influence.

From the average rank-and-file members and delegates Murray receives a spontaneous reverence. Yes, reverence is the word for the feeling which these rugged steelworkers have for their president. They think of him as fair, just, wise, good and strong. They all have an affection for him; that is why Nick Migas was manhandled when he mouthed the Communist line that Murray has sold out to the companies. The delegates were outraged and the beating Migas got was spontaneous — no rehearsed affair.

Murray has no "goon squad." He refuses to operate that way. He saw the curse that this thing was in the United Mine Workers. Once you have a "goon squad," in a union, you can never have peace because the "goons" have to be taken care of and when there is no "work" for them to do, they will make some.

Commies in Steel

The great failure of the Communist Party in the mid-thirties was their failure to gain a toehold in Murray's steel union. They have never ceased trying to get in. They have a few little beachheads; they have strength in the big Gary union. They are in a few spots on the West Coast, and in a few scattered locals in and around Pittsburgh and Philadelphia. Murray and his leaders will clean them out with the new provision in the union's constitution that denies the right to hold office to a Communist. Murray does not want to deny them membership, but he does want to deny

them, and their stooges, the right to lead any segment, however small, of his beloved steelworkers.

Incidentally the Trotskyites are in a few locals. They are even more annoying than Stalinists because they are against all constructive moves.

PITTSBURGH CATHOLIC
May 20, 1948

Murray—A Great Man (1948)

Philip Murray is a great American. One of the greatest living. To understand his greatness you have to examine him from three points of view.

Take the United Steelworkers of America. This union is nearly a million strong. Murray built it to that strength in ten years. He did it against the opposition of the toughest, slickest and most resourceful corporation of them all, U.S. Steel. As he built the union, Murray taught trade union attitudes and fundamentals to the people. His union has changed, at his direction and by his desire, from a benevolent paternalism to a vigorous democracy. It is now a democratic set-up without the factionalism that has ripped and torn every other big union. This is a tremendous achievement. Any man who had this alone to his credit would be entitled to the appellation "great."

Built CIO

To examine the second phase of Murray's achievement. Look at the CIO.

When Murray took over the CIO in 1940 it was on the verge of falling apart. John L. Lewis had got out because he expected it to collapse, and he did not want the stigma of failure. The CIO was financially busted. Its unions were weak in membership and it was wracked by pro- and anti-Communist factions.

Murray saved the CIO. He held it together. He put it on its feet financially. He survived the loss of the miners; he kept the factions away from each other's throats and he kept the Communists from increasing their jurisdiction.

The CIO now is strong enough to afford a factional fight; it is strong enough to deal with its Communists and if the Communists pull out, they will hardly be missed. This achievement with the CIO by itself is enough to put the stamp of greatness on the man.

The final phase of Murray's career is his contacts in national and international matters as a man of great influence and prestige. It can be said that Murray's conduct has always been constructive. It is impossible to point to a single instance where he has acted out of personal pique or personal ambition. He has had the power to paralyze the nation; he has had the power to make unreasonable demands; he has had the power and the nerve to lead the nation to the brink of disaster so as to gain a point. He has never used his power in such a fashion.

You look in vain to see Murray take a stand in national politics or international affairs which is based on anything other than solid, Christian liberalism. He invariably takes the sound, progressive, constructive course. Witness his support of President Roosevelt, before and during the war and his opposition to the Third Party movement today.

In my opinion all this is the measure of a great man in the strictest sense of the term. A man not only great, but good!

PITTSBURGH CATHOLIC
July 15, 1948

Partial Victory (1949)

Although the entire battle is far from won, Philip Murray scored an impressive victory when he outmaneuvered Big Steel last week. It seemed apparent to observers that this first round of the battle was over as soon as the Big Steel people began to hem and haw over President Truman's proposal to postpone the strike and appoint a fact-finding board.

As soon as they began to haggle they were done. They were already in a poor position by first refusing to cooperate with the President. They could have saved themselves only by the most astute maneuvering and that they were unable to arrange.

A very, very significant development was the splitting of the solid front of the steel companies. The smaller companies have never before dared to disregard the leadership of U.S. Steel. But they did it this time and left the big company holding the bag. Murray's skill in splitting the ranks of his opponents is comparable to John L. Lewis' achievement in the coal strike of 1922.

After that strike the big coal companies proceeded to devour or ruin their smaller defiers. That may be tried in the steel industry, but it is doubtful, because you have big banking interests on both sides—the Mellons and the Morgans. Besides, the day of industrial freebooting is going fast.

Strike Eventually?

The strike is still not to be ruled out completely. Murray wants that pension, and his people will back him up. Pay no attention to all that talk about rank-and-filers opposing the leaders' decision to strike. The steel worker is not yet as rock-ribbed a union man as the miner; but he is pretty good, and he can enter upon and sustain a strike.

When the report of the fact finders comes in, Big Steel will balk. Then you may have a short, sharp strike. I have not met anyone who is not pulling for the workers to get a pension. Sentiment will be even stronger when the hearings are concluded because the steel union knows how to present its side of the case and knows how to get its story out to the public.

PITTSBURGH CATHOLIC
July 21, 1949

Morale (1949)

As the rank-and-file of the Steelworkers read newspaper accounts of the hearings before the Presidential panel in New York, their morale gets better. They are psychologically even better prepared for the strike than they were. For they very much resent the testimony of the corporations and they admire the ferociousness of the attacks that Philip Murray has been making against the Steel Citadel. If the steel corporations had sat down and tried to determine the type of testimony that would most anger the steel worker, they could not have done better. . . .

A Stab in the Back

As Philip Murray reaches the climax of his fight for pensions and security, the officials of Communist-controlled unions will be meeting in New York City on Aug. 30 to plan a dual labor movement.

This deliberate stab-in-the-back comes with full knowledge that it will weaken the cause of the workers. It is no coincidence that the Communists make their move at a time when Murray is locked in a struggle with the most powerful corporations in the country.

At their meeting the Communists may decide to pull out of the CIO and start a new national federation that will be affiliated with the World Federation of Trades Unions, a Communist movement. Even if they do not take the final step at this moment, they will lay their plans for this betrayal of the American worker. It will mark their downfall, but they will be serving the Russian interests of the moment and that is all they care for.

PITTSBURGH CATHOLIC
September 1, 1949

Steel Strike (1949)

It looks like a long one.

It looks to this observer as if the bankers who control U.S. Steel have determined to stem the rising tide of American unionism by provoking this strike and defeating the U.S. Steelworkers, at the same time damaging the prestige of Philip Murray.

The circumstances that made the strike inevitable may have been deliberately planned. It will be remembered that when the recommendations of the President's Fact-Finding Board were first announced, responsible officials of Big Steel, off the record, indicated that they were pleased.

The Steelworkers, who were not too pleased with the award, at first indicated that they might reject it and then, for the sake of peace, publicly announced that they would accept. "Big Steel" then changed the signals and began to talk about contributory and non-contributory pensions.

It is pretty obvious that they were looking for a handle, any handle to reject the Board's findings. Their moral position is weaker than ever after the Ford's acceptance of non-contributory pensions. However, in high banking and industrial circles, there exists a powerful group which advocates the necessity of slugging it out sooner or later with the unions. They feel that a defeat administered to one of the largest and most powerful of the labor unions will slow all of them down.

Morale

The morale of the Steel strikers is exceptionally high. I have made some personal checks. They are prepared to hold out, no matter how long it takes. Their confidence in Phil Murray was never greater. They feel he had no other choice than to take them out and they feel that he and they will win.

Murray's presentation of his case was effective with the general public and with his own members. In the past two months he sold them completely on what he was trying to do.

Steel and Coal

The Steel strike is hurting the coal strike, rather than vice versa. There is enough coal over ground for continued full operation for some 45 days. The longer the steel strike, the more coal available and the weaker Lewis' position. Lewis will now have to have his miners out in the cold weather and nobody wants that. The exceptional productivity of the mechanized mine is the factor that hurt the miners.

But Lewis is by no means reduced to impotence. He still can, and will, get something for his people, unless the coal operators are determined to fight to the finish. In spite of various dope stories to that effect—I don't believe it. Of course, if they beat Murray's union, they might feel able to handle John L., but they won't beat Murray.

PITTSBURGH CATHOLIC
October 6, 1949

Stumping the Country (1949)

Philip Murray demonstrates his usual directness and courage in stumping the country. Lewis does not face the rank and file directly when the heat is on. Few big leaders would have sufficient confidence in their hold on the rank and file to go right to them in time of strike. Funny things can happen in a strike and it takes a brave man to schedule large public meetings when the pot is boiling. Murray's tactics will pay great dividends, because they will bring the story not only to his own people but the entire public.

PITTSBURGH CATHOLIC
October 20, 1949

Steel Strike Aftermath (1949)

Viewing the matter calmly the magnitude of Murray's victory in steel grows every day. His union gained in solid achievement in the way of pensions and insurance benefits. More than this the victory for all working people in the country grows apace.

Senator Robert Taft has made a remarkable proposal for study of a universal pension of $10 a month. Other influential conservatives admit that they simply must swim with the tide. Murray's victory saves the pension idea which otherwise would have been set back for years. . . .

PITTSBURGH CATHOLIC
December 1, 1949

Annual Wage (1952)

Philip Murray wants a guaranteed annual wage for the members of his steel union. He wants this with the full realization that it will be a precedent that will benefit all the workers of the United States. He wants to make this great contribution to the welfare of the American wage earner. After he forced the steel companies to grant decent pensions, the Congress granted more liberal social security payments. You can be sure that the winning of a guaranteed annual wage will mean increased unemployment benefits.

The reactionaries in Congress fight tooth and nail against shelling out money for the workers and the poor, but they are always glad to open the box for the relief of the corporations.

PITTSBURGH CATHOLIC
February 21, 1952

Whose Ox? (1952)

The steel companies and their supporters are delighted when government powers are used to force men to work by way of injunction; they are unhappy when companies are prevented from a lockout by means of government seizure (technical seizure, at that). Which is the more important violation of freedom, forcing men to do your will, or forcing aggregations of capital?

Let us remember as Catholics that the big heresy of "liberalism" is the personalization of property and the regarding of property rights as equal with human rights.

Dilemma

We have a dilemma here. An industry like steel in a time of crisis is too big, in this complicated society, to be permitted a prolonged shutdown. Too many other things go down with it.

And yet there is some violation of freedom in any government interference. Technical government seizure is not always enough; in the railroad industry this technical seizure has frozen the status quo and permitted the companies to simply deny certain demands of their unions with impunity.

Seizure with teeth would be more fair than injunctions against working people. . . .

PITTSBURGH CATHOLIC
April 17, 1952

Hell, Go to, That Is (1952)

Philip Murray's use of a good sturdy colloquialism to describe his attitude toward the steel corporations disturbed only the Pharisees. In saying that the corporations could either grant the union the WSB formula or go to hell Phil was merely expressing determination and was making no judgment as to the ultimate disposition of the souls of the hard-faced characters who control Big Steel.

Phil's tough talk at this past convention is not surprising. He is not a gentle person. He is occasionally mild-mannered and he is generally jovial; but in labor negotiations and many other phases of his work he is a pretty rough customer.

He does not go into the mock Shakespearean orotundity of some of his contemporaries in labor leadership—but the rough edge of his tongue is quite rough. If this were not so he could not have achieved and maintained his pre-eminence in a very hard-boiled occupation.

I suppose it is true that he is smoother than most of his fellows, but that smoothness goes when the occasion demands.

Convention

I attended the last day of the Steelworkers' convention in Philadelphia last week. The bulk of the oratory, both domestic and imported, was over and the union was engaged in a business session.

Most of the speaking was by rank and file delegates. The payrollers did very little talking. Murray had a few sticky questions, e.g., dues increase, that he wanted put over. In other organizations the official spellbinders batter the mute delegates for hours before such crucial votes. Philip Murray simply let the delegates talk. Of course, his staff had previously done some spade work, but not so much as you might imagine.

In at least one instance Murray himself was swayed by the logic of the speakers and suggested a change in a proposed measure. It was really a democratic deal.

The brand of oratory from the floor was good. And, interestingly enough, more Colored than white delegates felt the urge and hit the floor.

I thought that it was about as democratically run as was possible. I do not believe that the delegates had any sense of being steamrollered, and yet Phil Murray dominated that convention, just as much as the more arrant bullies dominate theirs.

The big difference is that he is not afraid of his convention or his members. You would be surprised how many of the muscle men with the loud roars are afraid of their people — that is why they do not dare to let up for an instant.

Settlement

The strike? The Steelworkers will get their just raise or else. They will back Murray, because they know that he will fight their cause through to the bitter end.

PITTSBURGH CATHOLIC
May 22, 1952

In Memoriam: Phil Murray (1952)

I speak to you with a heavy heart this night concerning the death of a great and beloved friend of mine. Philip Murray died early this morning, died at the other coast of this continent, died in the midst of his work. Many thousands of America's citizens are literally heart-broken at his passing, as I confess that I am.

I regret his death because it leaves a void — his work, as we poor human beings see it, was not finished; he was needed! Needed for his million steel workers, needed for the 16 million men and women in the organized labor movement, for the more than 60 million workers of the United States, and for every underdog and every decent, liberal cause.

But the greatest regret, I feel, is a selfish one. I shall miss him as a friend. He was the friendliest man I ever met. His friendship was a warm and warming thing. It is hard that his strong gentle voice is stilled, that his hearty laugh and wonderful chuckle will be heard no more. The stories that he told so well will be repeated by other lips but they will not be the same.

I am glad that circumstances caused me to see a great deal of him, particularly in the past year and a half. I heard him at meetings, on television, over the radio, in small rooms and large, and at a great variety of gatherings. I saw him preside over his great steel workers conventions, two, the last twelve months. I saw him in private consultation with his leaders as they developed strategy and worked out problems. And many, many times I talked to him personally over things of interest to him and myself. I was with him as he visited sick friends and relatives in hospitals.

Not often have we the opportunity to observe the great ones of the earth as they go about their daily tasks, not often do we observe great, human, humble figures so close to us. Not often do we see those who "can walk with kings, nor lose the common touch."

There are many pictures in my mind of Philip Murray. I remember him handling angry brawling CIO conventions with unbelievable finesse, being gentle when necessary and then figuratively knocking heads together, scolding nationally prominent men as if they were school boys and making them like it.

He could control great unruly gatherings very well, and other men can do that also; but his way with other strong, and strong minded, men of prominence, had to be seen to be believed. How many times angry factions came into his presence for a knock-down-drag-out-showdown, with newspapermen and the curious standing around waiting for the excitement, and there was no excitement. The irreconcilable were reconciled; no one knew just how, but there it was.

I remember him among his more humble friends and his relatives and listening to jokes. He had a great interest in the foibles of people. . . .

He had utterly no regard for social life. He told me that President Roosevelt and Mrs.

Roosevelt used to pressure him to visit the White House socially but he could not bring himself to participate in that sort of social life. He never went. As he once said, he was more at home in the kitchens of his friends in the mining patches and the steel towns.

He lived most simply, though he could have afforded a more elaborate existence.

He told jokes on himself. Once he consented to attend a big fancy "blow out," in the days when he first took over the Steelworkers. He rented evening clothes for the occasion and when he got to the lobby of the hotel to his horror he discovered that he was the only one so togged out. He scuttled back to his room and changed, and later when Ed Stettinius [Morgan Bank] mentioned that he thought he had seen him earlier dressed differently, Phil said, he assured him it must have been someone else.

He had these humilities and his hatred of swank, and I must say that he balanced it. I never saw a man possessed of more natural dignity. He had the sort of dignity that an aristocrat might envy; it made itself felt when he entered a room or a hall. There was nothing solemn or long faced about this dignity. It could not be described, it was just there.

When he assumed presidency of the CIO that organization was on its last legs. No large CIO union had exclusive representation rights with the industrial giants that it dealt with. No CIO union had any treasury to speak of. They were all on a hand to mouth basis. The might of American industry was at best half organized and at this time the tide had already begun to turn against the New Deal.

At the time of Phil Murray's death all the big CIO unions are sound financially and represent the bulk of big American Industry.

During the war he was a peacemaker. He got everything he could for his own union and others, but he kept the no-strike pledge to the letter. Delicate and constructive labor states-

manship was his forte.

He waged a great successful battle against Communism in the CIO. When he took over, the CIO was riddled with Communists. They controlled a million actual or potential members. In the years since the war he met them head on.

There were many who thought that he did not move soon enough, but he moved fast and in deadly fashion when the time was ripe. He waited until the Reds were embarked on an arrogant and unpopular political venture and in vulgar parlance he pulled the rug from under them. There are little pockets of them left in the CIO, but they amount to nothing.

Phil Murray was determined to get rid of the Communists but determined not to do so in such a way as to create precedents that would establish dictators in his unions, or permit weak leaders to belabor all their opponents as Communists and inaugurate a reign of terror.

"Time" magazine some months ago wrote an excellent appraisal of Murray. It outlined his enormous power, rated him as the most powerful labor leader in the nation, and perhaps the most powerful single human being in the United States.

His labor power was this: there are other labor leaders equally powerful in their own unions, but no one else has anything like the six million CIO members personally, and through all their leaders, devoted to Murray. This power he used judiciously. Often his care in proceeding made the rash think that he was over cautious—his caution was the caution of the man who has enormous power, knows it, but does not glory in it, and has made his personal pact with God that he will not abuse the power given to him.

His work will not die. It seems impossible that anyone will be found to take it up, but leaders will come forth. He built so solidly that his institutions will go on.

Philip Murray was a good Catholic. His Catholicity was both simple and profound. He knew the deep strains of religious thought and they influenced his program and his conduct. In personal life he was unaffectedly religious. He would never dream of missing Mass; attending evening devotions when he could. In times of great stress he made visits to the Blessed Sacrament. . . .

In a great controversy Phil Murray once told a formidable foe that he lived to serve his union, his country and his God. Thus did he live and thus did he die. May God have mercy on his soul.

Exerpt from Radio Address on WWSW
PITTSBURGH CATHOLIC
November 13, 1952

Phil Murray leaving a Steel Worker Organizing Committee meeting in 1937. To the right is union publicist Vince Sweeney.

⚏ The Liberty Bakery Strike (1952)

The Liberty Bakery Strike marked Rice's last major public battle before he was "exiled" from Pittsburgh after the arrival of Bishop John Dearden. The strike prefigured his later labor involvements as he supported a rank-and-file insurgency against an entrenched leadership. Although the strike was crushed, it sparked a reform movement in Local 12 that eventually gained power and, through one of its leaders, Sam Papa, provided important leadership during plant closing struggles in the 1980s and 1990s in Pittsburgh.

Your bakery workers in Pittsburgh belonging to Local 12 of the AFL Bakery and Confectionery Workers are relatively underpaid. The strike they are engaged in is just. No offer was made by the Master Bakers' Association (the employers).

The union presented demands that were, of course, high; but the companies certainly could have countered with some sort of proposal and started the bargaining. This the companies did not do.

PITTSBURGH CATHOLIC
May 8, 1952

. . . My information on the bakery deadlock is that the baking industry in Pittsburgh has not yet made a reasonable offer. The last one they made was something like ten cents, all told. The A&P and Krogers have settled with the Bakers union for 24 cents. Even if you grant that the A&P can afford more than other bakeries, you still have a big discrepancy. This discrepancy is larger because the A&P and Krogers have for years given fringe benefits lacking in the other plants.

I believe that if the strike had been settled earlier there would have been some chance for the workers taking less than the A&P formula; but the longer the strike lasts, the less inclined the workers will be to go below the full formula. Many of the strikers have temporary summer jobs and are getting along all right.

There is an interesting controversy between the two unions involved. The inside bakers belong to the AFL Bakery and Confectionery International and the drivers belong, of course, to the Teamsters. The leaders of Teamster Local 485 have believed that the sensible way to handle this strike was to shut everybody down at once. In that way, they would avoid the situation of having some members working and some on strike. And also the pressure engendered would end the strike more quickly.

The Bakers Local Union 12, on the other hand, believed that the best possible way to handle the strike was to sign up as many bakeries as possible and thus, isolate the stubborn few, on the theory that the stubborn few would become less stubborn as their business began to go elsewhere.

The two locals were not able to agree on a common strategy. There is much to be said in favor of each method of proceeding, and the best labor men in the world find themselves in disagreement.

You will note that the steel and coal industries follow the strategy of shutting all down at once, while the automobile workers take company by company.

However, several of the big steel and coal strikes have been solved when, after the strike was in progress, one segment of the industry has been broken off and led to a settlement which the others later accepted. . . .

PITTSBURGH CATHOLIC
June 12, 1952

Your correspondent was deeply involved in a labor dispute last week. Judge John T. Duff issued an injunction banning picketing, or any interference, during an "unauthorized" strike at Liberty Baking Company in East Liberty. As an aftermath of the injunction a total of 63 employees of the bakery were jailed.

Six men were jailed at first and I was called on to help. When I arrived on the scene the six men had been released on $10 forfeits. Several score other employees had heard the news and came to the plant. They were herded into a tavern across the street from the plant because the police told them they would be arrested if they walked or stood on the street in front of the plant or if they stood on the corners.

I questioned the police and I telephoned the Judge in the case — I used the phone in the tavern — and I was told that the injunction was in force and the men might not picket peacefully or make any demonstration.

The strikers indicated to me that they planned to make a peaceful demonstration because Teamsters Local 485 was scheduled to haul in bread and make deliveries as soon as the picket line was taken off. I tried to dissuade them and suggested they wait until morning, but they felt the strike would be broken and their jobs would be in jeopardy if the trucks went through.

The strikers felt that a peaceful demonstration would result in only token arrests and that then the Bakery Drivers, as strong union men, would not make the deliveries. Bread was being baked in another bakery and wrapped in Liberty wrappers.

Shortly after I left them the men walked out into the street. They asked that they be allowed to picket or else be jailed. There was no rushing, no flying wedge, no threats. There were only six police. The puzzled officers eventually called the station. Then the excitement began. Word went out that there was a riot.

The strikers waited patiently until the patrol wagons came. They walked into the wagons. Several women strikers and some old men were ordered out of the patrol wagons by police, who did not want to arrest them.

I was called by the Superintendent of Police and by the Judge to talk to the demonstrators. By the time the police car took me to the scene everyone was in jail.

I called the Judge and the Superintendent of Police seeking for some way of getting the men out of jail; 57 men in jail overnight is not good. Their families were frantic.

I was told that the men had defied the courts and law and order and should be punished. I worked for some time seeking a formula that would release the men. Bail was out of the question. It was set first at $1000 and then cut to $200 per man. My attempt failed and in the middle of my efforts the men were split up into jails around the city.

The best that I could get was an agreement from the Judge that he would talk to the magistrate in the morning and have the men released on their own recognizance if they would agree to abide by his injunction. This was mentioned to the Superintendent of Police and he arranged to have me taken to talk to the strikers in each jail and inform them what they were to do in the morning. For some reason the Judge did not, or was not able to carry out the bargain.

That is why the men were mute and thunderstruck the next morning when Magistrate Stiba attacked them so strongly, fined them each $50 and held them for the grand jury.

The newspapers in their very first story spoke of "riot," "mob," "flying wedge," "attempt to rush the plant," "rushing the police." It has been difficult to get the truth to the public.

Then the comedy of errors began. The Magistrate admitted the fines were too severe according to law. He cut them to $10 and ordered refunds.

The sheriff's office admitted the injunction had not been properly served; therefore the men had not violated it. Note, injunction papers were served to the men only after they were in jail.

But that made no difference. It then was stated that the men were arrested for "disorderly conduct and inciting to riot," etc. Note, that not one incident of violence or abuse was adduced. One policeman even testified in court that the men gave no trouble. But the story of "riot" and "violence" would not die.

The men were completely innocent and if the case ever goes to trial there will be embarrassment in many places.

The strikers asked me to be their spokesman because they had no one else to turn to. They had to have an outsider spokesman because, in previous difficulties with their union and their company, "spokesmen" have been severely punished.

After a study of the case I would put the blame on poor leadership in Local 12, which has been in turmoil for years. Most important meetings feature police in attendance. Even executive board meetings see police called in to protect old guard officers. Men have been expelled from the union for their trade union militance. Over the years many have been fired. The turmoil involves shops other than Liberty.

The unfortunate company may not be too much to blame, except that good labor relations demand that you get along with your own employees first, and then get along with the union higher-ups later.

In spite of the fact that 57 men were in jail, Teamster 485 members did haul the bread. In trade union ethics a picket-line does not vanish when it goes to jail, it gets bigger and more inviolate—but not this time.

As of this writing the strike is effective. Only a handful of the bargaining unit involved has returned to work.

Although it was a headache and a heartache I am glad the men came to me, a Catholic priest. Where else would you have them go?

To the Communists?

PITTSBURGH CATHOLIC
August 21, 1952

Some time this week the crisis at Liberty Bakery Company will come to a head. Judge John T. Duff will have been forced to make his injunction permanent, or modify it, or wipe it off the books entirely. There is some chance that by the time you read this the issue will be settled, but it is hardly likely. It is possible that the strike will spread to other bakeries.

The status of the dispute now is this: the temporary injunction with all its sweeping provisions remains in force. The company is attempting to operate its plant with police protection. Other unions, in the absence of the picket-line are working, in addition, perhaps 35 regular members of Local 12 are working, but 125 or more are still on strike. It is reported that one man has been brought in from Ohio to operate one of the difficult machines.

PITTSBURGH CATHOLIC
August 28, 1952

An injunction is an ugly thing. It is a last-resort weapon. Injunctions were so abused in labor disputes that one of the first and most popular things which the New Deal did was to virtually abolish their use in such disputes. . . .

The Pennsylvania anti-injunction statute still recognized the fact that not only companies but workers can be injured. And so this statute required that when an injunction is granted to an employer he also must be enjoined from doing certain things.

To put it very simply, when the worker is enjoined from hampering the employer's business, the employer at the same time must be enjoined from employing people who will take the worker's job, or from transferring people into the jobs of the striking workers.

In the case of the notorious Liberty Baking Company injunction, this was not done. There are many other strange and odd things about that injunction. They are now all being fought out in court. . . .

It is almost unbelievable, but true, that for over two weeks, the striking employees at Liberty Baking Company were not permitted to so much as walk or stand across the street from the bakery. The Baking Company now employs Pittsburgh's most powerful law firm. A law firm with a reputation not only in corporate and tax matters, but also in labor, rather anti-labor matters. It is passing strange to see this gigantic, 65 lawyer, anti-labor law firm move contentedly in company with the counsel of Local 12 of the AFL Bakery and Confectionery Workers.

To say more might be to risk a citation for contempt of court.

PITTSBURGH CATHOLIC
September 4, 1952

. . . The bakery strike has narrowed itself down to a very simple proposition. The company, the Liberty Baking Company, and the union, Local 12, AFL Bakery and Confectionery Workers, have decreed that workers will be fired. The union demands the firing of 57. The company demands the firing of some but not the whole lot.

The company has some new people working, many of them sent by the union. The company is not in full production, but produces some. No picket line is permitted by the courts, and so the Bakery Drivers are delivering.

Some money has been collected to take care of strikers. They have been able to hire counsel. Your correspondent and a few local labor leaders are standing by them. Otherwise they are abandoned. The only thing that stands between them and complete defeat is their own determination.

It hardly seems possible that 57 people can be fired in this town as a result of a labor dispute. The determination of these humble people is something to behold. Their dignity and their calmness in the midst of provocation, slander and abandonment is amazing.

I feel that they will win because their spirit is not, and cannot be broken. The ones that are not absolutely sure of being fired still state that they will not go back to work until all go back to work, because conditions in the plant are now, and will be unbearable. No seniority, no questioning of the word of the boss—no let up, but drive, drive.

It is disheartening to see a union lose its soul, but it is heartening to see free American workers refuse to accept slavery and humiliation. I am convinced that the workers will win. And I for one will remain with them right down to the bitter end.

PITTSBURGH CATHOLIC
September 11, 1952

I got back into Pittsburgh in time to see only a small portion of the hearing on the Liberty Baking Company's injunction. . . .

It was pathetic to see the bewildered strikers — honest, decent workers — faced by union and company bound together by hoops of confusion. Company and union lawyers and principals huddled together more than once.

Company and union counsel . . . cooperated in baiting and badgering the strikers. The attempt was too obvious — to make certain individuals stand out as leaders. Why? So that they could be fired.

What have these men done? They have been militant union members and officers. They have fought for seniority and against the speed-up and stretch-out. They have fought to make Liberty Bakery a place where a man could earn his wages without dulling his mind and wearing out his body. They fought to remove the conditions which make the baking industry of Pittsburgh a disgrace.

Some have committed the additional crime of showing that they have aspired for union leadership, and that they believed all the slogans about freedom and democracy. It was a shock to know that a conspiracy existed to drive this wonderful leadership material out of the union movement.

A most poignant moment came — the papers of course did not get it — when one striker after another was asked his years of service at the Liberty Baking Company. The least was nine. There were two with ten years. The rest went up to 24. Most were between 17 and 20. Something is wrong, very wrong somewhere, when such men are goaded into revolt.

The hearing was bitter on the part of the company. Attorney Unkovic tried hard to establish this writer as the cause of the strike. He carried his attitude outside of the courtroom and nearly provoked a riot in the corridor when he approached a bunch of the strikers and told them he would turn his collar around and lead them. He made other remarks to them of the same nature. The intent was obvious: to provoke more violence by a contemptuous attitude. . . .

PITTSBURGH CATHOLIC
September 18, 1952

It has been my contention all along that on the famous night of August 14, when the 63 Liberty Bakery strikers were arrested, there was no violence. The men were arraigned in the court room of Judge Louis Kaufmann, County Court Judge, last Friday. From the testimony given under oath it became apparent that there was no violence whatsoever, and the city, in order to sustain its charge of disorderly conduct, had to fall back on a technicality, namely 57 of them, standing together, blocked the street. Judge Kaufmann released five of the 63 immediately. The other cases he is holding under advisement.

Other new developments in the strike are these: Local Union President Sam Wehofer sent a letter notifying the two executive board members from Liberty that since they are no longer employed by the company they cannot be board members. A careful study of the by-laws and the constitution of the union makes it difficult to ascertain how he, the president alone, can make this determination. . . .

A day after Mr. Wehofer informed them that they were fired and no longer members of the executive board, the Liberty Baking Company sent them a notice that they were fired and their insurance was no longer in force. Something went wrong with the timing because they should have got the company's letter first. It is strange company-union cooperation. . . .

On Friday a young woman testified in the court of Judge Kaufmann as to the peacefulness of the scene on the night of the alleged riot. She and a companion were informed on Saturday that they were fired. In spite of injunctions and firings the Liberty Baking Company apparently is far from full production. Some 75 to 80 workers are still on strike and matters cannot be described as normal.

PITTSBURGH CATHOLIC
September 25, 1952

Twelve hundred members of Local 12 of the AFL Bakery and Confectionery Workers signed a petition asking the International to enter the present mixed-up situation here and if necessary impose a trusteeship. The workers were from Hankey, Kroger, Clark, A&P, Bauer, and Ward Baking companies.

Police were called in again by Sam Wehofer, president of Local 12, to enforce his will at the Local's executive board meeting Saturday last. The two board members from the Liberty Baking Company have been discharged by the company. Mr. Wehofer maintained that he had the right to remove them from the board and appoint somebody else. Last month he adjourned the meeting when they refused to leave it. On Saturday he sent for the police to eject his political foes. The police should refuse to act in cases like this unless there is disorder, because it is not the function of the City police to serve as a sort of sergeant at arms.

Some fifty people remain away from their jobs at Liberty Baking Company. Most of the fifty are fired.

PITTSBURGH CATHOLIC
October 23, 1952

The blacklist that has been drawn up against the strikers of last August by the Liberty Baking Company and Local 12 of the AFL Bakery and Confectionery Workers operates in various ways. The first and most obvious way is employment. Liberty gives a bad reference for any of the strikers from working at any other bakery. It goes further. At least one of the strikers, when he appealed for unemployment compensation, found Liberty's lawyer fighting against him down at the Board's office.

PITTSBURGH CATHOLIC
December 18, 1952

The Liberty Baking struggle ended in defeat for the affected workers. The struggle would sow the seeds however for the long-term renewal of the local. Analogously for Rice, this experience would germinate as something that would flower in the 1960s and 1970s. Then too, he would embrace dissidents and unpopular causes while distancing himself from institutional unionism and many of its leaders.

Rice teaching at Braddock Labor School, 1950

Leading Pittsburgh March for Peace and Justice, May 24, 1969. From left: Byrd Brown, Rennie Davis, Donna Allen, Rice

CHRONOLOGY

☎ 1958
Rice becomes the pastor at Immaculate Conception parish in Washington, Pa.

☎ 1959
Rice resumes his column in the *Pittsburgh Catholic.*

☎ 1966
In January, Rice becomes pastor of Holy Rosary parish in Homewood.

☎ 1967
On April 15, Rice marches arm-in-arm with Martin Luther King Jr. to protest the Vietnam War at the UN. On October 21, he is a speaker at the March on the Pentagon.

☎ 1969
August and September, Rice plays a prominent role on the side of black demonstrators demanding more opportunities for construction jobs from the building trades unions.

☎ 1971
Rice runs for Pittsburgh City Council. He places seventh in a field of twenty-eight.

Justice and Peace 1960 – 1975

4

☎ African Americans and the Building Trades

Immediately upon the renewal of his regular commentary in the Pittsburgh Catholic, *Rice began to write in support of the struggle for equality and jobs by African Americans. He became a leading white spokesman on civil rights issues while he was pastor of a largely white parish in Washington, Pennsylvania. When he was appointed pastor of Holy Rosary parish in the black community of Homewood, he became an articulate and controversial interpreter of the African-American community's concerns to Pittsburgh's Catholics. His advocacy for minorities, especially his support for the entry of African Americans into the construction trades, lost him the affection of many old friends in the labor movement.*

Negroes and Unions (1961)

In common with other friends of the labor movement I am distressed and embarrassed by a grave inconsistency found in the section of the movement that is strongest and most durable, the old line crafts. These unions contribute to the repression and deprivation of the Negro by virtually total exclusion of him from membership. In this, of course, they merely typify our whole country at its worst and weakest; but since they exist to seek justice and are the human end of the management-labor equation, their guilt is greater than that of others.

The very traits that made them strong and durable produced, and now prolong, their sins of racial injustice. They are practical and clannish. They survived in troubled times because they had a simple objective, the protection of the economic interests of a craft or a group of crafts and a simple code, stick together. At one time they regarded the Negro workman as a threat, an importation from the South by the employers to destroy their unions. To an intense degree they traditionally have nurtured the hostility that most White workers have had against the Negro, chiefly that most pernicious feeling that if the Negro should share their work they would somehow lose caste.

These people are not evil, but they are set in an old evil way. In other matters they have become forward looking and have contributed to the social advancement of all Americans, including Negroes. They are, however, fanatically determined to protect their enclaves. To be sure, they protect these enclaves against others than Negroes, admittance to many of the trades being almost a matter of heredity, certainly, of clan and friendship.

I have discussed the problem with men who are leaders in the crafts, just and humanitarian men in the main. The weight of tradition hangs heavy on them and they say their members will provoke more difficulty than any other factor, however, they admit that exclusion of the Negro cannot go on even though none of them is willing to take strong steps to end it now.

As for the members, they are like all other Americans. Too many of them react to the idea of a Negro being a brother mechanic the way most White men react to the idea of a Negro being a neighbor; hysteria, malice, selfishness and irrational prejudice war with feelings of decency and justice.

The facts of the exclusion are easily given. Men get into the crafts through apprentice training. Negroes do not get into the apprentice programs, or, if they do get in, it is in token numbers which in the aggregate are meaningless.

Now this is not the only field in which the Negro is prevented from earning a living, but it is almost the worst, and it has a quality of absolute exclusion that is intolerable. . . .

It would be wrong to leave the impression that the old line crafts in building, printing and railroading are alone in their violations of Negro rights; if that were so, the Negro would not be nearly so desperately off economically. He, in fact, is victimized along the entire economic front, even when unions in the field are in his corner, the decision makers are White and nearly always they are equipped with prejudice.

But the old crafts do present a special problem with their degrees of official and quasi-official discrimination and a breakthrough must come. For the sake of labor's honor and respect and, even, survival a remedy must be found. It is my fervent prayer that the decent men who lead those unions will provide the remedy from within.

PITTSBURGH CATHOLIC
April 20, 1961

Bias in Building (1969)

Pittsburgh is in the midst of its greatest construction boom, $200 million worth. The boom is so great that it exhausts the local supply of skilled craftsmen. As you hardly need to be told, those worthies have strong unions; they and their union manage a great measure of control because of their monopoly of skills.

They cope with the present shortage of labor by working overtime and by permitting the entry of union men outside the area; they have no intention of doing anything so naive or idealistic as developing more skilled men from among their fellow Pittsburghers. They are consumed by thoughts of eventual job scarcity but they also love the very heavy paychecks that come from guaranteed overtime at double the normal rate.

This adds to the cost of construction but it is not of itself a prime maker of inflation; costs have climbed even for that construction which is not dominated by the building trades. I do not quarrel with the high wages, my quarrel is with the exclusiveness which keeps Negro workmen from having a crack at that big money. It is obvious that this greatest construction boom in our history is passing the Black man by.

Look at any of our construction sites, U.S. Steel, the Stadium, any of them: you will see a few Negroes lifting, or wheeling or carrying but you will not find them among the chaps laying the tile, fastening the girders, pulling wire, wrapping asbestos or doing any skilled job other than a token here and there.

Black exclusion is bad for everyone and I should think that the crafts would realize this

*Black demonstrators confronting police in riot gear during construction
jobs demonstration, August 1969. Byrd Brown is in center.*

themselves. It is ugly sociologically and harmful economically that a certain segment of the population is cut out of a good thing.

At the moment it becomes very dangerous for the crafts that they are excluding Negroes because it makes the totality of their exclu-sionary policies very visible. The white men who have been excluded, and are still being excluded do not stand out by their absence, but the Negroes do.

In the past they did not because in those days Negroes were invisible; now that they are visible their absence is noticeable and calls attention to the whole system of practices, rules and contracts by which the building trades union maintain a monopoly, not so much of skill, as of access to skill. These days that monopoly is not nearly so impregnable as it was in the past, since a continuing technical revolution within the construction field is changing the realities.

Personally I am not hostile to the crafts and do not mind their peculiar mores, but I draw the line at sympathy for their racialism; . . . I do not want them to be destroyed but they may bring destruction on themselves.

It is apparent that the Negro has been excluded so long that construction is an alien world to him; even if the unions cooperated and stopped obstructing it would take more time than we have to settle it all. If they are smart they will turn around and do everything they can to find and hold Black craftsmen; until they do, their unfair exclusiveness will cry to heaven for remedy.

That a day of reckoning may well be at hand appears from several signs: people like me who have been union friends for decades are beginning to fight on the other side; extremely militant Blacks are beginning to see construction as a good issue and to see the construction site as a good target; moderately militant Black men such as Nate Smith and Rev. James Robinson are beginning to push harder because "responsible" tactics are getting them and their people nowhere.

Pittsburgh Negroes have been very patient about all those construction jobs excluding them; the boom is more than a year old and it is almost lily white. One of these days plain ordinary Black folk, neither militant nor non-militant, are simply going to appear quietly around all construction sites in such numbers that they cannot be hauled away and they are going to clog the jobs and bring them to a halt.

No one can organize such a movement; it is the sort of thing that has to happen by itself, but it will happen after the militants challenge, expose and sufficiently develop the issue.

The gingerly handling of Nate, Jimmy Joe and their followers after they were arrested the other day indicates that the explosiveness is well understood by many people but careful handling cannot keep the lid on forever. . . .

PITTSBURGH CATHOLIC
August 15, 1969

Race and Labor (1969)

. . . There is now a Black Construction Coalition, which is united and respected; it is a development, a growth.

Community attention has been called dramatically to the lack of Negroes in crafts and pressure is mounting. I have no way of knowing what direction the battle will take but, if I were plotting Black strategy, I would demand that the construction system itself find, train and accept black workers in every craft. I would not have black people agree to do this for the system. The system discovered how to excluded the black man, let it discover how to include him. I would not be patient with the system; I would not wait and I would insist that the responsibility rest with the unions and contractors and their interlocking association. My reasoning is that the whole system is a gigantic exclusionary device and it will take in black workers only when reality forces it to want to take them in. Black pressure backed up by decent white opinion can hasten the day.

Pressure will call constant attention to the inequities of the system and will put it in danger; the unions have the most to lose and they cannot afford to waste much more time in putting the house in order. At this juncture I would not care to prophesy as to whether the system will reform or be destroyed, but I do know that the time is past for Negroes in the big cities to be passive as enormous construction projects go on and on in their midst with them excluded from the worthwhile jobs. I cannot imagine there being any more peace on this issue until there is change; as I implied two weeks ago, the construction sites are obvious and open targets.

As confrontation time approached the Master Builders and the craft unions began moving and making mistakes; it certainly was a mistake to present a rather small apprenticeship program guarantee with three unions missing. It was an even greater mistake to work the thing out with public authority but no recognized black spokesman present.

However, that is the direction a solution will take: guaranteed entrance and acceptance for black people, but the number has to be sizable and the burden must rest, not on the black community, but on the crafts and the builders.

As for the three union holdouts, one is a tiny craft, but two are quite sizable. The asbestos workers could be forced into line very easily because other crafts could do their work without trouble but the steamfitters and electrical workers are bigger and more difficult to handle. Of the two, the International Brotherhood of Electrical Workers Local 5, is number one tough guy, and significantly enough IBEW locals are the toughies all over the country.

Local 5 is strong, tightly knit and wealthy; it has a high proportion of contractors in its membership and it has a very small membership proportionate to its working force. That is, possibly there are three outside permit holders, all white of course, to every local

> **"I do know that the time is past for Negroes in the big cities to be passive as enormous construction projects go on and on in their midst with them excluded from the worthwhile jobs."**

member working on construction — it might even be four to one but the figures are not available. Local 5 had one black member, or apprentice, who used to be moved from job to job when it got hot.

Local 5 is so tightly structured and controlled that only legislation can bring it to judgment and that legislation might do as much harm as good; nonetheless it may have to come if there is no substantial give.

The legislation could classify Local 5 and similar organizations as devices or conspiracies to restrain trade or perhaps to restrict employment or hinder access to skills — that could blow up all the crafts and it would be a pity; it is a weapon of last resort, but we may come to the last resort before we know it.

The old men who control the Local 5s of this nation may be beyond caring and they may even speak for the generality of their members, but if the labor movement of this country gets a staggering legislative belt in the near future it will be they who will be the causes.

PITTSBURGH CATHOLIC
August 29, 1969

The Demonstrations (1969)

Pittsburgh made some more labor history last week as black and white marches shifted the construction race problem out of the conference rooms and onto the streets and front pages. That problem can hardly be ignored anywhere from now on.

129

Drama and tension mounted as black people and white allies marched for three straight days to the accompaniment of an official mood more changeable than the weather: one day the mood was tolerant and helpful, the next angry and impatient, and the next full of love and understanding. At all times most of the police were grim and unsmiling; their smiles broke out only when the white workers took to the streets — then it was mutual love and kisses, confetti too, as the white office people demonstrated that, although they might not know the issues at stake, they did know white from black.

The great stadium and the monstrous U.S. Steel office building are in the process of changing the look of Pittsburgh, but the drama that swirls within and around them may make a change every bit as deep and permanent in the working lives of the human beings who will use or gaze upon them.

The quarrel over admittance of blacks into the construction unions and companies has simmered for years, but the simmer changed to an angry boil as a tremendous building boom rolled on and on in Pittsburgh and the black worker remained out of it. Pittsburgh made the history because we have very tough and unco-operative unions and we had some half-hearted industry attempts at solution which fizzled; above all, we have this boom, this highly visible and highly discriminatory building bonanza.

The 13,000 construction workers are a lot for an area this size and that was not all of them, merely the ones laid off when the bigger projects shut down; two or three hundred is a tiny token of blacks in that number particularly when the more dramatic of the buildings tower over black areas where unemployment and under-employment remain critical.

As you so well know, the construction sites were closed on the initiative of Mayor Barr; there were two closing. The first on Monday was universally acclaimed, or almost so; by the

way, that took the steam out of the first black demonstration; James Slusser's police put the steam back in on Tuesday and stuck our fair city on the TV sets of the whole world with their club swinging (those big clubs are really not lethal — too clumsy — but they make a horrifying picture and look like murder when raised in the air); the second closing (Thursday and Friday) had the impact of a second coming as it caused angry white workers and their women folk to erupt. . . .

The white workman's counter marching over lost pay was a first, because that sort of workman in that sort of union is not the marching and demonstrating type; classically the craftsman hire a business agent whose job it is to handle such matters, the idea being that the union takes care of the craftsman who pays a good stiff price for the service.

I am sure that the business agents suffered through the whole thing because they saw where it could go. Some of the eruptive force came from the pressure of rebels in the various crafts who claim that they could get still more money, better conditions and, now, freedom from black and liberal interference. Not a happy scene for the traditionalists.

Incidentally the business agents and other union officers kept their end of it as cool as they could, just as the black leaders did; I saw a number of indications at crucial moments when the leadership, all of it, opted for the less abrasive, but the leadership did not always win and each time that the vox pop [voice of the people] prevailed, regardless of whether it was blacks, whites or police, the blow was toward trouble. . . . The turmoil in the long run helps my black friends who cannot do worse than they do in times of civic tranquility. . . .

I must say that I am not happy over the probable loss of my erstwhile title of "Labor Priest" and I regretted the absence of labor chaps from our [Labor Day] Mass. I appreciate those men and I wish I could be on their side.

Sorry I cannot be with you, men; you may not miss me but I shall miss you. . . .

PITTSBURGH CATHOLIC
September 5, 1969

Construction Talks (1969)

There is more white support for the black job drive than most of us realize, but it is an almost underground phenomenon; the loud mouths in the saloons and elsewhere are anti-black but the other sentiment can be discerned by experienced observers in the quiet ones. Within the ranks of labor itself and right in the building trade unions there is a strong current of sympathy for the black job hunter, and a touch of realism. However, the gloomy fact remains that most construction workers are more interested in protecting their personal job security and high income than in anything else under heaven, and perhaps over heaven at that.

Construction union leaders are in confusion locally and they are not nearly so strong as they pretend to be; continued pressure can crack them. At the moment they are trying to stall and shift the burden; they want their international leaders to come in and order them to do what they know is right and inevitable, and in the meantime, they grasp every chance to stall.

Clifford J. Jones gave them a beautiful stalling gimmick when he very naively said, "let us make a survey"; "absolutely," said the crafts, "a survey, we want a survey, a two, three, or four-year survey, that is better even than a long, long apprentice program"; but the blacks exploded so fiercely and unitedly that common sense came back into the negotiation.

One hears conflicting stories about the attitude of the national union leaders. From a very good source I hear that an emissary from the top came into Pittsburgh and prevented the locals from agreeing to specific numbers; on the other hand, a local paper reports that the national leaders say that they have no power to force a settlement.

Ironically, there is virtually no chance that blacks will flood the construction industry no matter what is agreed; with everyone working hard and "sincere" it would take perhaps ten years to reach ten percent black skilled men. The reason is that you have to turn the average black around so that he aims for construction and sees it as an acceptable way of life and work. Those white leaders who, with due deliberation, oppose any concessions to blacks are doing so partly out of fear that many of the poor whites whom they have excluded in the past will slip through. A few are using the racial issue to try to keep their people solidly in their own pockets and away from internal rebellion.

A sensible concession to the black coalition could actually save the building trades unions, but, conversely, the longer this drags on without resolution the more likelihood that the law and its administration will be aimed and adjusted so that the hold of the crafts on construction will be broken. It might be as hard as cracking the atom but it can be done; unfortunately any law that will hurt the closed construction unions is bound to hurt many other unions that are being more decently operated.

The Black Coalition also has its internal stress and strain, and it must avoid certain pitfalls, chief of which is acceptance of the proposition that black leaders and the black community must find, train and motivate suitable black candidates for construction. Even legitimate training programs under black auspices can serve to shift responsibility from where it belongs, the white contractors and unions.

PITTSBURGH CATHOLIC
September 26, 1969

*Rice marching arm-in-arm with
Dr. Martin Luther King, Jr., at spring
mobilization march to the United Nations,
April 15, 1967*

Marching Against Racism

Rice participated in numerous demonstrations, picket lines, and meetings protesting racism. An early and consistent supporter of the nonviolent tactics of Dr. Martin Luther King, Jr., Rice totally shared the civil rights leader's view that the struggle against racism and the war in Vietnam were intimately linked.

Eyewitness (1967)

I walked arm in arm through the heart of New York with Martin Luther King and I was the first speaker at the gigantic peace rally that gathered under the title of Spring Mobilization. Like St. Paul I glory in my infirmities because no one seemed to give a care whether I walked or spoke. The show was King's and Stokely's [Carmichael] and [Floyd] McKissick's and [Rev. James] Bevel's and [Cleveland] Robinson's. It was not even the show of the charming and handsome Harry Belafonte (a man much handsomer than even his picture shows.) It was not the show even of lovely Mary Travis . . . of the team of Peter, Paul and Mary. Even the great and beloved old genius Pete Seeger got only a footnote.

It was black men leading white men. Ordinary white men and women. All ages, but mostly of the uninteresting age of 20 to 30. Kids were there but they were not important. Nuts right and left were there but they just caught the eye of the color coverers.

The meat and potatoes were King with a routine speech, Stokely with charm, sparkle and artificial venom, Bevel and Robinson with a wild logic and McKissick with honest, reasonable white type good sense. It was their show. The media made it their show and the logic of events made it their show.

As I said on local TV, there was no outstanding churchman of any denomination. No Catholic bishop or cardinal. I was just a guy that was available. Even all the usual ecclesiastical peace cats were off premises for reasons

good or bad. Berrigan was really sick they tell me. The sad point is that, and I say this most solemnly — "they were not missed." The only ecclesiastical cat that might have truly made the scene was our own colorful John J. Wright. He might have moved in. The others would have been wasting their time.

Dr. Ben Spock made it, but he is no ordinary white spokesman, even Linus Pauling spoke and was lost in the shuffle, as was Bill Pepper, who had written a great Ramparts article.

The papers and TV gave a poor picture of it. They used numbermanship. If the cops love you, they double the figure. If they do not love you, they divide. Long, long division. The police did not love us. They did a superb job of keeping order. All hail to them for that, but most of them had an aversion to our intestines. I noted this. Before I spoke I kidded around with them and was met with the special warmth the New York policeman gives to the normal Catholic priest. After I spoke, it was freezeville, all the way, but I understood. They were doing their job. They did not dig us, or if they did they suspected themselves of unpatriotism.

The crowd was much larger than 150,000, the maximum given us by a Sunday paper. It was 300,000 at least. I strolled the walled off space along the UN grounds and looked down six streets — all packed, absolutely packed with people. At 5 o'clock — we started to speak at 1:30 — people were still leaving Central Park. I know the parade route was two miles. One of the Indians had to leave for the men's room after a mile. He just knew when

Rice at press conference on August 29, 1967, in New York City announcing the march on the Pentagon. Speaking in the center are H. Rap Brown and Jerry Rubin.

we had made a mile. Indians have a superb sense of time, distance and bladder tension.

The old Indians were charming. They sang a peace song, complete with wild Yip, Yips, but it may have been a rain dance because we got rain to cool us all, and get the paraders away in peace and quiet.

The speeches were not terrific. They were more of the same but the crowd came to listen and not to be entertained or to cut up. It was a quiet crowd. Rarely was there a wild cheer. There was some repetition of slogans but it was easy, quiet and earnest. It was not that the loudspeakers were ineffective. I wandered through the crowd and the clarity of the sound was exceptional. It was not a hippy crowd but a deadly serious crowd that believed the messages given. No murmurs of disapproval but murmurs of approval and occasional applause. The quietness and order were really a prime part of the story. Antics were exaggerated not to ridicule the march but because the American media have the weakness of seeking the bizarre and unusual. They often miss the forest for a few outlandish and exotic bushes.

King is a calm man. He accepts his position and has no pomposity. He did not cavil at the extraordinary security but accepted it. He made no grandstand gestures and did no waving to the crowd, just said hello to a few acquaintances.

Carmichael is different. That lad is electric. Above average height, he is a charming good-looker. In anyone's book he is definitely upper class, but an upperclass Negro. He appeals to all Negroes and to alert whites. While waiting to go on he was not a bit intense and joked pleasantly as he watched every detail and made sure that his place on the program was appropriately timed. He was not afraid to follow King. As I mentioned, Dr. King did not make a great speech but spoke for the record. Stokely stirred the crowd and hammed it up. A delightful heavy.

My little speech received polite applause and nothing more. I stressed that I was there in default of someone more important. I mentioned Popes John and Paul as my authority for speaking peace and I said, as I often have, that we must get out and get out now. Our choice is to kill those people or leave and pay an indemnity.

I forget whether or not I said, as I said later on TV, that so much rides on President Johnson. If he is a saint, he may save us. He has the potential of true greatness. He is big enough to decide deliberately to lose an election and save the world; in Christian terms to suffer the loss of the world so as to save his own soul and the entire world. . . .

PITTSBURGH CATHOLIC
April 20, 1967

Martin Luther King (1978)

Dr. Martin Luther King . . . in life made whites squirm when they were not frothing at the mouth. He was a strong, controlled Black man, utterly at variance with the old and the new stereotypes. A man, not a character; certainly not an entertainer.

King was far from alone in the fight against segregation and abuse, and there were effective forces that owed nothing to him. However, he rightly dominated the scene and, without him, less would have been accomplished.

He brought people into action whom nothing else, and no one else would have activated. Most Blacks tend to be inert politically, as do most whites. He reached the religious Black masses and the cautious hard-working survivors. If you are Black, that is what you do a lot of, plain surviving.

There was a type of young, very angry Black that turned against Dr. King as time went on. They were impatient and in a way jealous not for themselves but for their brand of action. . . .

Many of the chaps I dealt with in Homewood had this slant. They thought that they were more practical than Dr. King and his nonviolent insistence, but they overestimated their own power and their staying power. They seemed to be riding high at the moment but their day was brief. . . .

I met Martin Luther King only once and was with him for just a few hours, but it was no ordinary meeting. As part of the Spring Mobilization for Peace in April of '67 there was a march from Central Park to the UN and a rally.

Dr. King made his strongest antiwar statement by participating. He led the march, spoke at the rally and entered the UN to make a declaration. As a member of the national steering committee and a speaker at the rally, I was at the head of the line beside Martin.

There was more to it than that. Threats had been received and there was fear of an assassination attempt. My assignment was to walk arm-in-arm with him and never leave his side. I remember police peering protectively over the parapets of the buildings which lined the way and the abusive pro-war cadres which tried to disrupt the march.

*Rice, Coretta Scott King, Mrs. and Dr.
Benjamin Spock, and Dick Gregory at the
March on the Pentagon, October 21, 1967*

Incidentally, this was a most gigantic rally but it was played down and actually reviled by the total news media.

As we chatted pleasantly of nothing in particular, Martin, as his followers were calling him that day, seemed unfazed by all that was going on. What a cool leader!

He was not tall but squat and very muscular. . . . He had a Buddha sort of face that was not expressive. His voice did it all. God gave him a glorious vocal instrument that could sing and soar; joined to what he had to say and to the great and poignant issues that he addressed, it all added up to some of history's most sublime oratory.

PITTSBURGH CATHOLIC
February 24, 1978

A Good Man (1968)

Martin Luther King was a good man, a rarely good man. Not a simple soul, but a modern man, who was sound and true. His great fame did not spoil him, although it came almost overnight and was an enormous fame; one hears no stories of him being difficult or demanding. He became an institution gracefully, allowing himself to be institutionalized for the sake of the cause but having no airs or arrogance because of it. Future generations will appreciate this more than we do because they will have the whole story on many famous men. When they look for the real Martin Luther King they will find the man we all know. Reassessments will but add to King's stature.

Martin Luther King lived long enough to see his work and worth questioned — his consistent advocacy of non-violence did not go down with everyone. In his espousal of peace he was a paragon; he was for peace in every sphere and with everyone; he set a good example and that example was a rebuke to certain white people. There was bitterness among some southerners

Rice waiting to address a peace rally in Point State Park in the early 1970s

because a Negro was obviously a good man and was at the same time, militant and brave; the combination infuriated. They could adjust to a Negro saint, but not to one who carried himself so beautifully, and led his people with such brilliant militance. Other whites who are far from being racists were shocked that Martin Luther King would dare to criticize America's foreign policy, expecting him to be submissive in this grave matter so that he could do more for his people; but Martin Luther King knew that Negroes had a right to equal treatment and should not have to earn it over and over again by being nice and complaisant.

Most of all, his Christian pacifism was so integral that he could not remain silent on the war if the heavens fell.

A year ago, I walked arm in arm with him through New York City and I spoke from the same platform in front of the United Nations. From the amount of abuse I, as a small participant, received, I can imagine what his mail looked like. As we walked along we shared our wonder that Christian ministers in an allegedly Christian country should be expected to apologize for demanding an end to a war.

Martin Luther King was a fiery orator, one of the century's greatest, without a trace of demagoguery and he was a militant without hatred. He was catapulted into fame and leadership almost by accident, but he was no accident; he had the requisite talent, stability and integrity.

The sad aftermath of looting and unease was inevitable. As the Kerner report tells us, we are two nations, one fat and the other lean. Those people who are involved in the looting are largely young and they are as bereft of real hope as if Martin Luther King had not lived and worked at all. That is the tragedy, not just that the looting goes on, but that the whole thing is so unnecessary, such a waste; if only the nation had moved in time! If only! . . .

PITTSBURGH CATHOLIC
April 12, 1968

Cholly, Not Hoovah! Not Hoovah! (1989)

Mike [Levine] had me on his KD radio show often in the turbulent 1960s. One of those times I fired a shot heard — if not around the world — at least in FBI Headquarters. You must remember that J. Edgar Hoover was still an icon, one of the most highly respected people in government service. Also he was one of the most feared. Not by me.

Mike and I were discussing Rev. Martin Luther King, along with whom I had just led an anti-war protest, when a woman called in to say that J. Edgar had branded Doctor King a communist. My rejoinder was that Hoover was "A punch drunk old man, and totally unreliable."

FBI files reveal that the revered FBI director was informed immediately and reacted angrily. The Most Rev. John J. Wright, Lord Rest Him, was our bishop and generally approved my tough stances, but this was different. I met him the next day at a confirmation and he

said: "Cholly, not Hoovah! Not Hoovah!" I then laid off.

Obviously, before the rest of us knew the ugly truth, John Wright did, namely, that we were dealing a with man as evil as he was powerful.

Later, when I allowed the Black Panthers to use Holy Rosary's cafeteria to serve breakfast for hungry black kids, Hoover again reacted angrily. Handwritten and initialed by him was the injunction to consider using "CoIntel Pro," that is, disruption, sabotage, slander and wire taps. I'm glad it was not used.

PITTSBURGH CATHOLIC
September 29, 1989

Marching in Boston (1974)

If one were free to choose the time and place for a protest march, one would not choose Boston in the middle of December, but there we were last Saturday, thousands of us, shivering in damp Roberto Clemente Park, wondering what was holding up the start of this March Against Racism.

A motley coalition of Marxist and non-Marxist radicals and moderates had pulled the thing together and in spite of luxuriating confusions and strange oppositions it was working. The marchers, divided a hundred ways, were united only in their opposition to racism.

Except for one brief flurry of violence the day was uneventful. The violence came not from an attack by racists but from a clash with the police over the route of the march. The authorities wanted us to walk through a quiet residential area, we would have preferred a busy commercial street.

While the leaders jousted verbally with the police, a few of the more daring rank and file tried to pierce the barricades and were repulsed. It was a bit more than a token skirmish but not much more.

Rice speaking at Vietnam War protest in Boston, January 1968

I can understand the police being adamant and reacting strongly; continually they are called upon to be firm and tough in restraining racist mobs made up of "their own kind" in South Boston. Really they had no choice.

Certainly the police were not the enemy we were marching against, except in the extended sense that the total society had done wrong and was a racist enemy, and the police its agents. The direct enemy was American racism as typified in South Boston.

We were marching against racism itself and against all of its proponents, including the Irish and Poles of South Boston. We were marching to serve notice for what it is worth, that we do not acquiesce in the move to shut Blacks up in their ghettos and to stall their progress.

We protesters of today have a complicated task, more difficult in a way than that of the greater fighters of twenty years ago. The struggle against racism has settled in the North, and the enemy is not official nor palpably villainous. In the front line we do not see the hulking Southern sheriffs backed by evil laws, but angry poor people who are themselves victims of society. In the background, and hard to confront, are crafty legislators, employers and bureaucrats who plot to circumvent or repeal good laws.

PITTSBURGH CATHOLIC
December 10, 1974

Homewood Tales

After Rice moved to the African-American neighborhood of Homewood, one of his most important tasks was to explain the viewpoint of his adopted community to the white working-class Catholics he had left behind. In particular, he often took the highly unpopular position of advocate for African-American prisoners and analyst of the violence that was often recorded superficially by the newspapers.

Recollections of Homewood, 1968 (1978)

1968 was such a year of destiny. . . . That was the year of the long hot summer. We had predicted that it would be so and that there would be rioting and trouble. There was indeed. Upon the death of Martin Luther King, Jr., we had our ritual riot in Homewood and remained in turmoil. Continual muggings, break-ins, daylight robberies. It seemed as if the writ of law ceased to run.

I was no longer privy to the councils of the militant Black leadership in Homewood. It was a time when Blacks were determined, and rightly so, to control their own destinies and to have no white leaders: but I was in communication with the leadership and knew a strong faction of them wanted the neighborhood to cool down.

The civil authorities did not know this because such was the mood of the Black community that the police force had temporarily lost the cooperation of its informers. In spite of being frozen out of the meetings of the militants, I could always get vital information. So for a while I knew more than the police and the civic powers.

As you may recall, I then was pastor of Holy Rosary Parish in Homewood, a Black ghetto. My parish was beginning to become unstuck. The whites had fears which were rational enough. They moved out in droves and some who remained in my territory would patronize parishes in nearby white ghettos. A valiant remnant, however, held firm.

I really did not blame those who left but was concerned over their departure and was deeply concerned over the white attitude in general. Naively I thought it possible to get your average white person to understand and make allowances for his Black brethren. Anything that would add to white irritation, especially white Catholic irritation, bothered me.

On the Fourth of July we had an incident, a big, bothersome one. The St. Vincent de Paul Store went up in flames. That store was on the main street within the shadow of our great Gothic church. I got the word after Mass, and, when I stepped out to look, was greeted by dark greasy billows of smoke scudding overhead as the fire raged out of control. One more shock in a Summer of shocks.

The store sold old clothes and furniture cheaply, it performed a service and was popular with the poor. But it was full of rags and other combustible material.

When the fire chief, now dead, Lord rest him, hastened to proclaim that the blaze was started by a fire bomb, I was alarmed. Fire bomb meant Black militant and that contributed to the white backlash which was coming on strong.

So I challenged the Chief and we had a public row. My checking convinced me that the fire was due to arson all right, but another sort, a torch job.

I hesitated to say bluntly that it was an insurance fire, and my statement was "a fire due to spontaneous combustion."

For some strange reason the Chief and his department kept insisting and insisting that it was a fire bombing and promising apprehensions. These never came, and a few years later a chap who occasionally sups with the mob told me with a chuckle that I had been right. It had been a torch job by some well-known practitioners of that art.

I am convinced that not only this fire but many others at the time, which were blamed on fire bombing, were nothing of the sort. Now ten years later the truth is obvious and arsonous burnings of ghetto buildings is out of hand. The crime does not get the attention it should have and is costly socially as well as financially.

That is not the only time, may I state humbly, that I was right while the world and its powers were wrong.

PITTSBURGH CATHOLIC
August 25, 1978

The Billy Hines Case (1970)

When I heard the names on the three-judge panel that would decide the fate of William Hines, my heart sank; my premonition proved to be justified as the fifteen-year old black boy was sentenced to life imprisonment for a crime of impulse and passion that took the life of a white girl. Hines has a third-grade education but is physically strong; it would appear that he did not have the intent to murder but killed the unfortunate girl in a clumsy attempt to ravish her.

Such a crime, involving as it does, a black male and white female, presents a troubled white social and legal structure of white judges, white jurors and white lawyers with a grave problem to which the only acceptable solution is the treatment of the black male, regardless of age, as if he were a white male of "good" family —in this case that did not happen. . . .

My concern with the case was intensified by

several circumstances: the crime occurred within two blocks of where I live; the lad was one of an annoying pack of teenagers who hung around our property and were, some of them anyway, winos at an early age (they were not of the drug culture nor of the militant Afro culture); finally, the girl's father was not only a friend of mine but was actually assisting me on a matter.

In a strange roundabout way, Hines contacted me six weeks ago; he did not quite remember my name but something he once heard indicated to him that I might be the sort that would try to help him. His case was being pushed to early trial and he feared that he was being set up for electrocution; would I visit him?

I went to the County Jail and met the young man for the first time. It is easy to forget how completely alone a black youth can be. He belonged nowhere and to nothing except whatever structure there was on the streets among boys his own age, and that gives no support at all when trouble comes.

There was no force and no institution to be summoned; Billy, sitting in the jail, was naked

Rice visiting with Billy Hines in prison

of resource, and for advice and counsel he had only his fellow inmates. . . .

There was not very much anyone could do for Hines short of providing a lot of money to buy counsel. If the lad had money, or if the case had more publicity value, one of our criminal court experts would take it and do wonders with the facts, the lad himself and the jury, but, as matters stood, there was no chance of that.

Life imprisonment was a bad sentence in its severity (it was really the most severe that could be imposed, execution being out of the question) since the convicted was a young black man, the victim a white girl, and the crime sexual. Such trials are, in a sense, political trials in which the white system is on trial in the eyes of all black people. Every case of this sort either promotes or impedes reconciliation between ruling white and alienated black.

The dominant whites fear black physical strength and violence, they also fear, and have odd ideas about, black sexual aggressiveness, thinking it different from the white brand. White judges are pressured to respond in a white fashion, which is what our three worthies did.

The black public, on the other hand, is supersensitive to the white sexual double standard with ancient memories of savage reprisal and repression on this very score; the black public also has a stored-up resentment ready to be released when it appears that the law or the system regards any black life as unimportant. Our black-white murder trials have all gone one way of late and this is not escaping sharp and angry notice. . . .

PITTSBURGH CATHOLIC
October 9, 1970

Dead by Mistake (1971)

Death in the streets of Homewood from a policeman's bullet was the fate last week of Ernest T. Williams, nineteen years of age and black. He is dead because he was mistaken for another young man and ran when challenged.

White authorities and news people were sobered by the tragedy and walked softly. Anxiety was obvious. What would Homewood do? Riot? Violently begin a long hot summer?

The policeman was suspended and placed under a general charge of murder. (Blacks wryly noted that he was freed with no bail.) The FOP [Fraternal Order of Police] leadership maintained an admirably tactful silence. Over and over it was stressed that Leonard Moses, the man for whom the young Williams was mistaken, was an escaped convicted murderer. . . .

Young Ernest Williams had no way of knowing how he would be treated if he halted. He could not possibly know that he was mistaken for someone else, and had no assurance that his person would be respected or his rights honored.

A question arises from many whites professing a difficulty in telling blacks apart. Were and are, hundreds of young black men (who might resemble Leonard Moses in the eye of a police beholder) in danger of instant death if they panic and run?

Suppose that the youth running and refusing to halt had really been Leonard Moses, would it have been right and moral to have killed him? May any policeman now kill him on sight?

Young Moses, part of a cluster of horror and excitement in the riot of Holy Week, 1968 [King's assassination] threw a fire bomb into a white home and struck an aged woman who, poor soul, died of burns. A horrible occurrence and an evil deed!

Should the law in its majesty, acting in the name of our total society, have refused to consider the ugly excitement of the moment and the youth of the sinners? Might it properly have considered the life patterns of Moses before and after the event? Those who maneuvered Moses and his companions into life imprisonment, well after the event, appear not to have considered anything but vengeance, punishment and a lesson.

Leonard Moses is not a mad dog but a person who made one dreadful mistake, yet he suffers the same penalty as the adult and hardened James Earl Ray whose premeditated murder of Martin Luther King set off the chain of events that resulted in the Homewood deaths and scores of others. . . . Blacks know and understand perfectly the sort of thing I have just taken pains to spell out. I took the pains because I write for a white readership and whites, since they aren't the victims in these instances, need to have them spelled out. . . .

I went to the funeral of Ernest Williams not as an observer or reporter but as a mourner. The ceremony was an African rite and it was short, simple and moving. The theme of the one brief sermon was positive with little anger, no hate and much hope.

Handsome young men and women wore white mourning costumes and the women hummed softly—no hymn. Once during a moment of quiet after the casket had been closed and the family had poured out its grief a woman's voice cried out: Jesus help us.

PITTSBURGH CATHOLIC
July 2, 1971

A Chase (1972)

Last Tuesday night as I was going to an ACLU meeting, our new dog was growling and barking in a manner to indicate that he was disturbed over something that was "going down" back in the alley. Sure enough, as I edged out

the back door I saw a sight.

Police and police vehicles unobtrusively filled the alley in sufficient numbers to startle me, let alone an impressionable dog. Ten vans and cruisers, no less, with attendant men in blue.

I inquired politely if they were after the IRA and they in friendly fashion informed me, no, but a couple of armed bandits were reported as having dashed into our gym.

The gym was open as our students were playing a game, and so I steered the officers in the direction of the entrance and departed on my way. These days one does not get excited over reports of the scurrying of armed men.

Next day in school I suddenly remember. "That was a false alarm, wasn't it?" I ask. "No!" "Two men did come dashing in."

It transpires that the dudes never got past the door, however. Mrs. Bonnie Murdoch, one of our demurely pretty black teachers, was on the door extracting quarters from all who desired to enter and spectate.

She dialogued with the alleged armed bandits as the massive fleet of police equipment converged on our premises, their sirens silent as befitted the tense situation.

The two brothers would not pay a quarter and she would not let them in. They left. End of incident.

I do not know if Flaherty's finest ever did apprehend their quarry.

PITTSBURGH CATHOLIC
February 25, 1972

A Story That Was Ignored (1973)

Franco Harris is a large, fast man who has attained sudden fame as a result of his derring-do on the playing fields of professional football. He is not easy to interview because he is reserved and finds it hard to talk about himself.

However, James Crutchfield of the Post-Gazette got a marvelous interview out of him on the subject of his interesting ancestry. Mr. Harris is the son of a Black GI and an Italian war bride. His quiet and understated reflections on growing up in America in a military atmosphere were a social document with the impact of volumes.

It started me thinking about an Italian war bride who came to see me twenty-five years ago. Her husband had called and asked if I would talk to her. She was a woman about thirty who had married a Black officer of the same age. She was not pretty, but she was a trim, nice-looking person who came from a middle-class family in Northern Italy. I am not much for noticing women's clothes but she was dressed in marvelous taste, subdued, but expensive clothes, shoes and umbrella.

She had been employed in Italy in an office and had lived with her family.

She loved her husband very much, and had simply not believed that she could not make a life with him in America. She had been told all about race prejudice in the United States, but could not imagine the reality.

They were living in the Hill District, near where I was then stationed, and the quarters were bad. Her husband had not been able to find a civilian job to match his Army job and pay. To be stuck in a slum staggered her, and to have no friends was killing her.

Her English was very good, but communication with her neighbors required more than English, and her husband had no relatives in Pittsburgh.

Over and over she told me that she understood prejudice of class, she had that herself, but prejudice of race or color was incomprehensible to her. I met her several times and

> **"Over and over she told me that she understood prejudice of class, she had that herself, but prejudice of race or color was incomprehensible to her."**

tried to help; she had no place else to run.

The end of the story is that some months later she phoned and informed me through tears that she was giving up and going back to Italy. She still loved him but was arranging for a divorce. She was anguished, very bitter and unable to make sense of the tragedy that had befallen her and her marriage.

I have encountered other war brides of Black soldiers and officers who stuck it out but they all suffered terribly and often they got it from both sides. Sometimes the husband's family was mean or indifferent, to add to the pain.

Franco Harris's family made out better than most, but they were protected by living in an Army situation, along with similar families. His saga will help us with our prejudices, a little.

PITTSBURGH CATHOLIC
January 19, 1973

Officer Wallace's Death (1974)

Homewood was deathly quiet on the Fourth of July, the normal fire cracker exuberance being absent. In the past we had been very lax in our attitude toward laws that ban firecrackers; this year there were no bangs the night before nor all during the day, just a few at dusk.

A white policeman had been killed in Homewood and the black young man accused of the murder was at large along with two companions who had figured in the tragic incident. No young black men strolled or strode the streets of Homewood, because there was fear and anxiety in this neighborhood. Parents kept their young men home or sent them to picnics in the parks; unattached young men simply laid low.

What were they afraid of? Shocked and angry policemen were searching grimly for the suspects. There had almost been a shootout when they cornered the wrong chaps in a house in East Liberty. On that occasion there was some disturbing talk on the police band, not racial stuff but a cryptic remark or two, into which you could read what you wanted.

Young black men did not want to be hassled and they did not want chance involvement with the searchers so they kept out of sight until the heat abated. Our police did not run out of control but in the aftermath, as they were searching, they treated our black neighborhood in a cavalier fashion. Following tips they did not bother with warrants, although they would ask for permission before they searched a house. So if you were black, you might see a carload of men, in or out of uniform, heavily armed, rather grim faced, looking over your house. If they asked permission to come in, even if you knew all your rights you would think twice, in the presence of all that firepower, saying no.

Patrick J. Wallace, Jr., the murdered officer, was a zealous professional who seems to have enjoyed his dangerous occupation. He was fearless but not brash; he was aggressive in the pursuit of his duties but not a bully. There are indications that he had the respect of most blacks who encountered him. An honest man enforcing the law is deeply appreciated in the ghetto and Wallace was uncorruptible.

Blacks can sympathize with the passing of a vigorous young male because so many of theirs die young or are destroyed one way or the other. The destruction of the black male is one of the saddest features of ghetto life. Many a lonely black woman raising a child understands what the widow of Patrick Wallace must face.

Those of us familiar with the black situation in Pittsburgh and especially us whites who live by choice in black communities dread this sort of incident. We hate its effect on race relations and we know that innocent blacks and whites may suffer on its account. We also wonder what it means for the future. Is this a new pattern, could it be a trend or is it an isolated incident?

My inquiries indicate that this was a special incident and that we are not likely to have an epidemic of cop killing. Officer Wallace and his partner were pressing a group of young black men who were considered prone to major crime and who were being blamed for recent bank robberies and other major stick-ups. They are not a gang but they associate with each other and generally go about armed. No more than twenty of them all told and several are in prison.

Those young men are not saint material but if they were white, or if this were not a racist society, they would be pursuing business careers flamboyantly, or they would be into the non-violent, safer sort of crime, the white collar variety. . . .

The hunt for the killer goes on because the network of informers on whom normally the police can depend is not hitting. That could be ominous. Do the informers know nothing, or are they afraid or perhaps disinclined to tell?

If the searching goes on and on and civilians look out their windows day by day to see men with rifles running through alleys and across vacant lots the community tension will become oppressive. Our black communities have been calm and our police have been safe; too much pressure exerted unwisely could turn around and cause us big trouble.

The young blacks of my area are free men in a free country, that they should have to cower in their own homes because a member of their race committed a crime against a policeman is more evidence that we are still a racist state and city, and we had better do something about it.

PITTSBURGH CATHOLIC
July 12, 1974

The Late Bouie Haden (1974)

William "Bouie" Haden died this week and we are burying him from Holy Rosary's beautiful church. Mercifully a heart attack took him. I say mercifully because he had cancer of the bladder and bone and at times his suffering was intense.

The pain at the end matched the pain in his life. The pain of a tough sensitive man existing in a society where he was not considered fully a man because of his race. The pain of a Black man who would never back away.

When he was just a lad in Virginia the family slipped into poverty; down there before he was twenty he barely escaped a lynching party; he revolted against the Army's automatic degradation of the Black soldier and was punished severely time after time; he was shunted aside in the steel mill and pushed out of his seniority line; to survive in a system he could not stand he conducted petty hustles in the Ghetto for years.

He was thrown in jail fifty or more times and did his time without a whimper but with a lump of anger in his heart because he was bright and well-read and knew that loftier men did greater wrong and suffered not a whit.

And then, as the Ghetto stirred, he stirred. He could always charm crowds, particularly

> "**A**nd then, as the Ghetto stirred, he stirred. He could always charm crowds, particularly young crowds and he began to talk of freedom and justice and the Black's rightful heritage."

young crowds and he began to talk of freedom and justice and the Black's rightful heritage. After some years of this he attracted the white media and he was wonderful copy when civil rights was NEWS. That leonine head, roaring out its anguish and anger, filled the TV screen (one of the networks used him in full tide of oratory to keynote a major special on the Black revolt) and he was terrific copy in the print media.

He read a great deal, he knew poetry, scripture and history. He was up on world and national affairs and economics. That is why his rhetoric was usually effective; also he knew the Street and the Black condition. Oh! how he knew that!

I learned that he regretted the hatred he roused in so many white breasts. He was merely trying to shock the Man into doing right; he did not hate white people and he did not love violence although he threatened violence over and over.

In actuality he kept the peace and he kept faith with the Black movement; final proof being that he died a poor man. Others amassed wealth from the struggle or gained comfortable jobs, he would not accept the cushy jobs that the establishment offered because he would not be bought.

Bouie accepted a grant from the Fund for Neighbors in Need, which Cardinal Wright had instituted, and that set up an amazing and shameful episode. There was an explosion of anger and hatred. Cardinal (then Bishop) Wright was hanged in effigy on the Cathedral lawn, and to this day some Catholics hold back financial support.

They thought that Bouie was ready to lead an army against them to dispossess them, perhaps, or they may have been shocked by the bitter truth he so eloquently expressed: The classic Black angry male rubbing the white man the wrong way.

In a short column I cannot relate all his adventures. His wild newspaper; his center that was sabotaged from the beginning; his attempt at self policing of the ghetto; his many attempts to revive Homewood-Brushton economically; his successful finding of jobs for scores of Black men and women; his acts of kindness and protection; his successful negotiation with radio and TV stations for more Black presence; his many-faceted drives for Black dignity, pride and self sufficiency.

He was not a Black separatist or a Black nationalist and he did not lead a squad of bully boys although he could easily have done so. Haden wanted to dialogue with whites, and he recognized the pains and sufferings of the white poor and working class.

In his heyday Bouie was hated by the police, especially the police brass, and they eventually broke up his organization. They did not understand that when he confronted them he was not seeking to overcome them but to change their attitudes and procedures. He counseled against fighting them. "The police never stop coming," he said over and over, "against them you cannot live." At the height of militance and madness he said that you could not have a community without police and law.

I saw him at work, reasoning with angry, violent and dangerous young Black men and cooling them. He was the major influence in tempering Black fury during the riot of 1968, which was mild in Pittsburgh.

Among his qualities was total courage. He risked death and beatings several times. Regardless of that silly story white men reassured each other with, he was never intimidated; the Mafia did not mess with him,

nor he with them. His courage extended to meetings, verbal confrontations and non-violent risks.

When the Black revolt was no longer fashionable and the opinion makers decided he was not news, he did not slacken but plugged away in poverty and obscurity. Indomitable.

From way back he had the Black militant's scorn for the Planned Parenthood campaign; the Pill and Abortion. "Black genocide": he roared. The dirty, snide inference that his opinion was influenced by Catholic money disgusts and infuriates me.

In his later days he regretted his extreme flights of oratory and some of his militant actions because of the hatred and fear they aroused in whites. He was convinced that cooperation between the races simply had to be and it bothered him that he might have hindered that cooperation. I think he did much more good than harm but he was not sure. He was hoping to last long enough to get a new movement of cooperation going.

When he first arrived on the scene I was almost intimidated by him, although he was friendly to me from the start. In time I came to lean on him and trusted him as much as I ever did any human being. I believe that he trusted me and trusted the Catholic Church. I respected Bouie and loved him as a man of honor, principle and compassion.

When he realized how sick he was he asked me to pray for him and I did that often. I knew how painful his disease was, having seen its ravages close at hand. Characteristically he would not take pain killers, he did not accept the pain but raged against it — his own man to the last.

It is with heavy heart that I see him laid in the grave and say a few last words.

PITTSBURGH CATHOLIC
August 2, 1974

Vietnam: Sinned and Gone Mad

The only other issue that would vie for Rice's attention with the same level of urgency as the racial crisis in the United States was the war in Vietnam. Rice began to speak out against American interventionism following the invasion of the Dominican Republic in 1965, and then threw himself into the struggle against the Vietnam War with a passion that greatly upset many readers of the Pittsburgh Catholic.

Do We Belong in Vietnam? (1965)

Vietnam is a dirty and dangerous business and we have to get out. The dirt and the danger lie not so much in what may happen to the United States, but in what is being done by us against other people and in what additional evil we may be led to inflict.

Long before we got directly involved in the conflict we supplied our allies with truly dreadful weapons and directed their use. Napalm and phosphorus bombs are an inhuman product of modern technology. While they are not so bad as the nuclear bomb and not so nauseatingly destructive as bacteriological weapons, they are murderous and should be outlawed. It was bad enough to use them against technologically advanced peoples such as the Japanese and the Germans, but to use them against jungle fighters is unclean. The anti-personnel shell with its cruel needles of death is no better.

It is said that the enemy is unfair because he has used terror to get support and respect. What are we doing? What is the jellied gasoline which clings, burns and tortures? What of the phosphorus which eats into the bone? What of the miserable victims of napalm, phosphorus and steel splinters who continue to live in unbelievable agony and helplessness? Is this not terror and are we not guilty?

Are we repelling an invader? No, we are not. The Viet Cong are not invaders. They may be Communists but they are native to Vietnam. We are the invaders and we are the only invaders who are there in force. The Chinese Communists are not present in force, nor are the Russians.

The North Vietnamese do not want Chinese domination, but we may force it upon them.

We have misunderstood the facts and have misread the past every step of the way. We have seen, and we see, parallels where they do not exist and we draw foolish conclusions.

The situation now does not parallel the European situation during the rise of Hitler. Appeasement is not the danger here. . . .

Some say, it would be awful to let Vietnam and Laos and Cambodia slide into Communism. I say, let the people decide. If the Communists can win their allegiance we cannot really do anything about it. We who do not understand their ways. We are growing more hated every day as we kill more and more of them.

I do not fear that we will lose. I fear what we will do in order to win. It looks as if we are ready to destroy the industry of North Vietnam. That industry was built up with sacrifice and heroism, however misguided. What right do we have to destroy it even if we intend to build it up again?

So this was done under Communist control, so what? It was done and the people like it.

Is it not better to be dead than Red? Let the Vietnamese decide that for themselves and we will decide it for ourselves.

Finally: We will lose face if we leave. Which is worse? Lose face or lose your soul?

PITTSBURGH CATHOLIC
April 22, 1965

Rice addressing anti-war rally, 1969

At the Pentagon (1967)

Between the Lincoln Memorial and the Washington Monument an immense reflecting pool glistened in the gentle October sunshine. Both sides of this pool were packed with people, and for the four hours that I was there more people flowed in as buses finally made it from New York and New England. Behind us, on the steps of the Lincoln Memorial and in the roadway, thousands more stood or sat.

No great national figures, other than Dr. Benjamin Spock and artists such as Robert Lowell and Normal Mailer, dared to appear but the people were there. The turnout was not as large as at the UN in New York six months ago, but it reached the figure credited to that April march and would have been larger had not bus companies in New York cancelled without warning.

Airplanes roared in the skies continually and they were not all of the routine passenger variety. The sky seemed to teem with helicopters (army, police and journalistic) and the profusion of metallic birds made speaking and listening difficult.

The crowd was younger and lacked the rather settled look of the earlier one, but it was not a boisterous or a silly crowd and it certainly was peaceful.

Shortly after the speaking began, a husky man made a sudden rush and overturned the podium with its cluster of microphones. As always at these affairs, the violence and the bad manners come from the war-loving opposition, and, as always, there are cries from the peace demonstrators of "Don't hurt him." How different from the cries of, "Get him," that greet similar incidents in all other crowds!

No orator really stirred the crowd although there was frequent applause and a few times there was chanting of slogans. The sound system did not work perfectly and many in the vast crowd could not hear, but they remained patiently. Singers solo and in groups, performed but there was no mass sing-along. A marvelous puppet show was presented by a group called, "Bread and Peace Puppets."

On the platform there was much going to and fro and the whole lacked the precision of the New York demonstration. We were delayed in our march to the Pentagon because the authorities did not follow through on their promises. A fence that was to be taken down was not, and the line of march was changed to a tortuous route, through spots that narrowed, an underpass, over broken ground and so on.

On the march itself thousands walked before us and at the sides and after we left the Memorial Bridge the march lost its organized character and each person got to the Pentagon parking lot as best he might. It was a tribute to the nature of the crowd that there was such little disorder; another sort of crowd might have turned ugly, or disorderly or might have panicked.

Police to protect the marchers or smooth the route were very little in evidence. A small group of right-wing nuts with a sign "Red Clergy Go To Hell" were able to hold us up for nearly a half hour, something totally unnecessary that should not have been permitted by the authorities.

As we neared the Pentagon we saw the great fence topped with barbed wire that had been newly erected to keep us under control. Military men and police in full battle array peeped out at us from behind the fence. I understand that there was a shoving match at one small part of the fence but no attempt was made to knock it down. Thoughts of the Berlin Wall crossed my mind as I looked at the new and sudden barrier.

A strange thing happened at the Pentagon. We had assumed that few people would relish direct confrontation and that the marchers would automatically crowd around the speaking stand until, at a certain juncture, a few of us would detach from the main body and proceed to the squat threatening home of rampant militarism. What actually happened was that thousands of the marchers just kept on marching past the speaking area and right

> "A small group of right-wing nuts with a sign "Red Clergy Go To Hell" were able to hold us up for nearly a half hour."

down for their own confrontation. We waited for a long time as various speeches were given and reports exchanged and, then, it became obvious that we, the official confronters, had best get to the battle line.

The front door and the great steps were already engaged as we drew near. MPs were in rows as the crowd eddied and flowed in front of them trying to get in but not really pushing or being violent.

Dave Dellinger was the leader of those who had elected civil disobedience and he proposed that we proceed to a line of soldiers some distance from the main entrance and address them with a view to changing them from war to peace. After his brief introduction I was the first to speak and I told of the foolishness of escalation which takes more and more lives, of the evil we were doing to Vietnam, and of the true patriotism which dares to censure mistaken and evil national politics.

The soldiers were really done up in battle dress, helmeted, armed and equipped. We were only a small group but they were ordered to advanced slowly upon us. When I was in the front they did not push us back but flowed around us.

They isolated our little group and at a slow pace swept back the crowd behind us. Another line of soldiers was moved into position and it was the turn of Dellinger and Spock to address them. This line again marched forward and Dellinger, Spock and some others sat down in front of the line. As the line reached these people the soldiers began to shuffle into them trying to kick them aside. I saw a non-com grab Dellinger by the hair as he screamed "Get up, get out of there."

Spock and most of the others eventually got to their feet but Dellinger and one of the women leaders were dragged away and arrested. Some women were crying; but there was no panic, and no one was really hurt. In another part of the field tear gas was used but,

there again, no one was badly affected. Some of the soldiers got more of the gas than the protesters because no one had told them to put their masks on.

It was strangely quiet and undramatic. As we walked away, Lowell commented on how ugly it appeared to him. I saw it as disciplined soldiers overcoming a peaceful and undisciplined group of civilians. Perhaps a dress rehearsal for both.

Certainly the soldiers were not needed, and it was not necessary for them to walk into us. Had they let us alone we would have had to leave after saying our say.

The soldiers were there so that their commanders would learn how to deal with civilians such as us, and soldiers will be used more and more for this sort of thing. That implication is uglier than any action of the day. The victimized class who are being drafted into the army are now impervious to the logic of the intellectual peace promoters but they may not remain so forever.

PITTSBURGH CATHOLIC
October 26, 1967

Kent State Will Live in Infamy (1990)

On May 4, 1970, I was part of a large chanting, sign-carrying picket line that was protesting at the Federal Building against Nixon's brutal Cambodian incursion. Demonstrations were on all over the country. In the midst of ours, we got word of the burst of gunfire 100 miles away that will "live in infamy."

At an anti-war demonstration on the campus of Kent State, the Ohio National Guard had fired into a crowd of students. Some were noisy and abusive, but the demonstration was winding down and the Guard was withdrawing. Guardsmen turned, knelt, aimed and fired. Four students died, two of them women. Nine were wounded, some seriously. None of the victims were armed and all were too far from those who were armed to be a threat of any sort. Some of the victims were not even protesting, just watching or crossing the campus.

There was an instant cover-up and obfuscation. We cannot discover whether or not an order was given to fire (it probably was), but no one, either officer or man, was punished.

Blame must extend beyond the Guardsmen who had been pumped full of hatred for the protesting students.

The odious Nixon and his loathsome vice-president, Spiro Agnew, had been spewing inflammatory rhetoric against all student critics of the Cambodian escalation, and the crass governor of Ohio had thrown oil on the fire when he sent in the Guard. The governor savagely attacked the Kent State protestors going so far as to call them the equivalent of Nazi brown shirts.

Those who pulled the trigger suffer privately except for the ones who are subhuman. James Rhodes, state Governor and Commander-in-Chief of the Guard, was finished politically. Nixon and Agnew escaped scot-free; when they were tripped up, it was for other crimes and misdemeanors.

On the recent anniversary, it was disgusting to glimpse Richard M. Nixon on PBS getting two hours for his smarmy, self-serving justification of a squalid career. The man is entitled to tell his story and get away with as much as he can, but on that day? . . .

As for the Kent State incident itself; it did not take the heart out of the anti-war movement whose men and women remained brave and fiercely determined to end the slaughter in South East Asia. It is fashionable in some circles to sneer at the students involved, but I knew hundreds of them. They were not playing games but were serious and committed and fully informed. They knew about the horrors being perpetrated by our side and dared to express bold disapproval and to oppose the popular will.

I am proud that I was part of the leadership of the anti-war movement, a leadership that was not distant from the action but went into the streets themselves.

My contribution was enhanced by the fact that I was two generations older than the bulk of the activists, and, as Monsignor, member of the Bishop's Council and pastor of a major parish, I brought weight and credibility. I was able to give support and often protection to the protestors as I marched at their head and addressed their rallies. For a couple of tough years, in terms of age and prestige and ecclesiastical standing, I stood alone not only locally but nationally.

Another telling factor: the protestors were called Communists and my anti-Communist credentials were impeccable. I may have earned those credentials in somewhat dubious fashion, but they were useful, as was ruefully recognized by our Left Wing contingent.

PITTSBURGH CATHOLIC
May 11, 1990

Kent State Incident Brings War Home (1990)

In a predictable reaction, super-patriots blamed the Kent State victims. But the nation as a whole was shocked. Killing Blacks or strikers was one thing, but students, white ones at that! Rebellious students were a new and disturbing phenomenon and America did not like them, but shooting them was unforgivable.

The venom displayed by the Guardsmen who pulled their triggers was not surprising. The Ohio National Guard had its share of slacker/slickers like Dan Quayle who were in it

Rice addressing anti-war teach-in at the University of Pittsburgh, 1965

to avoid the draft and Vietnam. We know now that many of these dodgers mouthed patriotism and were furious resisters.

However, most of the Ohio Guardsmen were not that type but were sons of blue-collar families. Such families were doing very well because their strong unions had brought them good wages, heavy industry was booming, and well-paying jobs were plentiful. There was wartime prosperity because Lyndon Johnson had opted for guns and butter and no economic sacrifices.

Revelling in that false prosperity, the families of workers had reason to feel very good about their country. Anyway, they were inclined to be patriotic in an unquestioning way. The fathers were big in Veterans' organizations, and the sons gravitated toward the Guard even in times of peace. Many had brothers in the real army, some in Nam itself.

No wonder the Ohio Guard members as a whole had been bitterly angry at anti-war resisters even before they were inflamed by their bombastic commander, Gov. James

Rhodes. In examining what happened and why, one has to consider the military quality of the Guard from top to bottom and figure that into the equation. Not judging them as human beings, but as the officers and men they were professed to be, they were about as far from an elite corps as one can imagine. Discipline was poor and so was morale. It was criminal irresponsibility to throw them into confrontation with anti-war protestors.

Blue-collar trade unionists and the like carried their attitudes into the Reagan era and many of them deserted the liberal New Deal coalition. Their reward for supporting the war and then buying into Reaganism was the Rust Bowl and the precipitous fall of most of them out of the middle class. Their pension funds are in some jeopardy, and their children face a future of poorly paid deadend jobs, but they still may not have learned a lesson.

Of course, in 1970 none of this was foreseen, and the white working class was fat and sassy, patriotic as all get out, and contemptuously angry at all peaceniks. So a Kent State of some sort was waiting to happen.

PITTSBURGH CATHOLIC
May 18, 1990

Good Friday 1971 (1971)

On the first Good Friday, as the Gospel tells it, "the people" chose a convicted man of violence in preference to the Prince of Peace and they gave the man of violence his freedom. The Prince of Peace they disposed of by the cruel expedient of crucifixion.

Who were "the people" on that first Good Friday? All of us. We are all guilty of the death of Christ, as Christian preachers have been pointing out ever since it all happened.

On Good Friday 1971 we can meditate on how "the people" have spoken once again on the subject of good and evil, of the killer and his victim, of God and man.

The outpouring of sympathy for the dapper little Lieutenant who was convicted of killing women, babies and old men in Vietnam is an extraordinary expression of human sinfulness by a civilized populace. There is everything in that wave of protest. Hatred of the victims or contempt of them. Justification of evil when it is our own. Exaltation of war and soldiering. Rejection of truth. Denial of the unity of the human race and the brotherhood of man. Reversion to savagery.

It is all obscenely logical, fitting and to be expected, however. We have consistently worshipped a strange set of heroes in this plastic American age and finally have an ultimate in that odd little lord of life and death: our Everyman? For centuries we have exalted country above every other value; we waged cruel war and maintained cruel oppression against human beings who have differed from us, do not match our mold, stand in our way or merely seem ripe for submission. The slaughter of Indian and buffalo was a figure of great romance, still is. For a full generation the men who rain death from the skies have been acclaimed paragons. The hero worship of Calley is a twisted thing, but that the people of America spontaneously should create a Calley cult is poetic justice, it fits. He is the sort of hero we deserve. . . .

All in all it is an amazing subject for meditation to recall that Sergeant York of World War I and Commando Kelly of World War II have been replaced by Lieutenant William Calley. He is in the history books to stay, he and his deed are emblazoned on the shocked consciousness of what passes for the civilized world.

That is one way of looking at it. Another, somewhat altered and perhaps more in keeping with Holy Week and Easter, is to emphasize the pity that we should have for the vast American public which, like the public in Jerusalem long ago, is conditioned by its leaders. Generations to come may well spare a little pity for a people so confused and totally at sea that it took to its heart a convicted killer of the helpless.

Some pity let us now spare for the man himself. He was conditioned to the task and his statements indicate that he may not be as proud of himself as are his bewildered and brutalized American loud-mouthed cheering section.

PITTSBURGH CATHOLIC
April 9, 1971

Smug, Evil West (1971)

Four years ago when I participated in the Spring Mobilization for peace and against the killing in Vietnam, it was a nightmare of almost constant vilification and alienation. I fought back and I didn't whimper, but it was not at all pleasant. Most of all, the alienation from an entire constituency of friends (even intimates), allies and supporters was tough to take.

The process had started much earlier as I began to first, suspect, and then, condemn, the Vietnam adventure. In 1967 I was part of the national leadership and remained in it, but as it shuffled and reshuffled I drifted to the periphery. I intend to be in the march tomorrow, April 24, and I believe in it, although it has become what [radical philosopher Herbert] Marcuse calls acceptable dissent and it may well be "used" by our ineffable President in his own obvious fashion but, he uses everything, or tries to.

These days I have to force myself to read about Vietnam and our continuing atrocities from the air. It is repulsive reading and one gathers from it disgust, rather a cleansing indignation. Only my disposition keeps me from sinking in a miasma of depression or a copout. My copout would not be drugs or revivalism, but it could be reading. That is the

temptation but I feel I shall be saved by the tendencies God implanted in me to get angry at injustice or stupidity and to be willing to try hard regardless of the prospects of reforming the unjust or enlightening the dense.

PITTSBURGH CATHOLIC
April 23, 1971

That Times Story (1971)

Pittsburgh is being cheated by that long newspaper strike because without newspapers the ordinary Pittsburgher is missing, among other things, the full impact of one of the great news stories of our day: the New York Times' publication of that Pentagon study of presidential power, deceit and Vietnam.

That story itself is the story of a massive cheating of the total citizenry. It barely touches the basic infamy of the war which is the destruction of a land and its people by a blind, selfish and self-righteous foreign power, us, the U.S.A.

Significantly the horror goes on even as we debate the revelation. Apparently our reigning President is more concerned with protecting presidential power than he is with the implications of his present use of that power.

The study which the Times is struggling to release to us was commissioned by Robert McNamara when he was in charge of what is euphemistically referred to as the Department of "Defense." He wanted to see wherein we blundered. It would appear that a young man who had been involved in some of the evil decisions that are described in the study picked up a copy of the thing and brought it to the New York Times.

Rather courageously the Times decided to publish in full with commentary. The Times had been cozened and deceived as had all the established papers, services, broadcasters, and networks.

Let me insert that the Times need not have been so easily deceived, and had it and other news organs been doing what they are supposed to do, they all would have caught on almost immediately.

The revelations are old hat to those of us who read the radical press and even to those who read the liberal press with care. Tonkin Gulf was a put on. The President, cabinet members, generals and academic specialists have been lying to us. It is said you can boil a frog without the frog knowing what is being done to him if you increase the heat slowly enough. Well, the public of the United States was one gigantic frog and it has been boiled.

Gentle readers who wonder why I react with such furious contempt toward government officials and other wrongdoers on the Vietnam business may now understand. I have known for years that we were being fed lies and garbage and have been killing babies and women and fields and a whole society in Vietnam for the shallowest of reasons — we did not know how to let on to ourselves how evil and foolish it was without top politicians being destroyed and their place in history being the barnyard rather than the hall of fame.

The whole adventure was pointless and some brilliant men have acted as nasty idiots. Power has corrupted everyone down to the comedians and clergymen who still reinforce the lies with laughs and prayers.

PITTSBURGH CATHOLIC
June 25, 1971

Our Greatest Mistake (1972)

Our American government has been interfering in Indochina for at least twenty years and that is not only the greatest mistake of our history but also the most shameful and most cruel of our actions.

There was shame and cruelty in our treatment of our own Indians, of the Mexicans and the Philippinos, but Indochina tops them all.

We have a national fault in that we associate shame only with losing, and our maturity will come, if ever, when we realize the shameful deed is to misuse our strength against the weak, win or lose.

We are obsessed with national honor and we associate that with winning wars and dominating other human beings; in the last twenty years the more we strive for honor the more we tarnish what we have left of it.

We have been immoral in that we have put our own national interest, often a very remote interest, above humanity. We have gone against our own democratic principles in that we suppress movements of liberation all over the globe and support dictators and militarists in Korea, Greece, Turkey, Taiwan, Latin America, and Pakistan.

We have sinned and gone mad.

We are beginning, merely beginning, to pay for this sin and madness. Our cities rot, our young people are deteriorating, our religions are slipping and our minorities lie sick and neglected, our workers are demoralized and lose their motivation, our system of government totters on the edge of tyranny, internal order moves toward chaos, and our vaunted economic powers are waning. All of which is only the beginning.

Neither the evil old men who launched this military enormity nor the arrogant younger technicians and cold scientists who have pursued it will themselves pay the penalty, this side of eternity, but generations yet unborn most surely will.

To understand it might help to realize that our nation is not sacred or privileged or endowed with any divine mission; it is to be judged on what it does, and its people in these days of comparative freedom and participation are to be judged on what they permit as well as by what they commission.

Rice accepting draft cards,
December 7, 1967

Our President is a desperate and angry man who in order to punish the soldiers of North Vietnam, who are beating his allies, can order an action that will not affect the present fighting but will certainly kill civilians. The bombing of Hanoi and Haiphong harbor by B-52's must have killed hundreds of old men, women and children, and its only justification was a disgusting desire for revenge.

More immoral than that is the bombing that has never ceased all over Indochina and which kills more civilians every day than military personnel. We do it because we have the tools and can think of nothing else to do. . . . After all our sins and cruelty we have nothing to show and will have less in a short time.

The question is: will we cease and desist or we will keep on hastening the decay of our own country and killing additional thousands of civilians pointlessly? There is no chance of us winning anything but shame and unglory.

PITTSBURGH CATHOLIC
May 12, 1972

The Christmas Bombing (1972)

Incredible is a risky word to use when one is referring to actions of the current president of the United States, but it close to being the right word to describe how Richard Nixon has chosen to mark this Christmas season. After all, we are told that he is a very religious man and we can observe that he has prominent religious types in to pray in his august presence, and, conversationally, he loves peace as much as he loves God.

So, why do most Americans not find it incredible that he, by his personal edict, would order an unrestricted bombing of North Vietnam at a time when his nation was in the midst of its annual chanting of peace on earth, good will toward men?

I am trying to discuss the matter calmly, and I hesitate to use superlatives in describing Nixon's Christmas action, but the terse communiques which announced the action used certain superlatives. It is the heaviest bombing of any place at any time: a new first for America. The target is not a powerful, industrial, well-developed nation but a weak, third-rate nation whose great friends have lost their enthusiasm. A cheap shot, if one may borrow one of Mr. Nixon's favorite expressions: there is no chance that this small nation will be able to hit back at our country. It is safe to beat up the Vietnamese who have no long-range bombers, no nuclear submarines, and no bases outside their own borders.

In that undeveloped country there never was very much worth hitting, and one must wonder what justifies the massive raids of B-52's whose patterns obliterate oblongs measuring a mile-and-a-half by a half mile. One has to conclude that terror is the object of this bombing and people, not installations, are the target. Even if Nixon is not trying to kill by the thousands he is certain to kill and maim by the hundreds as he scorches the earth.

We must leave off superlatives and look to the trivial as we examine the reason for the renewed assault: the pique of a most powerful man who cannot have his own way. The peace talks went a bit sour, the North Vietnamese negotiators were tough bargainers and Nixon, operating through Professor Kissinger, could not hurry them up or force quick compromises that might save his face. So he said: no more gradual escalation, let us hit them at once with all we have got and see how they like it.

It still will not work. My gloomy prediction that the pre-election peace would prove to be a phony was correct, to my regret. I predict that after the present spasm of destruction the North Vietnamese will be as tough as ever and have even less to lose by continuing to hang tough. What have we left other than the nuclear bomb, and Nixon is mean and petty but hardly mad enough to let slip the dogs of nuclear war — I think. . . .

PITTSBURGH CATHOLIC
December 29, 1972

POW's (1973)

About those prisoners of war and their stories of mistreatment: remember what they were doing; remember the stuff they dropped on people — napalm, fragmentation bombs, etc.; remember that prisoners from the other side were being tortured by our allies while we stood by; such prisoners were sometimes dropped from our helicopters so that others would talk and that hardly made pilots lovable; remember that many My Lais were witnessed by the enemy and the word was passed around.

Killer aviators are heroes only to the peoples who possess planes, ground troops always have had a poor view of them. Back in the twenties when France was subduing North Africa and used planes against the natives, Abd El Krim was inconsiderate enough to spread-eagle captured pilots and light fires on their tummies — the "civilized" world with its planes, bombs and machine guns was, of course, horrified.

Our military lost the battle of propaganda, along with some other battles, while the war was going on, it is renewing that battle now. I do hope that a bit of counterinformation will squeeze into print or onto the tubes.

PITTSBURGH CATHOLIC
April 6, 1973

We Ignore Stench in Vietnam (1974)

Sakharov and Solzhenitsyn, as they fight their very good fight against Soviet Russian abuses, often bewail the suppression of knowledge in their country and long for more openness because now even the intellectual community knows too little of what goes on and criticism is unable to have its salutary effect. They seem to think that more information would be bound to help.

Maybe so, but one wonders about the saving of power of knowledge as one contemplates the United States today. Among us knowledge is not suppressed, we have as free a press as there is anywhere, and even the other media in their own way convey at least a glimmering of the truth. There is distortion, of course, and selective emphasis but if you want the truth, you can find it.

Yet in the United States the public knows only what it wants to know. It has been deceived and misled but there is every indication that often it wants that. At any rate, a whole people, all two hundred million of us, with access to the pertinent information can and do ignore monstrous truths; it can virtually will them out of being as it were.

That is how we cope with the unpleasant reality of Vietnam today. For years we handled

it by simply lying to ourselves and the whole world; meanwhile we treated with contemptuous hostility those who insisted on the truth, the whole ugly truth.

Finally the lie came to its logical climax; we fashioned the lie of lies and called it peace. We said the war was over. Oddly the President who proclaimed that the war had ended and that we had achieved peace with honor gave as a finale the obscene and unnecessary bombing of North Vietnam, and then after the phony peace was declared, insisted on bombing Cambodia until Congress made him stop.

More than a year has passed and most of our own fighting men have been withdrawn, but fighting, destruction and killing persist. We keep our faction well supplied with money and material; we even maintain 6,000 advisers over there to help with the sophisticated equipment we lavish on the death trade.

More Vietnamese were killed in one year of "peace" than Americans were killed in ten years of war. All the frightful and ingeniously murderous weapons and devices that we used to use, as well as some newly developed ones, are now at the disposal of the regime we have been supporting so expensively and sinfully for so many pointless years. . . .

There is no peace in South Vietnam and no freedom. Thousands are in jail on suspicion of wanting to mount political opposition. Detention without trial is a commonplace. Torture is routine. Imprisonment can itself be torture, as witness, the tiger cages which cripple men permanently and which are built by American companies to Thieu's specifications; the U.S. pays the bill, of course.

Now we are handling this running sore, which is a stench in the nostrils of all decent men, by ignoring its existence. The knowledge is there. Even the standard newspapers provide detailed information, but it has no impact. Vietnam has vanished from our minds. College students, unthreatened by the draft, are exposing themselves, or contemplating such exposure, rather than against Vietnam and the ghastly hell that we continue to sponsor for its people.

PITTSBURGH CATHOLIC
March 22, 1974

Viet Agony "Made in USA" (1975)

The civil war in Vietnam would have been resolved with relatively small losses but for our clumsy intrusion and our constant raising of the ante. And Cambodia, before we struck, it was a happy little land that fed its people, even exported food, and had few problems. After a few years of our kind attention it is disrupted, torn, hungry and laden with the wounded and dead.

Critics of our evil adventure in Vietnam foretold what would happen. They knew, and they said, that nationalist anti-imperialism was an idea whose time had come in Southeast Asia, and that our enemies would keep going long after we become weary, and that all our wealth and power would not avail. That prophecy is come true.

Does it feel good to have been right while so many others were wrong and reviled one so bitterly? No, it feels awful to see the tragedy. During Lent and Holy Week I often saw those pictures of Vietnamese women mourning their dead when I would read and speak of Mary holding her dead Son. There is only one consolation: apparently it is coming to an end.

Who is to be blamed? The critics who said that it is sinful madness and should stop? Nay, rather the leaders, whose arrogance and blindness urged them onward, and to a lesser degree the citizens who agreed that our nation had to win, right or wrong, and who were saying that lesser peoples and their poor feelings did not count for as much as our national pride. We were in it, and we might as well keep on. Five Presidents of the United States are to blame, and so are the Secretaries of State, and the bureaucrats, and the likes of Kissinger, Bundy and Rostow.

The lunatic fringe among the military and the rightwing ranters did not cause this; intelligent men, regarded as reasonable and respectable, caused it to our eternal shame as a nation.

PITTSBURGH CATHOLIC
April 4, 1975

We're Forgetting, But Not Forgiving Vietnam (1975)

Vietnam and its people are being forgotten by us, forgotten but not forgiven. After all we lost that costly war, and we are never gracious about losing.

When Kissinger and Nixon achieved their phony peace in 1972, they solemnly promised that we would help "to heal the wounds of war," but now Kissinger and Ford say that the promise is not operative or something.

Kissinger is said to be very bitter toward Vietnam, and he resents all attempts to help in the incredibly difficult reconstruction. Congressional hawks of both parties feel as he does. Humphrey, whom I was trying to like again, is very bad on the issue and is a major force in killing Congressional action. He has said of the Vietnamese, "what have they done for us?"

Not only do we refuse to help but we are interfering with voluntary agencies who are helping. We have an embargo which was quietly tightened so as to include the whole country. We use our veto to keep both Vietnams out of the UN. Our hawks lost the war and are determined to lose the peace in the same stupid way. Vietnam, if left alone, will rebuild with or without us, and one day we shall have to recognize that it exists. In the meantime we lose in terms of prestige, honor and commerce, but that is not all important.

What is all important is that we are not alleviating a human misery for which we are responsible.

There are problems to be solved and matters to be negotiated before our government moves but our present leaders are being petty, vindictive and obstructionist.

Our ignoring of obligations is almost as grave a sin as was our active conduct of the evil war, but neglected and suffering human beings are not so dramatic as war and there is no chance that our press and media will keep telling us and reminding us of them.

North Vietnam is not in as bad shape as the South, but it suffered dreadfully from the Kissinger-Nixon 1972 Christmas bombing, it is full of wounded and every family mourns its dead. In material terms it was impoverished and its development stunted.

Poor South Vietnam, the territory we tried to save by beating it to bits, is the real sufferer. Most of the 150 billion dollars that we spent in the struggle did its evil work in the South where we defoliated forests, massacred whole villages, dropped more bombs and napalm than everybody all together dropped in World War II, bulldozed away jungle, and moved millions of human beings off the land and into sick and swollen cities.

There is not enough medicine for those who were poisoned, deformed, and wounded. Not enough medicine for the spreading tuberculosis, nor the rickets and glaucoma, nor the gonorrhea which ravages a pathetic army of prostitutes that our military presence summoned into existence.

South Vietnam has unbelievable humanitarian needs. Medicine and related supplies is the obvious need but there is much more: food, tools, clothes, the sort of supplies that society needs for normal activity.

After World War II we rebuilt not only our allies but our enemies. We were most forgiving and generous, even to brutal invaders and butchers, even to the nation that massacred and practiced genocide. Why are we flint-hearted toward a people whom we invaded and came close to destroying?

There is a legitimate fear of strengthening Communism but that should not prevent humanitarian assistance. We even helped Red Russia after the first World War. Our American people do not hate the Vietnamese administration, but a lot of our leaders do.

The issue of those Missing in Action is being used to stall negotiations. It is unreal since Vietnam, North and South, have many thousands of missing people. Families have been torn asunder, and their radio is full of piteous pleas and advertisements of family members seeking each other. If they lose each other, is it surprising that they lose invaders?

Nothing we can do will erase the past or blot out our sin. And really we can do nothing about the destruction of the culture and social fabric of South Vietnam. We cannot put the people back on the land, we cannot find parents for a quarter of a million orphans, we cannot rehabilitate the like number of prostitutes, we cannot put a half million veterans back to work but we can give that nation a break as it copes with its heartbreaking and back breaking task of rebuilding.

PITTSBURGH CATHOLIC
November 28, 1975

> **"Our ignoring of obligations is almost as grave a sin as was our active conduct of the evil war, but neglected and suffering human beings are not so dramatic as war."**

Parallel: Kent State and Latin America (1990)

Kent State held, and holds, a horrid fascination because of its sickening resemblance to incidents which are almost commonplace in the Third World half of our hemisphere.

In Mexico City in 1968 military forces out-of-uniform killed 600 protesting students. There are haunting similarities. The students were children of the upper and middle class; the killers were recruited from the workers and peasants and imbued with hatred and envy of the protesters. There was no investigation and none of the killers or higher-ups was ever punished.

Then in Uruguay and Argentina students were among the tens of thousands who were rounded up without any legal process and slaughtered like animals in an abattoir. The military had taken over and had a free hand. Both officers and men were convinced that they were being patriots as they eliminated possible dissidents as revolutionaries. Uruguay was particularly disturbing because it had been a true democracy for years.

This is why the success of George Bush's flag waving and phony patriotism amid the echoes of Kent State now worries me.

We were fortunate that our institutions stood up under the assaults against the Bill of Rights of the Nixon years. Watergate was a spectacular assault that was thwarted and exposed. A less notable one came almost exactly one year after Kent State. At an anti-war rally in Washington, Nixon used federal forces to round up 10,000 peaceful protesters and intern them for hours. The courts in effect rebuked him when they awarded damages to the detainees. Who knows what else Nixon had up his sleeve if he had gotten away with Watergate?

We, in spite of our allegedly higher level of civilization, have more in common with our humbler and poorer neighbors to the South than we care to think about. We are all ex-colonials and we all treated our indigenous peoples abominably. We all squandered and still squander our natural resources. Like them we are afflicted with machismo. What else could explain the Ollie [Col. Oliver North] phenomenon or Grenada or Panama?

We are more violent than any other first-world nation, and thus less civilized. Not just the violence in the streets but official violence. Our courts display this by acquiescing to popular demand and reinstalling capital punishment and by other sentencings. The executives and legislators are more to blame, of course, but we expect less of them.

A president can get away with anything if he practices flag worship and engages in cheap foreign adventures against weak countries while dousing the media.

Now that we have a huge permanent military establishment there is a legitimate worry that the military may be tempted to fool around on their own with reforming the country. It was a grave mistake to get them into the drug war and give them a taste of messing with a civilian problem.

Eisenhower knew whereof he spoke when he warned against the military industrial complex. He was not all that good a president, but he thought as a professional soldier and not a gauleiter.

Since we have had the oversized military, presidents have not been oblivious of the domestic political advantage to be gained from relations with it. Johnson, Nixon and Reagan each had a trait or two that made him a bit dangerous to our freedom as he sat in the Oval Office. A person, man or woman, who had all those traits combined might one day enslave us, and turn us into a huge banana republic.

PITTSBURGH CATHOLIC
May 25, 1990

*Rice leading picket line for Pittsburgh hospital
workers organizing drive, early 1970s*

Reflections on Labor's Leaders

Though Rice became increasingly critical of labor officialdom on the burning issues of race relations and the war, he continued to write about labor issues. Frequently, he would evaluate the legacy of union leaders from the vantage point of his long personal familiarity with their careers.

In Memoriam Quill (1966)

Michael Quill was no ordinary man. To the public he was panache — flair and swagger. A man of invective and anger mingled with guile. He was that, but more.

I knew him very well and my heart sank as I heard the news of his sudden death. I had lost a friend, and a man was gone from public life who stood for so much that was worthwhile.

Quill was sincere and fearless. He did not want to die anymore than the rest of us. He enjoyed life and had a lot to live for, but it was characteristic of him that he would risk his life by being the principal in the unavoidable showdown with the powers that stood between his men and the good life.

The accepted, and superficial, view of the strike is that Quill started it for no good reason at all and was merely being difficult, seeking drama and excitement for personal reasons. But actually there was a true crisis.

New York newsmen have been merciless with the man, some in death as in life. . . . New York writers may have been tired of having Quill around, they may have been smarting from the lash of his tongue, or they may simply have been caught up in the general hysteria.

It is nonsense to blame Quill for the strike and for the misery of the poor. Oh! How they love the poor as a stick to beat with. . . . It was a twisted campaign that the newspapers waged. They damned Mike as an irresponsible author of this strike, and they inspired an hysteria that, in time, seized them and their writers. The low mark was when that excellent columnist, Reston [New York Times], said that Quill had done to New York what Vietcong had done to Saigon. Pathetic peddlers of phony whimsy such as Jimmy Breslin, the Irish Uncle Tom, bore down on Quill. They said he was despicable for striking now, and was equally despicable because he did not strike on earlier occasions. They accused him of having let his people down. Inconsistent while demanding consistency from him. My feeling is that they will not let him rest but will pursue him to the grave.

Michael Quill would not follow trends or fads in the labor movement, and he refused to become a member of any establishment. Other men, every bit as fiery as he in their early days, are now playing the dignified salesman. He laughed at such, and derided them in public.

George Meany, who was never a radical, sneered at Quill during the strike. [Walter] Reuther, to my horror and disgust, disavowed his own early turbulence and proposed taking the strike weapon from public employees. Does Walter not realize that he hurts every union member by such a timid stand? . . .

Michael J. Quill was a great dissenter. The labor movement and the country are poorer now that he is gone. He was a sincere champion of the people, particularly the distressed and disinherited. He loved the labor movement and wanted it strong, honest and efficient. He ran a good union with complete honesty, and had no care for personal wealth or luxury.

I never met a man who more sincerely hated injustice, prejudice and bigotry, or so longed for racial decency. . . . There will never be another Michael Quill. The same set of circumstances will not arise again. The men whom he developed to succeed him will do well with their heritage, but they are the first to admit that something extraordinary died with Mike. He will not be reincarnated but his spirit will survive because it is the spirit of all the honest and colorful rebels and battlers for unpopular causes that ever lived, or will live.

PITTSBURGH CATHOLIC
February 3, 1966

Reuther — R.I.P. (1970)

If Walter P. Reuther were starting a career today in the labor movement he would be wasting his time and would have no hope of achieving leadership; more significantly, a young Walter Reuther would have no interest in today's labor unions and would not desire to lead or be involved.

He would be caught up with the race problem and would be eyeing, and perhaps, controlling a phase of the student revolution with its drive for peace and reform. He might flirt with politics, but labor, ugh.

Reuther disbelieved in violence, actually he hated it and would not even contemplate its use, and yet, violence dogged him and often intruded into his life. Beaten expertly as he moved to organize Ford, threatened constantly, shot and almost killed by an assassin, finally he died from violence, the impersonal, technological violence of a jet airplane crash.

He was a man of the machine age, loving and accepting, but never totally trusting machines; plans for their social control, production and use dominated his thinking. Perhaps fittingly, a complicated, beautiful modern machine killed him.

Reuther got into the unions forty years ago at a heady time which was perfect for him. Strong men and powerful forces were con-

tending for the favor of the workers. American capitalism had finally lost its tight grip and the open shop industries of the nation were seething with unrest.

The established labor leaders and organizations were moving clumsily but powerfully to take over and the key men who emerged and lasted were either part of the old system or quickly became part of it in loyalty and attitude. John L. Lewis for all his vision and vigor was fundamentally old school, so was Phil Murray. The Communists were new and so was Reuther, the socialist, who was not completely a socialist, and never was to be typed, owned or absorbed.

The hundreds of thousands of men in the automobile plants were the prime target and everyone went after them: the craft unions, the Communists, Trotskyites and Socialists, the professional unionist of old AFL and the new CIO, everyone.

Within the auto plants there was a great supply of potential leaders whom the Depression had dumped there. Detroit, the auto center, produced a mad assortment of right-wing nuts and theorists from Father Coughlin to Gerald L. K. Smith.

Reuther had to fight them all, and the companies, but in time he emerged as the top man. It took fifteen years but in 1946 he won the presidency of the United Auto Workers by a narrow margin and then, in the next election, simply wiped out all his opposition and ruled unchallenged until his death.

Reuther was a superb tactician and a tough customer in political infighting. He controlled the union through his Walter Reuther Caucus which met openly before conventions and existed at other times as a visible entity.

In a non-violent way, Walter was ruthless, and, not surprisingly, he was bitterly hated by the high and low whom he had run over. Of course, he was an object of adulation to many in and out of his union. His peers in labor

In 1971, Rice ran for Pittsburgh City Council, in the Democratic primary, finishing seventh in a field of 26.

HERE'S ONE THAT'S ON YOUR SIDE

Charles Owen
ELECT **Rice**
TO CITY COUNCIL
PULL LEVER 42-B

Monsignor Charles Owen Rice

HERE'S ONE THAT'S ON YOUR SIDE

CITIZENS FOR CHARLES OWEN RICE
Joseph Sabel, Rev. J. A. Williams, Co-Chairmen

leadership did not love him; Walter tended to lecture, and brilliance made some uneasy and others jealous as blazes, he was never just another labor leader.

As an orator he was merely good, not great. The voice was clear but not deep or melodious and he used it no better than adequate. Content carried the speeches, not style.

By nature a planner, he had a way of producing plans for all manner of problems and occasions; Phil Murray used to joke about all the plans, and would wonder when Walter would produce a thousand year plan for everything and everybody, everywhere. Phil liked and respected the man, however.

When Walter was running for his second term as president of UAW, many observers thought that the Communist and their allies would beat him. Phil Murray asked me to call upon Cardinal Mooney of Detroit and ask if the Cardinal would help. Detroit's Association of Catholic Trade Unionists, which the Cardinal helped and sponsored, was deeply involved in the fight already and the Cardinal sent me back with the message that "the Red Head" would win easily, as in fact he did.

Walter was a disciplined planner in his private life. Money meant nothing and luxury was despised. No drink, no smoke, no gamble, nothing. No weaknesses nor vices, neither the charming nor the disgusting kind — merely a hard-working, no-nonsense chap who drove himself, expected much from others, and was hated even more cordially by his enemies for this type of virtue.

Reuther was a friend of mine, and once I was able to do him a family favor; it involved an educational opportunity for a relative of his and I enjoyed doing it. He never was asked to return the favor as all I would have wanted would have been support for some cause, and he was on the right side anyway from his personal momentum.

It is a shame that Walter Reuther missed the top slot in organized labor because he would have been good and different from the lesser man who kept him out. It is because he would have made changes that he was denied the post. He certainly would have dismantled labor's international spy ring and would have ended the nefarious corrupting of labor unions in the undeveloped world. Labor would not, under him, have domestically remained a lackey of militarism.

Withal, Walter P. Reuther, regardless of position, could not have changed the direction or fundamental attitude of the trade unions and their members; even he could not have brought them heart and soul into the great spiritual revolt of these times. I am afraid that for some time to come the working man will remain prisoner of a materialistic society which he wants to enjoy, not change. The students and intellectuals will have to do their best without him.

Poor Reuther, Lord rest his soul, achieved great power over working men's associations, but the working men's minds and affections went a way other than his, or mine.

PITTSBURGH CATHOLIC
May 22, 1970

George Meany (1970)

George Meany, president of the AFL-CIO is indisputably top dog in the trade union movement today, and more's the pity because he is denuding the movement of its idealism and aiming it in the direction of total conformism with power. Of course, Meany is being consistent with his past.

He came out of the construction trades in New York City, where he followed his father into Local 2 of the Plumbers, became a business representative, and before too long progressed to the point where he was president of all AFL members in the state.

To make his way he needed to be a politician and a power broker, which he was, and in time he became secretary-treasurer of the old AFL under Bill Green and finally head of the combined AFL and CIO.

Meany is not a bad man, but he is a practical type who brags that he never led a strike or walked a picket line, and he would now like to have all labor give up the strike as a weapon. . . .

George Meany is a strong man with a tough and simple nature, and, whatever else he may be, he is not one who expects perfection in this life. Hard simple solutions, with his friends and beliefs coming out on top, are favored by him. He is a narrow-minded man, some of whose instincts are good, but who gets credit for a great many more good instincts because he possesses power, and a lot of intelligent people make excuses for him. The AFL-CIO bureaucracy is full of old-fashioned liberals (Meany never was one) most of whom have dreamed of converting Meany and others of his general type, and now must be almost suicidal as old George makes eyes at Richard Milhouse Nixon carrying on what must be the clumsiest, and least attractive flirtation in the history of either love or politics. Only a specialist in hippopotami could view the squalid affair without revulsion.

Actually George and the other President belong to, and with, each other; George, in sum, is a bit less enlightened than J. Edgar Hoover but a bit more enlightened than John and Martha Mitchell, while he is the full equal of Spiro in delicacy of feeling and expression.

> **"Meany is not a bad man, but he is a practical type who brags that he never led a strike or walked a picket line."**

There was a time I thought Meany was nobly brave and that was when he threw Jimmy Hoffa and the Teamsters out of the AFL-CIO. I rather naively thought that it showed great courage, but in retrospect, I see it as a superb manifestation of Meany's feeling for power: Hoffa was one of two men within the AFL-CIO who could challenge Meany, and Hoffa, beautifully for Meany, had become the pet hate of a power greater than Meany's and meaner than Meany's, Robert F. Kennedy, Lord rest his soul, brother of the President of the United States. Please note that I do not say Hoffa was right and Bobby wrong, I merely note, well after the fact, what was going on.

I spoke of two men who could have challenged Meany's power within the "house of labor," the other was Walter Reuther. Meany, who had soothed Reuther into merging AFL and CIO by promising to step down after a decent interval, appealed to the late Walter's puritanical streak and got him to call for Hoffa's return or removal, thus splitting potential allies into isolated trouble makers. . . .

So, Meany has control and the labor movement, that was once the voice of decency, has retrogressed to what it was before the New Deal and what a portion of it never ceased to be: Selfish, xenophobic, and in love with power rather than justice.

It is painful to see the utter triumph of unrelieved bread and butter unionism, and to see the great CIO internationals, which once stood for something else, fall into line and become indistinguishable from the others.

PITTSBURGH CATHOLIC
October 2, 1970

Miners' Union Reform

Rice was intimately involved in the early 1970s struggle for reform inside the United Mine Workers. This involvement was intensely personal because of Rice's long relationship with the originator of the reform movement, Jock Yablonski, at whose marriage and funeral he officiated.

Jock Yablonski the Rebel (1970)

Last Friday I said the funeral Mass for a murdered friend, his wife, Margaret, and daughter, Charlotte; Joseph A. Yablonski, an officer for the United Mine Workers of America for nearly forty years, has been shot dead in his own house in the dead of night and the killers had with chilling efficiency rounded out their crime with the two other lives.

Miners and their families are used to death and the danger of death but this was different. A shudder went through the mine patches, and many of the men who work the mines in that district and nearby districts abandoned work in reaction to the brutal murder and in tribute to the slain rebel.

Yablonski was a rebel, a newly constituted rebel; after being part of the ruling apparatus of the UMW for a lifetime he changed. Jock was never your ordinary labor skate; he was an intellectual—a play and a novelette are to his credit in collaboration with his wife—and he truly cast a cold eye on life, death and politics in the coal fields.

When Jock and I both were young, late twenties, we met and liked each other, so it was that back then I was the priest at the marriage of him and Margaret in the little chapel of St. Joseph's House in the Hill district.

Jock was beginning to rise in the Mine Workers and he was different from most of the young labor men of the era in that his heart was with John L. Lewis and the UMW's not the larger Congress of Industrial Organizations. Lewis was president of the UMW and of the CIO, which he had founded and funded with UMW money.

Phil Murray was Lewis's great lieutenant in the UMW, CIO and every activity and Yablonski had begun his rise under Murray and Murray's solid supporter, Pat Fagan (still living, thank God). But when Murray and Lewis split, Jock stayed locked into the miners and Lewis. The Fagans went with Murray but in the fight for the local district, Number Five, they were defeated, and Yablonski was the architect of their defeat.

I was very close to Murray, and while Jock and I did not fall out, we ceased to have much to do with each other until almost twenty years later I was assigned to Washington County where Jock was a sort of uncrowned king.

He was loved and hated depending on whom you talked to; there were few neutrals. You reacted positively to the likes of Yablonski, either caring or not caring for the cut of his jib.

The miners' union was but a skeleton of its former self, but Yablonski who had become the top man in the district and its representative in the national union was still a man to be reckoned with. Things continued to go badly with the union as employment dropped, pensions failed to keep pace with the rising cost of living, safety fell behind extractive technology and the whole union lost its muscle tone.

As long as John L. Lewis was alive Yablonski remained quiet; even after the old man retired and his successor, W. A. "Tony" Boyle, began to snipe at him, he still was quiet. It was inevitable that when Lewis died the strong

Rice giving sermon at the funeral for United Mine Worker reformer Jock Yablonski, his wife and daughter, January 1970

man of the Pennsylvania soft coal fields would try for the top and so it was.

Joseph A. Yablonski had his allies in the fight. Ralph Nader, Joseph Rauh, Jr., Congressman Hechler and many others saw to it that the white spotlight of publicity beat down on the union during the election but still the old system and the old tradition were too strong, too ingrained, and Boyle won two-to-one, or at least that was the published result.

Finances were an issue in the campaign; the strange story of the miners' bank and its relationship to the miners' pension fund and, above all, safety and the union's sorry recent record were still more powerful issues, and even when the campaign was over Jock kept on fighting and insisting that he would carry on from within until something gave.

It is obvious from what his sons and other friends say that the man was out to make up for lost time and was truly interested in delivering the utmost in service to his beloved miners. One never heard him criticize Lewis or the other leaders of the past but when he heaped scorn upon the heads of the present men, heirs all of Lewis, one could draw one's own conclusions.

The United Mine Workers will probably not regain their old strength, would not have even if Yablonski had won, but they yet may regain their respectability and become a union rather than a facade of a bank and a trust fund.

Young men may appear to pressure the leadership and eventually become the leadership.

It is idle to speculate on who did the evil deed. Probably the killers were hired but one cannot be sure. One cannot even be sure that the union on any level was connected. I would incline to think that the doers of the evil deed were known to Jock or there would have been more evidence of a struggle. He was talking to them (he talked magnificently) and he was probably talking for his life and the lives of his wife and daughter.

It is my hope that we will learn the truth behind the murders, if only to allay suspicion and fear and bring some measure of tranquility to the troubled coal fields.

I ask my readers, as I asked the people at the funeral Mass, to pray for the souls of the dead, to remember all brave men of principle and the women who loved and supported them, particularly those in trade unions.

PITTSBURGH CATHOLIC
January 16, 1970

On the Eve of the Miners' Election (1972)

Three years ago I said the Funeral Mass over the bullet riddled bodies of Joseph A. "Jock" Yablonski, his wife and daughter. They died in the aftermath of an election within the United Mine Workers of America. Jock had run for president against the incumbent, W. A. "Tony" Boyle; it was a bad campaign and he had to contend with terrorism and fraud: he lost.

Yablonski was no ordinary rebel trade unionist but an insider, and he both knew and was furious at the tactics used to crush him. Instead of creeping back for forgiveness he declared war. In COAL PATROL he was quoted as saying: "They think they can make some kind of deal," but the only thing he would agree to would be "a complete, comprehensive audit of the United Mine Workers of America and turn the results over to the Justice Department and let Tony Boyle go to the penitentiary, where the hell he belongs."

Yablonski spoke thus in mid-December, and, on the very last day of the month and year, assassins gunned him down, killing his wife and daughter for good measure.

The deaths hit me hard because I had married the Yablonskis and was a family friend, Jock and I having become close when we were young, the miners were building the CIO, and I was talking union in the coalfields and elsewhere.

The Yablonski murders shocked the nation and a massive manhunt was launched which is not over but has accomplished much. In Cleveland a grubby set of suspects was flushed, all of whom were eventually convicted of murder or complicity after a spectacular and drawn-out series of trials and confessions. It was a contract assassination but the mysterious higher up, "Tony," who was said to have paid for it, has not been identified. However, Kentucky Mine Union District 19 has lain at the heart of the horrible story. Those sentenced for the crime are natives of the dark and bloody ground, one was a lesser functionary of the union, and two new suspects have been arraigned and await trial: these last are officials of some stature in the UMW and its Kentucky fiefdom, which has been notoriously loyal to Boyle and headquarters.

Within the troubled United Mine Workers Union itself, Yablonski dead accomplished what Yablonski living could not do: he brought the once hesitant U.S. Department of Labor crashing into the picture with an exhaustive investigation of the fatal 1969 UMW election, and widespread terror and fraud were uncovered. Backed by the courts and after a full legal review, a new election was ordered; that is proceeding now and the ballots will be cast during the first full week of December.

Criminal and civil charges against W. A. "Tony" Boyle and his fellow UMW officials of high and low degree are in various stages of litigation. Boyle's conviction for misuse of union funds in his own campaign is under appeal. He is under fire over the union's bank, and the union's pension fund. Some of his district officials have been convicted of misuse of union funds on his behalf; fined, given probation from jail and barred from office for three years.

The rerun election is under a new set of rules which give the opposition a chance. Still, the system and tradition favor the incumbents, in spite of everything.

Miners for Democracy, the reform heirs of Yablonski, held a convention and picked Arnold Miller, 49, a disabled West Virginia miner, to run against Boyle, 70, for president. Mike Trbovich, 51, a working miner and local union president from Western Pennsylvania, is the vice presidential candidate and Harry Patrick, another working miner from West Virginia, runs for secretary-treasurer.

The rank-and-file candidates are pushing for a reform of the union and want all Districts to have the right to elect their own officers; only a few of them have that right now. They want to cut down on the high salaries and perquisites of the union leadership and claim they will return union headquarters to the coal mining area. They pledge to cut out the corruption which the courts have found.

A strong pitch is safety: weak legislation and soft enforcement have resulted in disasters and a continual, less publicized, death rate in twos and threes. Other countries mine coal with far greater safety.

The Boyle slate is running strong and has advantages. As is customary in union elections, the incumbents say that the opposition

> **"The Yablonski murders shocked the nation and a massive manhunt was launched which is not over but has accomplished much."**

is criticizing the union when it criticizes them. An old tactic, but one that is useful.

Miners more than other unionists have a mystique about their union and the organization that runs it, and since they are isolated in their own communities they tend to be suspicious. Boyle talks of outsiders who want to hurt and take over their union. Some are listening.

About forty-five percent of the voting miners are retired and there are many locals composed entirely of the retired. These men are fearful of change and cling to tradition. They are hard to reach because they are not at the work place where the rank-and-file opposition is campaigning.

Miners in the South are more isolated even from other miners and they hear nothing about the campaign and little about the Yablonski murders or other relevant matters from their local newspapers or TV. Very hard to reach, they are another element of Boyle strength.

In the Southern fields the Boyle supporters use the accusation of Communism against their opponents and it may work down there. The Communists are not in this and the reform ticket is about as anti-Communist as it is possible for normal Americans to be. I should mention that I have found no trace of powerful outsiders being involved on the reform side. Yablonski's sons are non-miner advisers and the people who aid them have battled tyranny wherever they find it. The great corporations are doing the rank-and-filers no favors and, if Boyle goes out, those coal operators can look forward only to harder bargaining and tougher legislation.

Fear of the rich and powerful organization, now headed by Boyle, has been a constant in all UMW elections and it has by no means vanished. The rank-and-file slate must contend with fear and favor: the organization can do things for and to you, and although its teeth have been pulled it still has claws.

The official Mine Workers Journal has been commanded to carry material from both slates and miners have the rare experience of reading what the factions say about one another. This is an element of opposition strength.

The election must be rated a toss up, but whatever happens in the contest itself a loyal opposition will be a feature of coal trade unionism for the foreseeable future and that can only help the people of the coal fields.

UNION DEMOCRACY REVIEW
December 1972

Tony Boyle Isn't Guilty (1977)

When W. A. "Tony" Boyle was released from Western Penitentiary on St. Patrick's Day, reporters were amazed to hear a muffled sound of cheering through the thick wall of that grim pile. Some speculated that the convicts were elated that anyone beat the system. But that is not the way it was.

Tony Boyle was popular in the Pen. Both guards and guarded liked him and were convinced that he was not guilty of the brutal murders for which he was convicted; in that cynical community they are used to claims of innocence and virtue and are not easily impressed.

As everyone knows, Boyle was the last of a number of people convicted in the killing of his union rival, Joseph A. Yablonski, and the rival's wife and daughter. That shocking crime attracted national attention. In its aftermath Boyle was unseated as president of the United Mine Workers; I did my little bit to defeat him. You may remember that I offered the Yablonski funeral Mass and had officiated at the marriage years before. I have been no fan of W. A. Boyle.

Nonetheless when I met an old friend of his at a conference in Arizona, I dropped him a note as the man requested. To my surprise Boyle sent word that he would appreciate a visit from me.

The last time, the only time, I had seen him previously was at an elaborate Miners' pow-wow at the William Penn Hotel early in the fateful year of 1969. At the luncheon he gave a long, long speech. I was seated beside Jock Yablonski whom I was never to see again.

What a contrast between the feisty union leader of eight years ago and the pallid prisoner of today! Of course, sick as he was Tony was still alive and Jock was dead.

In passing, Boyle's popularity in the Pen came from the way he conducted himself; undemanding, quiet, friendly. Many famous cons isolate themselves and appear to look down on the common herd. Not he.

As for their estimate of his guilt, the denizens of the Pen speak from insight and information. They followed the case more intensely than the rest of us. They have special feelings about prosecution and justice and they have had a chance to observe in their midst some of the other actors in the Yablonski tragedy. Their conclusion is that Boyle is not guilty.

Now he is out on bond and will be tried again. The Supreme Court of Pennsylvania overturned his first trial because vital evidence which might have helped his case was excluded by the trial judge.

Richard Sprague, the superbly talented and deadly prosecutor who won the conviction, was not able to tie Boyle by direct testimony to the smoking gun nor put him in a room with the plotters, but he easily tied him to the blood money. It is in attempting to prove that Boyle simply had to know what the money was for that Sprague may have

> **"I oppose the sort of union that Boyle led and I oppose his sort of leadership, but I do not believe that he ordered the murder of Joseph Yablonski or even connived at it. He wanted to crush Jock but not kill or even maim him."**

slipped. Defense attorneys wanted a chance to prove that the devious way in which the money was shuffled was not unique with this piece of lethal skulduggery but had been done often enough for relatively harmless purposes. They were squelched improperly and so the resultant conviction was thrown out as tainted.

I always felt that Boyle was convicted as much from climate as evidence. Few murders have so outraged and disgusted the American people, and few were as publicized. If Boyle were guilty we had, for once, the top man. He had the power, the man was his enemy. Little evidence, but a mountain of inference.

My reluctance to accept Boyle's guilt has come from my knowledge of the normal legitimate labor leader's mind. Messing around with ballots, slugging opponents and rebels, mistreating the truth, and roaring violently may be accepted — not killing. I have not met one of the breed who felt that Tony Boyle was guilty. . . .

Let me emphasize that I oppose the sort of union that Boyle led and I oppose his sort of leadership, but I do not believe that he ordered the murder of Joseph Yablonski or even connived at it. He wanted to crush Jock but not kill or even maim him. In my opinion, W. A. Boyle is not guilty of the murder of Joseph A. Yablonski, his wife and daughter.

PITTSBURGH CATHOLIC
March 25, 1977

Freedom in the Church

Despite his consistently controversial career, Rice never directed his barbs and protests at the Church or its teachings. He felt a great deal of affection and loyalty toward the institution which fed and sheltered him while providing him with a pulpit to fight for the causes nearest his heart. The only deviation from this course was when church-related institutions like schools, nursing homes, and hospitals resisted unionization.

Fear Nothing (1971)

The late blooming radical has his problems and those problems are intensified for the priest or bishop who knows only his institution. I consider myself blessed that I fought all along and, not only that, but became intimately involved with many persons and institutions outside of the Church. I thus appreciate the freedom the institutional Church has given me to wage my fights even if it has not listened to me much. I know that few men in other institutions or professions, even, have been equally free. There have been consequences for me but they have not been dire.

Our bishops were a bit cowardly in their last meeting in that they ducked the moral issue of Vietnam and I am glad that they are being so forcibly rebuked, although in the main they are of my generation and I understand them. They are suffering from shock since the whole flipping thing turned over just as they stepped into the batter's box. I have reason to believe that they are capable of learning hard lessons, and changes will come even before the attrition of death makes its change.

I will never take a walk myself, and I do not mind being in the minority as I do my small bit to instill in the minds of our people what it means to be free men under Christ, free of tyranny of conventional wisdom and custom, free of the idolatry of the state, the national and all systems. As a Catholic priest, a man has more chance than most to fight and fight "not as one beating the air" against principalities and powers and the monsters of cruelty and indifference.

The thing is to fear nothing, not even failure, frustration or obscurity. One must have confidence that one can recognize the higher cause in its major dimensions and one must use what lies to hand to serve it.

PITTSBURGH CATHOLIC
July 9, 1971

Nuns and Unions (1968)

My first brush with hospital unionizing came 20 years ago when a union tried valiantly to organize Pittsburgh's healing houses and made enough progress to mount a strike at West Penn Hospital. The State, County, and Municipal Workers (CIO) was allegedly Communist-controlled at the top and, of course, that was used to hammer the strikers.

I was in the midst of a long campaign against communism in the unions but, thank God, I had sufficient sense to realize that the Red issue was irrelevant in the Hospital strike. All that were relevant were the ability of the union to represent the people, the needs of the people, and their desire to have the union represent them.

To all three relevancies the answer was positive and so I supported the strike in my column, did a brief stint on the picket line, and did as much as I could behind the scenes, that is, talking to the police, the District Attorney, and Catholic hospital authorities, soliciting help from other unions and, finally, appearing publicly on behalf of the union at a court proceeding.

The strike was lost because no one would touch it. After all, in that day a strike against a hospital was unthinkable. Even normally courageous and forthright labor people and labor friends ducked the battle. Mine was a lonely position and the position of the strike leaders was even more lonely. The key man had a legitimate background of youthful delinquency; the papers dug it all up and simply destroyed the young man while no one lifted a hand or a voice to save him.

The whole bit did me no good. Combined with my support of a very unpopular Teamster struggle against the department stores, observations about a Cardinal's strikebreaking, it took me out of the pages of the newly official Pittsburgh Catholic and deposited me in a small parish up-the-river.

I was on good terms with Mercy Hospital, which had been good in every way to me and my men at the House of Hospitality, and so I ventured to approach the hospital's top nun. I can never forget her cold fury when I asked her to give the union a break, nor can I forget the leading ladies of the various orders as they sailed full-rigged past me at court to effuse over the superintendent of the struck hospital while I huddled with a forlorn group of strikers and strike leaders. Made one feel quite like the Outcast of Poker Flat.

Now, 20 years later, a hospital union has a shot, but still it meets resistance of a special sort from Catholic hospitals. Among hospital Sisters the doctor is King and the good sisters specialized in keeping the working stiffs, including nurses and technicians, on the mark. Not all our hospitals shine in new techniques and advanced medicine but they are apt to be more orderly and clean, and you have less chance of getting one of those incurable hospital infections in one of them.

Today, among the orders, personnel is so thin that hospital Sisters do little more than administer and they are tempted to approach unionism as administrators rather than nuns. Actually there is a great deal of pro-union sentiment among them, more so than if they were a collection of middle-class Protestant holy women. However, the doctor is the key man and nuns feel grateful to their doctors. It must be added that the doctors are grateful to the nuns and very loyal. Each one is prone to kid himself that he is protecting the other from pesky unions.

The doctors do not want unions for two strong reasons. One, they are personally very conservative and, while they love their own little shop, the AMA, they have no use for the other unions. Two, they are fiercely independent of their work. A doctor should be able to move as he wants with all the supernumeraries leaping madly to assist while the explicit assumption governs at all times that the doctor knows best.

In New Castle the hangup is a doctor, a most excellent man, who feels that the union will be interposed between him and his patients. Unconsciously he wants machines rather than men and women as his auxiliaries; but, if the

> **"I can never forget her cold fury when I asked her to give the union a break, nor can I forget the leading ladies of the various orders as they sailed full-rigged past me at court to effuse over the superintendent of the struck hospital while I huddled with a forlorn group of strikers."**

work is human work, the human personality of each person in partaking in the work must be recognized.

When the nuns get letters asking why they as Holy Women do not follow the encyclicals of the popes they get upset, and their friends get upset. My reaction when I hear someone say, "Sister why do you not do what is right?" is "Why indeed!"

PITTSBURGH CATHOLIC
February 9, 1968

. . . A Catholic hospital can be in a hopeless position because it is so easy to hide behind the skirts of the nuns and to clobber trade unionists while at the same time beseeching understanding and sympathy. What cause do dedicated women serve as mere administrators of healing factories, where doctors make money, board members polish images and workers eat the sullen crusts of substandard pay and dignity denied.

PITTSBURGH CATHOLIC
March 1, 1968

Hospitals Need Union (1970)

Hospitals are big business; hospitalizing is an industry, a major industry, it may even be our largest. Millions of people make their living from the "sick" industry and, for most, it is a rather good living. Doctors and other technicians prosper; makers of medicine and their workers do very well; nurses are tolerable; administrators have no complaint; those at every level who construct hospitals and those who finance them, and all hospital suppliers together with their workers and salesmen make a living comparable to what they would make in another line of business.

There is one big exception to all this and that is a class of workers who are very intimate-ly connected with hospitals, namely the working staff, the people without whom the hospitals could not function.

These people are very important to all of us and we need them; it is to our interest that they be content, competent, stable, amenable to direction, personally healthy in mind and body, and efficient. Can they be as we want them to be, if they are not properly paid and decently treated? Hardly!

Most workers who have attained a half decent standard of living have done it through the assistance of collective bargaining, and their achievement and use of such bargaining has been protected and aided by government; hospital workers by law are excluded from such aid. As a result morale and efficiency are low; hospital quality suffers because of the condition of the laborers and hospitals are more expensive than they need to be.

Hospitalizing needs to be rationalized, streamlined and aimed at the patient and his real needs; just as schools are built and run for the convenience of teachers and supervisors, so are hospitals built and run for the convenience of the administration, the doctors and perhaps the nurses. Patients can only benefit from a rethinking of the American hospital and better payment of the lowly hospital workers who will become a more efficient and manageable force when they are compensated as they should be. The certain way to have an occupation regarded as little account and unworthy of one's best efforts is to fix the pay below the level of occupations that are desirable.

We are in the midst of a serious drive to organize all local hospital workers into a union and this is the first in a generation; Sam Begler of the laundry workers tried last year but he ran into some tough luck. Now 1199P is trying and seems to have a better chance at success. It is a New York organization, part of the recognized labor movement, is endorsed by the widow of Martin Luther King, Jr. and other important people and has, so it seems to the observer, momentum and the proper feeling for the job. The travelling organizers who come here are black men of skill, diligence and eloquence, and that is most important because the bulk of your hospital employees are black.

A generation ago in the midst of the last strong hospital organizing campaign I was embarrassed at the unenlightened attitude of the various Sister-administrators in the Catholic hospitals—not one bit better than their secular counterparts.

But this is a new day and our nuns are post-conciliar and very gung ho ho ho for the new Church, the Church in the Modern World, no less — so, what are they going to do? In other cities recently the chief-nuns-in-charge have been every bit as hard-nosed, unyielding and uncompassionate as the unreformed and unaerated ladies of the old Church Triumphant. . . .

PITTSBURGH CATHOLIC
January 23, 1970

Ecology Versus Burial Customs (1973)

It is quite incongruous these days at funerals, especially in the diocesan cemeteries. At the end we take a spoonful of dirt and pour it on the casket saying: Remember man . . . that you are dust and unto dust you shall return!

The incongruity lies in that we say this snug inside a chapel, not standing on the earth, and we say it over a body that is fanatically protected from returning to dust. The blood has been drained out and replaced with chemicals so that the body will resist nature's honest attempt to recycle it. Generally the casket is watertight and airtight, thus resistant to

nature. In addition, the casket will shortly be placed in what is called a vault but is really a cement box that is impervious to anything but a direct hit from an atomic bomb. Return to dust, indeed; fat chance.

The "vault" gimmick and the embalming have been legislated, I believe, by our state legislature which is ever happy to heed special interest groups such as morticians, beauticians, clam diggers, lawyers, doctors, police, firemen, tavern keepers, or judges who wish to limit access to their trade or increase public expenditure on their specialties.

An assault on the vault . . . is being made in some areas by ecology people who want to give nature a chance and let her recycle us along with other living and dying organisms. The trade, on the other hand, would give us plastic and longlasting bodies in death even if it cannot manage that in life, and hardly desires to.

This fits in with what the public wants, or it would not go down. There are a couple of trends in the matter. One set of folks wants to cremate the body and get it out of the way as quickly as possible; the other reaches for permanence. . . .

Ecologically, the traditional method of simply putting unprocessed bodies in the grave encased in biodegradable wood and fabric is much better than burning with its consequent air pollution and loss of organic fertilizer.

PITTSBURGH CATHOLIC
May 4, 1973

Tots in Church: Wail of a Problem (1974)

It is not easy to preach in a noisy church: by the way, it is even less easy to teach in a noisy classroom. I never mastered the second, although I tried; when Holy Rosary was a wide-open school I completely failed the challenge, longing to murder in most painful fashion the darlings who were acting out, and in restraining myself from this, suffering mentally and physically.

However I can preach, no worse than usual, to an unsettled congregation in which there are squalling infants and disruptive senior infants. It does wonders for the psychological balance of the children and it does not disturb mine.

Apparently I come by this tolerance honestly. I was told by my late beloved father that I posed a sort of ecclesiastical problem as a tad. I am not sure that they took me as an infant but, as soon as I became half ambulatory, I joined the family at Sunday Mass. My parents always wanted the whole family together as much as possible, at meals, at Mass, whatever. In those early days in New York they had trouble with me in church; I was one of those squirmy kids that was bad even when he was good. Still they managed to keep my ecclesial disruption to a respectable minimum. . . .

I favor tolerance of the noisy infant and encourage parents to bring him along. If he gets completely wild and raises unshirted hell, they should take him out for a moment, but I would never tell them so. If you feed the child just before Mass he will be drowsy and non-combative. You can feed him during Mass too and that will quiet him. . . .

When I was a young priest (looking back I wonder if I was the obnoxious young prig I now judge me to have been) I was as stuffy as the stiffest anent the adult chatterer, especially during my sacred sermon. Once at St. Agnes in the long ago, while I was preaching there was a disturbance around one of the back entrances and I expostulated. It turned out that the newly appointed pastor, Father

> **"I remind them all that I have the microphone and sound system and will complain about a wailing infant only if someone hands the kid his own mike."**

Edward Moriarty, on his first Sunday in charge was pushing and shoving the recalcitrant into the available seats; he had a thing about the Wall Flowers and Vestibule Loungers, as he called them in those happy days of the faith. He also had a thing about brash young assistants; all in all I was a trifle abashed. Father Moriarty was a voluble and tempestuous Celt and the incident did not minister to my detente with this not totally peaceful member of the same tribal entity.

Even in my salad days I did not wage war on the caterwauling babe and that was due to the influence of another clerical Celt, my beloved priest-uncle, Father Peter Rice, who was a peppery but most urbane Irish gentleman; he loved children and he loved to see families worshipping together. His favorite was the old missionary who said he could outshout any baby that ever lived and yowled.

At Holy Rosary these days I am glad to have anyone in church at all, young or old, and even if I were a confirmed warrior against the cries of babes and sucklings I would temper my winds of oratory to the unshorn lambs of Homewood. I am not unconscious of the older folk who comprise half of my congregation, but I tell them that they should be happy to hear sounds of life. . . .

And I tell them that I can carry on over the child noise, and I tell the young mothers to bring the babies to church without fear, and I remind them all that I have the microphone and sound system and will complain about a wailing infant only if someone hands the kid his own mike.

To the young priests who argue that they

Photo by Lynette Molnar

Rice on picket line at Jefferson Memorial Cemetery, May 1978

prepare their sermons with great care and deserve the opportunity to present them to those who want to listen to the word of the Lord and the fire of the Holy Spirit, I can only subjoin that our sermons are really not that important. They take second place to our example. So, if you lose your train of thought, no harm, steel yourself and struggle on. Very few in the congregation will notice one way or the other, but everyone will notice if you make an uncharitable spectacle of yourself, and that goes for us all.

In the days when we did not have quite enough to worry ourselves about, many priests got worked up over people, women especially, coming to church in scanty or otherwise unsuitable attire. Apparently in this more grim and somber day there remain a few clerics who are absorbed by the gravity of this problem.

I never bothered my head about that, and when I see signs in resort churches grumbling about respect for the House of God, I shake my head and wonder about the thought processes of some of my fellow Laborers in the Vineyard. I do not care about what people wear so long as they come to Mass. Whatever is street attire is fine for church, even men in pants and T-shirts or underwear tops would be all right. Mass should not be a social function or a dress-up occasion because that can keep people away. I am sure it keeps some of the young away now.

In depression days and later, how often, when taking census, one would encounter sincere people who were ashamed to come to church in the only clothes they possessed.

Come as you are and God love you! If no one else will let you in, you can always come to Holy Rosary and relax.

PITTSBURGH CATHOLIC
August 16, 1974

Rice marches with Methodist minister Charles Rawlings and the Tri-State Conference on Steel in protest against steel mill closures at U.S. Steel stockholder's meeting in Pittsburgh, May 1981. Mike Stout and Matt Bartholomew carry the coffin.

CHRONOLOGY

☎ 1976
May 15, Rice becomes pastor of St. Anne's Church in Castle Shannon south of Pittsburgh where Philip Murray is buried.
The steelworkers union contributed a bell tower to the church.

☎ 1979
March 27, the Tri-State Conference on Steel is founded at a conference called by the Episcopal bishop of Pittsburgh, Robert Appleyard, to consider the social impacts of plant closings.

☎ 1981
August , President Reagan crushes the PATCO strike by firing most of the nation's air traffic controllers.

☎ 1985
November 23, Tri-State's organizing efforts lead to the announcement in the office of Pittsburgh Mayor Richard Caliguiri of the formation of the Steel Valley Authority by nine communities in the Monongahela Valley.

☎ 1986
June 15,Rice retires as pastor at St. Anne's. He remains in residence as pastor emeritus.

☎ 1992
The *Pittsburgh Press* tries to break a coalition of unions, but is forced to sell out to the *Post-Gazette*. The centennial of the formation of the Homestead Strike is commemorated.

☎ 1994
June 17, Rice celebrates the 60th anniversary of his ordination to the priesthood.

Reflections on Decline 1976–1993

5

▚ The Collapse of Steel

The steel industry around Pittsburgh was in decline long before it collapsed. Both industry and union were afflicted with a myopia induced by long years of prosperous stagnation. Few people in Pittsburgh had carefully observed the situation for as long as Rice. He supported noble but unsuccessful efforts to reshape both the union and the industry.

Steelworkers Face Change (1974)

This may be the Last Hurrah of the old toughly benevolent USW as fabricated by my dear, dead friend Phil Murray with his miner background and his superb sense of control, a control that was more than even a good man like him should have had, and a control dangerous and harmful in the long run, which long run is running right now. . . .

The delegates were relatively quiet and the [United Steelworkers of America] convention smooth because prosperity sits upon the steel industry, a great prosperity second only to the prosperity of the oil industry, the fundamental reason being that steel is in short supply and steel capacity cannot keep up with the current surge in demand. The shortage is world wide and so foreign competition is negligible: the foreigners need their own steel and more. Steel people will tell you there has not been a boom like this ever in peace time.

Steel workers are making money, they are working long hours with overtime, their pockets are bulging and of course the companies are doing far, far better.

I. W. Abel is on his own without a referendum of the members since he gave up the strike weapon and made an arrangement with the leaders of industry, namely, the Experimental Negotiation Agreement, (ENA) guaranteeing no national steel strikes. He also set up productivity committees whose function is to get the workers to work harder, more efficiently and with less fuss over issues. Stakhanovism the Russians call it. . . .

In the past 25 years the steel industry and the union have done poorly by minorities and women. A federal decision came down against them, they are cooperating to blunt its effect, northern whites are being stirred up and blacks are waiting for justice and getting impatient. A mess.

Internal democracy may be the greatest

183

issue of all. The USW uses its power with federal agencies and the courts to preserve its traditional way of life, which is mighty comfortable for its elite. . . .

District directors are big men, key men, and they possess power and money. Uneasy lie their heads. They are sometimes toppled but almost never by rank-and-filers. At the very top in 1965 there was a palace revolt which put Abel in the saddle. I was more active in labor than now and I did not support him because I thought the shuffle meaningless, which it proved to be. Not that his predecessor was a friend of mine or a spectacular leader. But he and his crew appeared better for trade unionism than Abel's crew and that has proved out, I think.

The district which turned the tide for Abel then is big 31. Chicago-Calumet, whose absolute ruler, Joe Germano, retired and did not run last year. The administration candidate squeezed through according to the official count. The loser, Ed Sadlowski, former staff member, would not accept the "verdict," but fought all the way to Federal Court. The Labor Department, which treats all big unions tenderly, made a deal in which it dropped its court action, refused to interfere in a few other tainted contests, and agreed to a new election. A court trial would have exposed some strange goings on.

The official family of the USW is battling hard against Sadlowski, raising a formidable "voluntary" campaign fund among other tactics. Mr. Abel appealed most eloquently for a change in those dreadful federal laws which strive to make unions honest in their internal affairs. One hopes that Sadlowski wins and, having won, will not do as nearly all previous rebels have done, submit to the warm and lucrative embrace of mother USW's happy family and father Abel's kindly rewards for good boys.

Sadlowski has his eye on the international

presidency and may win it. I hope again that he can change the union which has grown so great that it is almost pure establishment, having supported all the worst doings of George Meany, such as his benign neutrality toward Richard Nixon and his malign support of the devastation of Vietnam.

As I once said of the old United Mine Workers: What a sad day when that which was erected with blood and sweat to protect the workers from industry, now protects industry from the workers!

Joseph Rauh and Ken Yablonski (Mine Worker reformers) are engaged on the side of the steel rebels; they will find less out-and-out villainy and violence but more power and a more subtle but no less tenacious tyranny.

PITTSBURGH CATHOLIC
October 4, 1974

. . . The USW was devised by coal miners, Murray and Lewis, according to a formula that had ministered to survival of the Miners Union. Important in the formula was control by a strong internal organization, a machine actually. Here is the rationale: To contend with ruthless capitalists you need unity, which you maintain by force and purchase if necessary. What is good for the organization is good for the union. Men who entered the UMW organization knew that if they played by its rules it would care for them, if they did not, "it took care of" them. What happened to Jock Yablonski was an extreme case of such a taking care of.

The Steel Workers' controlling machine has not been so rough and ruthless as the Miners', but it has not been gentle, and it has endured. It changed its leaders, when Abel ousted McDonald, but little else.

Today it may be facing substantive change, if not termination.

Two years from now Abel must retire, and

his hand-picked successor does not look like a winner. The machine has other strong chaps who will offer themselves but they will not walk in. You may recall my brief mention of a challenge that was mounted by an outsider, a mere staff man, in the largest USW district, Chicago-Gary. This man, Ed Sadlowski, in a supervised new election, easily beat the anointed representative of the hierarchy. The original election two years ago was so odoriferous that the U.S. Department of Labor, which has a very strong stomach, rejected its results and ordered the re-run.

The Department of Labor is charged with seeing that various laws, enacted by Congress to preserve the democratic process within unions, are honored. Like virtually all regulatory agencies of the Federal Government, the D of L has more sympathy with those it regulates than with their victims, customers or subjects. . . .

THE PITTSBURGH CATHOLIC
January 10, 1975

Violence, money and power mix readily. In the tamer reaches of society the violent portion of the mix is figurative, but in labor it can be the real thing.

A struggle rages. After a long simmer it is beginning to rage, within the United Steelworkers union. Power, and to a lesser extent money, are what is being struggled for. There has been violence already. I guess you could call it violence when a chap has a bullet put through his neck while he leaflets a steel mill in Texas.

The man who was shot (thank God the bullet did not hit his spinal column and he will be all right) was campaigning on behalf of a rebel, Edward Sadlowski, who aspires to the presidency of that large union and its 1,400,000 members. Ed will probably make a formal declaration of his candidacy at the convention later this month in Las Vegas. In the meantime his friends are campaigning, and so are his non-friends.

Sadlowski is challenging the traditional leadership of the USW and his chances are excellent. He is a winner as well as a rebel, having beaten the organization to win the directorship of the largest district in the union, Chicago with 130,000 members. That was a rerun. The boys counted him out the first time and the Department of Labor, prodded by the courts, made them do it over. . . .

Sadlowski is unusual. There have been several in the past, who became directors in the USW as rebels, but Ed is the only one who remained a rebel after winning. He will not go along, he will not be coopted, he will not join the comfortable and powerful official club.

I fear what may happen in the South. That region is more violent than the rest of the country, and more of its men carry guns. There is another reason for alarm. Southerners are more likely than the rest of us to get excited about Communism and Communists. If you accuse a man down there of Communism and have some credibility yourself, you put him in danger. It is a place where the Red smear is still effective.

The smear was used in the various Mine Workers elections and it hurt the rebels. It was absolutely untrue, but it worked a bit, and it roused people.

Sadlowski is being smeared. Letters are floating around here, and are surely floating elsewhere, especially in the South. Sadlowski is about as much a Communist as the other doughty American Pole of great fame and acclaim, John Cardinal Krol. Ed has been checked out by experts and he is clean and clear. I'm sure the Cardinal is also but I have not seen the tests on him.

The United Steelworkers are ready for a change. The union is not corrupt but it is soft, pompous, dull, a bit lazy and distant from its membership. It is more than a little like the old ERP's, the Employee Representation Plans, which the Steel Corporations set up in the early Thirties to head off Phil Murray's organizing drive.

Sadlowski would be a tonic for the USW's tired blood. At 38, he is a veritable folk hero with an amazing gallery of admirers.

I see no sign that he is an extremist. Tough realists are good for this country, its people and its industries.

PITTSBURGH CATHOLIC
August 13, 1976

The Steelworkers' Election (1976)

When a trade union tyranny is threatened it yells, "Commie," and smears its opponents as outsiders trying to take over the union. That is an old and dishonorable tactic, but it can work. Apparently it is being used in the battle now raging for top office in the United Steelworkers of America, AFL-CIO.

The USW has become stodgy and its leadership is uninspired, but it is a respectable union with respectable leaders. One hates to see men of this sort stoop to a disreputable tactic. . . .

The Red baiting annoys and disturbs me, also the charge of outside influence. That is a divisive tactic, as well as a mean one, and it can hurt very good people. When it is successful, it makes for apathy, and often has been a screen for tyrants and crooks. They creep in when the militant voices are silenced.

Ed Sadlowski is running for president of USW and he is the target. Sadlowski is a breath of fresh air for the whole labor movement, and entrenched labor skates everywhere dislike him and the fresh breeze. He is a natural. A real worker right out of the mill, he can talk and operate. Workers like him and so do those who are not workers: writers, students, reformers, idealists and so on. The man inspires loyalty as well as affection, withal a

formidable threat to the old guard.

Men of his sort are always attacked as Reds or leftists and generally the attacks succeed in destroying them, to the detriment of the labor movement, which needs new men and vibrant leaders; without which it is withering.

When labor got a new lease on life with the New Deal and made its last great surge, it had many men like Sadlowski, and they were assisted by idealistic outsiders of all sorts who sustained the necessary momentum. Phil Murray and John L. Lewis had great personal magnetism, and they welcomed allies as they pushed aside the entrenched old guard of their day. Working with Murray for years, I was an outsider, as the Communists used to complain. I know labor and communism, if I know anything, and I assure you that it is false to accuse Sadlowski, or his opponent, of being under Communist, or leftist, or Maoist or any outside influence.

A recent piece by Ira Fine in the Pittsburgh Press set me off. Ira is not an old labor hand and he may having been hanging around the Steelworkers' International Headquarters too much — it is in the same block as his paper. Someone induced him to use the phrase Communist-oriented in his piece and fed him guff about a danger arising from college-trained youth getting jobs in mills and mines. Nonsense. Any living movement welcomes brains. When you mistrust intelligent young people, you are ready for the bone yard. . . .

PITTSBURGH CATHOLIC
November 26, 1976

Fight Management, Don't Pray with Them

May the Lord forgive me, but I am convinced that the working man has to be powerfully suspicious of suggestions that he engage in public prayer as a solution to his problems as a worker.

Do not be alarmed, my little ones, I am not taking a stand against prayer. I want workers to pray, I want all people to pray, but I grievously distrust and dislike the use of prayer as an industrial relations gimmick. I am leery of certain "Christian" approaches to labor relations. Promoters of this sort of "Christianity" have more in common with businessmen than with laborers. One does not hear them urging businessmen to tone down their aggressive competitive inclinations. They put the cart before the horse as they urge workers to vie with each other to produce and serve the master.

Life in the workplace, as they should understand, is tolerable only when the workers are concerned with one another, evening out strengths and weaknesses, and competing only as a unit and only with those in control. This is true for all systems, communist as well as capitalist, and the true Christian knows it in his heart.

PITTSBURGH CATHOLIC
March 9, 1979

McBride, Steelworkers Face Challenge (1977)

The Sadlowski insurgency was defeated. Its banner was seized by local union rebel groups like the 1397 Rank and File led by Ron Weisen in historic Homestead. Lloyd McBride, a decent but unimaginative leader, took power only to preside over the beginning of the worst crisis ever to confront the United Steel Workers of America. Rapid downsizing of the industry combined with corporate attacks and governmental anti-unionism created a nightmarish situation for the union's leadership.

Friends of labor were distressed by the news that the labor movement lost members between 1974 and the end of '76. The figures gathered by the Department of Labor seem to be accurate. The loss was not large, but it was a loss. The movement should be growing. It should have the strength and vitality to grow.

There are many explanations for the loss. Organized labor has been static for years. It has not been organizing the unorganized with sufficient intensity. Its leadership has been uninspired. Industry moving to the anti-union Sunbelt has hurt and so have recessions. One suspects also that ordinary people have become conservative and slightly anti-union.

Because of all this I find myself hoping that Lloyd McBride, whom I opposed while he was running for the presidency of the United Steelworkers, will be a success. He has a great union under his control, a union that has not been challenged or asked to extend itself for years and he might very well be the man to galvanize it into action.

If USW becomes aggressive and goes all out to organize the unorganized, especially in the Sunbelt, it can shake the whole movement into a new life. From all accounts McBride is efficient and possessed of what the athletic coaches call desire. He wants to prove that he is a man in his own right and did not need to be hand-picked by anyone. Good.

The union he inherited is torpid. It grew recently by mergers with other unions rather than by organizing drives. Making it taut and effective will not be easy. Unions are not like businesses because they are political. People get ahead for reasons other than efficiency (they do in business also by the way). An organizer is a salesman, but he lacks the incentive of a salesman, which is more money if you sell more.

Loyalty is the coin of trade unionism, and it binds both the leader and the led. Rarely are even the strongest of union leaders noted for their driving characteristics. John L. Lewis for instance did not drive his organizers and he did not punish failure.

Lloyd McBride has his hands full. Old allegiances and loyalties abound, so do old enmities and they all impede action. If he can roll the union on, he is good.

Can we hope for more militance or will we be fogged in with labor statesmanship? There will be more militance but not a great deal because the union membership has grown conservative, and the basic steel industry is not in great shape. The union and the industry will continue their alliance against imports and may well form a hard alliance against environmentalism. Not highly desirable developments but the drift is that way. . . .

PITTSBURGH CATHOLIC
September 23, 1977

What a dreadful time to be a labor leader! What a doubly dreadful time to be a big labor leader of a big union with a record of success. Take Lloyd McBride. A thoroughly decent man and a competent labor leader. Poor Lloyd, his industry is falling apart and his membership is crumbling before his very eyes. He is paying for the mistakes of his predecessor, mistakes that had seemed brilliant coups at the time.

I. W. Abel began the Experimental Negotiating Agreement, which was an arrangement with the Steel Corporations whereby it was guaranteed before negotiations that there would be no strike. The ENA followed upon the widely held belief that inroads of foreign steel were solely due to strikes and threats of strike in the American steel industry.

None of the heavy thinkers guessed that deep flaws in the industry might have been responsible for the loss of markets to foreigners. In short, both the union and the companies believed the same story and missed the same points.

The thought that if the top echelons of both unions and company were of one mind all would be well. Both knew what was best for the workers and the industry. Meanwhile the industry was getting slack and was not keeping up its plant, and,

on the vital lower level, workers and the bosses whom they encountered day by day were not getting along. Actually, the management attitude from the top to the bottom was not one of respect for the workers; lots of respect for the union chiefs but little for the working man whose wisdom was thought to be non-existent.

The Experimental Negotiating Agreement, which by the way was not ratified by the membership resulted in high wages but it was founded on the assumption that high wages were a cure all and that other problems would solve themselves.

Now markets fade, and multinationalism corrodes American industry. Concentration of money and brains on armaments takes a toll. The barons of industry fancy themselves as investors and financial wizards, their first duty to make money not steel, and men like McBride agree that this proposition is sensible.

So it is that the workers are going to make concessions, to give back. Many workers and rank-and-file leaders loudly cry that whatever they give will translate not into money that will sustain their industries, but money that will fatten or salvage, profit sheets. They cry out from bitter experience.

The pressures on McBride and his peers is intense and is compounded by the fact that, through the years, they have begun to think like the great captains of industry and finance with whom they smugly deal as equals. . . .

PITTSBURGH CATHOLIC
July 9, 1982

. . . The erosion of America's industrial base, the flight of industries, and now a world-wide industrial malaise, a virtual collapse affects the unions. Reagan is truly anti-union, no matter what he says, and the flight of capital out of production and into speculation are just a few of the unfavorable developments.

It is in light of all this that Lloyd McBride,

President of the United Steel Workers of America, is facing a crisis unprecedented for his union. The auto workers have to face the same crisis, so have lesser unions.

Due to mistakes and blindness at the highest levels of industry and commerce, and malign provisions of the Tax Code, factories are closing. The powers in industry no longer lust to make things, they want a hand in the game of finance, playing with vast sums of money on an international scale, getting high satisfaction out of predatory takeovers and the like.

McBride's predecessors never had it so bad. Of course Phil Murray went through this sort of thing in the Twenties when he and John Lewis struggled to keep the Miners Union alive. Lewis ran the show; he took the line of no concessions, no backward step and the union virtually disintegrated.

McBride, in my opinion, is trying to do the right thing. He wants to preserve what he can for steel making in the United States. He cooperates with the industry in fighting foreign imports and one cannot blame him even if he and they are missing the point.

In the matter of concessions, he is taking a hard road. Tough dissenters such as Ronnie Weisen, my friend, will pounce on him, but he is right and they are wrong. The idea is to keep as much of the industry functioning in the United States as possible and to keep it union. When bad times are over there is the chance to win back what you gave up.

Men like Weisen would not be in such hot opposition if they, the ordinary rank and filers, really had a part in the decision making. It is unfortunate that they now feel it is the union and the companies against them. Not McBride, but the USW tradition of negotiating is to blame.

Considering what he inherited, McBride has been a good president. In a political organization, and that's what unions are, you cannot have perfect efficiency or perfect tolerance. He and his advisors have taken the position that they and the industry are in the same boat; I would have liked it better if they had looked for independent solutions; maybe they could not have found them but it would not have hurt to explore.

I will do all I can to enable Weisen to survive, because his type of dissent is invaluable, but in the meantime I wish Lloyd well in his desperate struggle to save the union and the industry. Let him remember that the captains of steel and their academic allies have been on a disaster course for steel making in the United States; they are not all knowing. Furthermore as he negotiates, he should never turn his back. Scrutinize every line for fatal clauses that might help finance and industry but could kill his union. May he be sharp and strong. . . .

PITTSBURGH CATHOLIC
November 5, 1982

Lloyd McBride, who died last week, was a nice normal person to whom fate dealt a weird hand. When he died he was International President of the United Steel Workers of America, USWA, in its day the giant of industrial unions. Through no fault of Lloyd's it dwindled. Why did it dwindle? The answer is plain. Its Basic industry, for one reason or another, faded like the last rose of summer.

McBride joined the USW when he was struggling to raise a family in the days of his youth and the union's youth. This was in St. Louis, not exactly the heart of steel territory, but a great union town influenced by the soft coal miners of southern Illinois, much manufacturing and some steel.

McBride was good, decent, Catholic, working/middle class. His only son is a brother in the Marianist Order, and he lived simply all his life. Church, family, union. Guys like that are the salt of the earth, regardless of what church they belong to.

Panache, style, flamboyance, rhetoric? That was not Lloyd McBride. But he had a following, and fierce loyalties developed because he was honest, dependable, pleasant, decent, true blue. . . . When I. W. Abel retired as President of USW, Ed Sadlowski made a strong run for the roses, and, if he had won, would have changed the union profoundly. McBride always said that he got in the race to save the union from Sadlowski. My opinion at the time was that Sadlowski, whom I supported, would be good for the union. I did not know McBride at all.

At any rate McBride won after a hard race in which whips were out and flanks were wet. In victory he was magnanimous and would have been more so, but his supporters had a legitimate claim on him and he had to think of them.

Lloyd McBride was out of an honorable labor tradition that places loyalty to the union very high. Men of his sort have feelings toward the union akin to their feelings toward country or church. When a man has made the union his life, he not only loves it but becomes possessive.

Such men are hostile toward, and suspicious of, another honorable strain in trade unionism, composed of those who do not revere the union for what it is, but value it for what it can do, or be made to do. These men are not tolerant of union weaknesses or mistakes, and they are prone to dissent and rebel. I supported some of them even though I was fond of McBride. . . .

If Sadlowski had won he might not have run the union so efficiently, but he would have confronted the crises actively and with imagination. He might well have been able to save more from the wreckage by carrying the fight to the corporations and trying different moves. On the other hand, such a daring policy might have made matters worse.

Lloyd has died, Lord rest him, but the fight goes on and the union lives.

PITTSBURGH CATHOLIC
November 18, 1983

George Becker and Lynn Williams lead support march for Pittsburgh Press strikers. September 1, 1992

Changing of the Steel Workers' Guard (1994)

In 1984, a Canadian, Lynn Williams, was elected President of the Steelworker's Union. He provided an articulate voice for unions and dislocated workers in Reagan's America. He supported innovative employee ownership efforts to save jobs. He made peace with many local union militants. His successor, George Becker, would inherit a smaller union which had regained some of its equilibrium, but was still confronted by enormous challenges in a fiercely competitive global market.

Lynn Williams will retire as president of the United Steel Workers of America next month. During his 10 years in the office he has been a Pittsburgher.

Ontario, Canada, was his home and birthplace, and he is the first Canadian-born international president of the Steel Workers, but not the first foreign-born one. The first and founding president was Pittsburgh's Philip Murray, who was born in Scotland and came here with his family as a lad to work in the coal mines.

There is no physical resemblance between the two men, other than they are about the same height, but there are resemblances in their methods of operation. Like Phil, Lynn has an easy way with subordinates and colleagues, and no pomposity. But, again like Phil, he can be tough when necessary with both companies from the outside and challengers from within.

Williams is not from the working class; his father was a minister of the United Church of Canada, but he served mostly in areas where the workers and the poor predominated. Lynn inherited compassion and a strong social conscience from his father. For a while, he was inclined to follow his father into the church, but saw the work the unions did, and how they were needed, and deliberately set out to get into the labor movement.

When he asked how he might do that, he was told to get himself a job as a working man, and become a labor leader by serving his fellow workers and demonstrating leadership. That he did.

Back around that time, a lot of middle-class idealistic young men got the same idea. Several approached me and I gave them the advice Lynn's friends gave him, but none of them took it.

After finishing college and serving a year in the Canadian navy, Williams worked briefly in a small fabricating plant and, with much perseverance, got a chance at reorganizing various metal workers and turned out to have a knack for talking to such workers and gaining their respect and confidence. When his chance came, he ran for union office, and again did well. Over the years the jobs got better and better; he was able to avoid making bitter enemies.

When he was near the top, a couple of elections were close and hard fought; but the last time he ran, which was for re-election as president of the International, he had no opposition.

There never was a worse time to be president of the Steel Workers, or any union in industry, than when he made it. The industry went to pot and foreign competition had it for lunch.

Williams had a strategy: He sold cooperation both to his members and the employers. He would strike a company only when he absolutely had to. And he gave concessions only when he had convinced his members that there was no other way.

As president, his major task was to unite the big union itself, which had been divided by bitter elections for the presidency; and that he has accomplished.

Upon his retirement, George E. Becker, vice-president, administration, will take over in a smooth succession, which will be good for the union. The two men get along, and there are no factions.

They are different from each other. George is blue collar and is the son of a steel worker. Williams had to work himself into the labor movement; Becker was born into it.

His career path was labor gang, assembly line, crane operator, inspector. Blue collar all the way and, in addition, talented and intelligent. He is not flamboyant, but he stands out somehow. You notice him in a crowd, and he has that look which workers trust. I can't describe it, but I recognize it.

Becker is a Midwesterner and is from the Milwaukee District of the USW. As he moved along in the union hierarchy, he faced trouble and problems affecting all American unions: the Wagner Act, labor's Magna Carta, has been tampered with and almost crippled. It has been poorly and perversely administered. Congress must be induced and pressured to restore it. All labor must get in the fight. But big, harmonious unions like the USW have to go all out. Becker will be an energizing and unifying force in the battle.

PITTSBURGH CATHOLIC
February 11, 1994

☰ The Mon Valley Resistance

In the 1980s, mills and manufacturing establishments in Pennsylvania and Ohio began to close with numbing regularity, throwing many long-established blue collar communities into abrupt decline. Rice became a partisan of radical measures designed to revive the steel industry through governmental investment combined with an infusion of worker participation and community involvement.

We All Live in Pennsylvania (1979)

In Europe, protestors against nuclear power chant the slogan, "We all live in Pennsylvania"; they do this to demonstrate that the lesson of Harrisburg's near holocaust is not lost on them.

There is a slogan that we Pittsburghers might have occasion to chant, "We all live in Youngstown." This will demonstrate that the implication of a dreadful calamity which befell Youngstown is not lost on us.

As elderly steel centers, Pittsburgh and Youngstown are at hazard to the enormous changes happening in their enormous industry. Already Youngstown has been dealt a shattering blow; poor Pittsburgh has been suffering from lesser blows for a generation or two.

Youngstown Sheet & Tube was a fine responsible company that earned a good profit, employed more than 5,000 and appeared to have an excellent future. It was a good employer and a good citizen, but it is no more. How it was done in, is a shocking story.

It was in the time of Nixon that a predatory conglomerate, aided by New York banks, was allowed by the Feds to devour the larger and healthier Youngstown Sheet & Tube. Stupidity, avarice and grave flaws in our system made this reckless gamble possible. For reasons of their own, the banks pulled out and failure was complete.

The company was murdered (not too strong a word). Youngstown is much smaller than Pittsburgh and the death of Sheet & Tube has wounded the city almost mortally. Another mill, owned by the same conglomer-ate, is reducing its operations, thus intensifying the agony.

Can the Youngstown syndrome possibly affect the much larger Steel City of Pittsburgh? Indeed it can, and it well may.

The United States Steel Corporation, USS, employs tens of thousands in this Pittsburgh area and maintains many manufacturing establishments and mills. USS has purchased large acreage along Lake Erie to the North, and plans a gigantic facility, a complete steel mill with complete automation. The mill will straddle the Pennsylvania and Ohio border on what is now farm land and lake frontage. The Corporation, as they call it, is not doing anything sneaky and is discussing its plans openly. . . .

Within its own ranks its leadership is torn between Greenfields and Brownfields, that is, between expanding to land that is virgin land, industrially speaking, and modernizing or rebuilding in the industrial areas, the Brownfields. The Green costs more to build but less to operate than the Brown. . . .

USS's Greenfields project is so immense and disruptive that we should be alarmed. It is nothing to take in stride. The effect on Pittsburgh is only one factor but, since I am a Pittsburgher, I shall look at that first.

What the Corporation decides and does is more important to us than who will be our governor, our senators or our president for the next twenty years, and yet, we have very little to say and we have not been alerted. Our politicians are not on to the issue.

It is time to press for a change of law so that great private entities may no longer make unilateral decisions that can destroy lives and give pain to thousands. Capitalism is sufficiently resilient that it will not be damaged by government intervention in these grave matters.

I would not like to hurt U.S. Steel because that would hurt our people, but a change in the tax laws that encouraged rebuilding in the Brownfields would help the Corporation and our citizens, and would save our precious land from being "browned" beyond reason or necessity.

PITTSBURGH CATHOLIC
May 25, 1979

More on Steel Industry's Plight (1979)

Last week I noted the imminent danger of U.S. Steel's withdrawal from the steel business and the likelihood that this would soon be manifested in the closing of plants. Even as the piece was on its way, the giant corporation announced the closing of 16 plants of various sizes and locations, and the termination of 13,000 jobs.

Poor Youngstown, Ohio, was hit hardest with the loss of 4,300 jobs and two plants, along with the almost certain abandonment of facilities by other steel companies. Within a few years that means 10,000 vanished jobs! No wonder that Youngstown residents are shell-shocked and convinced that they are in a disaster area.

In the Pittsburgh area we are faced with the immediate loss of 1,900 jobs and the prospect

> "**W**hat the Corporation decides and does is more important to us than who will be our governor, our senators or our president for the next twenty years, and yet, we have very little to say and we have not been alerted. Our politicians are not on to the issue.
>
> It is time to press for a change of law so that great private entities may no longer make unilateral decisions that can destroy lives and give pain to thousands."

there is worse to come. Ambridge, in the Pittsburgh area, was hit, but there is a hint that a reprieve is possible.

To understand what is happening, you must first understand that U.S. Steel is out to do two things that are related. One is the closing of unprofitable operations (you might call this pruning). The second is a gradual getting out of domestic steel, disinvestment. The money realized from this would be transferred to other investments in search of higher profit. . . .

David M. Roderick, new chairman of U.S. Steel, lays heavy blame for his company's bad situation on the federal government and wants: more protection against foreign steel; an easing of environmental regulations; and a variety of tax relief including accelerated depreciation.

He is a decent man with a tough job and I do not see him as an ogre, but he is an accountant rather than a steel-maker, and he once did make a statement to the effect that the business of the corporation was to make money rather than steel. Mr. Roderick is really attempting a very radical capitalism, which is too ruthless for today's complex world and this fragile society of ours; he is to be resisted, where he is wrong, but without rancor. . . .

I belong to an organization which is trying to educate workers, public and legislators. Tri-State Conference on the Impact of Steel grew out of the efforts of the Catholic and Episcopal

Rice with mill worker at Jones & Laughlin's closed Pittsburgh works, 1982

FOR LEASE INDUSTRIAL PROPERTY

Bishops of Youngstown and Cleveland to save that area. We favor what may be called social innovation, and are firmly opposed to the building of the giant Conneaut complex, on the grounds of what that will do to both the communities abandoned, and the new environment to be invaded. Scholars, experts and lawyers join clergymen, workers and concerned citizens in the effort. . . .

PITTSBURGH CATHOLIC
December 7, 1979

Youngstown Ruling Historic (1980)

History was made last week in Youngstown, Ohio, when a federal judge gave a group of steel workers their day in court. In the end he ruled against them, but he did them a great service when he accepted their suit, in the course of which he permitted them to subpoena the two top officers of the United States Steel Corporation, cross-examine them, and spread their answers on the public record.

Judge Lambros would have set a beautiful precedent if he had ruled in favor of the workers, but entertaining their suit was in itself a nice precedent which will help in the future.

The court case was one more act in a continuing tragedy which will play for decades: the shrinking of American heavy industry; the

My belief is that the well being of US Steel is of no greater importance than the well being of traditional steel-making communities. And I am passionately convinced that for the sake of the nation a well paid, sturdy blue collar work force (for all its faults and narrow-mindedness) is more important than any and all companies. To save the communities and the blue collar class we might have to go to community-worker ownership backed by the federal government: a fine alternative to either communism or radical capitalism.

hemorrhaging of jobs — good jobs; and the death of communities.

Youngstown, you will remember, suffered three years ago from the folding of another large steel facility and is in danger of becoming a ghost town. Late last year when U.S. Steel abruptly announced that it would close its two big plants, which employed 3,500, the city was aghast, but leaders of the two Steel Worker locals involved were prepared.

They demanded a chance to buy and operate the mills, and when the corporation turned a deaf ear, they recalled a public meeting at which they had been promised by proper authority, as they recollect, that the mills would be continued in operation, if the men pulled up their socks and made a profit. The men claimed that they had done this, and produced some evidence to get them into federal court.

The judge, although he ruled that the men had no contract, recognized the total situation and the grave danger to the community. He pressed the corporation to consider an offer from the men to buy the mills within a reasonable period. . . .

My belief is that the well being of US Steel is of no greater importance than the well being of traditional steel-making communities. And I am passionately convinced that for the sake of the nation a well paid, sturdy blue collar work force (for all its faults and narrow-mindedness) is more important than any and all companies. To save the communities and the blue collar class we might have to go to community-worker ownership backed by the federal government: a fine alternative to either communism or radical capitalism.

This is a different world and it calls for improvisation and innovation. Our best minds are now mired down in industry and the professions. Let them think new thoughts and scheme new schemes to deliver us from the stagnation of the moment. . . .

PITTSBURGH CATHOLIC
March 28, 1980

A Protest Against Steel Unemployment (1980)

. . . The ultimate menace is the proposal that blue collar jobs be phased out of the United States and transferred to the Third World, where wages are abysmally low, workers are still docile, armies are for union busting, and profits are sky high.

That may make financial sense but it does not make any other kind of sense; it is radical capitalism at its worst.

I want the steel workers of Homestead to be prepared to acquire the mills, if they are to be abandoned, and run them themselves with government financing. If eminent domain can be used to acquire property for the expansion of PPG in downtown Pittsburgh, it can be used to acquire the mills of Homestead so that the community and the workers may survive.

Not communism but a different form of capitalism, and one perfectly attainable under the present system of law. It is far better than the manic capitalism, which would strip us of our steel and of all heavy industry.

PITTSBURGH CATHOLIC
July 18, 1980

Analyzing the Steel Situation (1981)

In his remarks to the shareholders, Roderick said the company's broad-based effort to make better use of its assets has generated more than $1 billion for redeployment into more profitable areas.

As reported by our morning paper in its concise account of the 80th annual shareholders meeting of U.S. Steel, does that not sound like a bland, predictable report by the chairman? Yet it was blockbuster, and more should have been made of it, particularly since about 75 of us walking around outside Heinz Hall were graphically telling what it meant.

Some of the protesters carried a coffin, wore mourning and chalk white faces. As they walked through town (without me) they created a sensation. Literature was distributed by the protesters, and with the literature was an excellent Counter Annual Report.

The point of the protest was that U.S. Steel was proclaiming the death knell of American steel-making and, like a tree, the industry would die at the top, the top being the Monongahela Valley where it all began. . . .

This Counter Annual Report pointed out that U.S. Steel was getting out of the steel business, and even its scattered modernization was directed toward contracting rather than expanding. Most menacing of all is that the great Homestead area (Mon Valley) plants are heading for the fate of the whole Youngstown steel complex — that fate is to shrivel and vanish. . . .

Among the protesters outside the U.S. Steel meeting was Ron Weisen, President of USW 1397, the largest local of U.S. Steel employees in these parts. Ron is running for director of his whole district and you may recall that he had a bit of difficulty getting on the ballot but that is straightened out now and he is in the midst of a hotly-contested election which seems to be a fair fight.

Ron and his opponent, Paul Lewis, the man

who holds the position, are both out of the local steel mills and are both decent, honest men, who want to represent the same body of workers. It is not a polite tussle, but the stakes are high.

The Steel Workers' International union itself is an issue in the fight and I am happy to say that that union is honest, however, it is political in that it helps its faithful incumbents — it would not help a jailbird and is nothing like the Teamsters' International. Lloyd McBride, the USW International president, has an enlightened stance on national politics.

However, in the present state of the nation and the steel communities we could use a more aggressive and imaginative USW, one that would give some healthy opposition to the steel industry's shutdown strategy and protect communities such as Homestead and Hazelwood. . . .

PITTSBURGH CATHOLIC
May 22, 1981

Mighty Steel Strikes Us Suckers Out (1981)

In the town of Findlay, O., there is dancing in the streets, but here in Mudville, (not only of Pittsburgh but of every steel town is the name Mud these days), there is no joy, because Mighty Steel has not so much struck out itself, as struck us suckers out. Findlay will receive much benefit from the $6 billion which the United States Steel Corporation has been amassing; the various Mudvilles had the $6 billion taken out of their hides.

U.S. Steel in a great financial coup bids its billions for Marathon Oil, and Marathon Oil is happy. Findlay is happy (this little city with its 27,000 middle Americans) because its citizens, its libraries, hospitals, churches, schools, and way of life will flourish rather than fade. Ours will all fade as steel-making fades and moves and concentrates.

I saw it coming and often sounded the tocsin, having been alerted by the Tri-State Conference on the Impact of Steel and its experts. . . . The media has parroted the line of the domestic steel industry, to wit; all of its troubles are caused by imported steel, and it follows that environmental restrictions must be reduced or stretched out, tax breaks will be fruitful, and the union must cooperate. . . .

Prodded by industry and media, the politicians and the union worked hard to get tax breaks and environmental breaks for steel, all without strings, believing, as promised, that the money saved would be spent for modernizing the domestic steel industry. We tried to get them to hold out for various guarantees, but in vain. . . .

PITTSBURGH CATHOLIC
November 27, 1981

Lack of Commitment (1982)

Speaking of dominoes, who expected all those gigantic steel corporations to fall like dominoes? For years it was customary to worry about the future of unions, would they last or would they fade away? Hardly anyone expected industrial manufacturing to be the thing to fade? . . .

When I, following the insights of the Tri-State Conference on the Impact of Steel, decried disinvestment in steel and diversion of cash and energy to relatively frivolous uses such as office buildings and Shopping Malls, I was scorned by purveyors of conventional wisdom, and the Tri-State Conference itself was granted little or no status by opinion makers and purveyors. Only now is what we have been saying getting some credence, and not all that much. . . . One pessimistic school of thought holds that the United States should give up on heavy industry and manufacturing while concentrating on high technology.

That is really foolish because it virtually ensures huge unemployment and widespread, low-wage jobs.

A way that may show promise is the transfer of ownership and control to the employees. We in Tri-State would like to have ownership and responsibility shared between employees and communities. The number of attempts and experiments at some sort of social ownership is increasing. In smaller enterprises it has been proved to be workable but there are always pitfalls. Old attitudes persist and sometimes the workers are not permitted to share control although they have ownership. It will take years before the thing gets a true test and by then American industry may have bled to death.

It seems to me that we cannot expect worker ownership to do the job. Government intervention, even to the extent of selective nationalization, may be the only hope of preserving more than a skeleton steel industry.

Nationalization in order to be effective has to go beyond industry and must touch finance. The flow of capital is the malign witch. Capital serves itself; it dominates, it has no heart, no morals, no patriotism. . . .

PITTSBURGH CATHOLIC
April 2, 1982

Rice with Mon Valley dissident Ron Weisen, President USWA Local 1397, in front of shut Homestead mill, August 13, 1986

The Militant Clergy (1984)

Often people ask me what I think of Ronnie Weisen and the idealistic ministers in whose company he is raising hell against the bankers and corporations and some religious entities. I like and respect him and them. Why then have I not joined them in their activities? The answer is as many faceted as the question.

I feel toward Ronnie and his friends as I do toward the IRA whose struggle I understand and sympathize with. I don't approve of everything the IRA does nor do I disapprove. As Bishop Mark Hurley said after his visit to Ireland: the IRA is not the problem. The problem is the underlying situation and its deep, deep built-in injustices.

Ron and the ministers have a clear understanding of the abuses and of the villains. They are not able to whop the real villains, but they get as close as they can. Mellon Bank is a reasonable stand-in for the entire multinational banking community which whipsaws the world as it moves its money about. Wealthy churches are a tempting target for radical churchmen and their allies.

Actually I do not like to see the churches of the Presbyterian denomination attacked because in the Civil Rights and Viet Nam turmoil, that denomination was absolutely beautiful and paid the price for its convictions.

The Presbyterian pastor generally has about as much influence over his wealthy and powerful members as I have over mine. None of these dudes has shown the slightest inclination to follow my lead which is given not from the pulpit but from this space.

The Episcopalians were marvelous in that crisis; although not as forceful around here as the Presbyterians.

Not much was heard from the Lutherans, but now they are in the forefront of the church most militant. Marvelous young men are risking their pulpits and their livelihoods. Catholics were on the cutting edge of the Viet Nam resistance and the racial fight and are still active, but we have not really joined the new group. This group has different names. There is the Network to Save the Mon Valley, and there is the perfectly marvelous, Protestant-sounding Denominational Mission Strategy.

Lutheran authorities are having problems dealing with their radicals because apparently their law is not that clear cut, and appeals to scripture are dynamite. Their rebels have a specific grievance with Biblical overtones. The workers at a Lutheran center for the elderly have been displaced and others hired in their stead for less money. So the rebels target a specific Lutheran Church where not only does the Bishop preach, but the man responsible for hiring the scabs preaches.

I am not crazy about disrupting Presbyterian services, but I see the point of hitting the Lutherans where there is a specific injustice.

The ins and outs of Lutheran law on the appointments and removal of pastors are not clear to me. Young pastors, David Roth and John Gropp, may have good cases. If so, they will win. I find that among young Lutheran ministers and many of the laity, there is surprising support and respect for the rebels.

As I keep saying, when the injustices over our society grow too great, and chaos and rebellion rumble, we shall be glad to have non-Marxist, militant, intelligent leadership.

Both Pastor Roth and Pastor Gropp are sturdy, and their religious faith is beautiful to behold. As they become more seasoned, they will become more formidable fighters for the Lord.

PITTSBURGH CATHOLIC
November 16, 1984

McCollester and American Workers (1993)

As steel plants began closing in the mid to late '70s we did not know what to think. At first, some feared that U.S. Steel was going to move its operations to a huge tract, acquired long ago at Conneaut on Lake Erie.

Then it appeared that the corporation might be planning to disinvest in steel, and then finally we began to realize that the American steel industry was in danger of collapse. There was no plot and no one had planned what was going on. Leaders of the steel industry did not themselves immediately recognize that disaster was a possibility.

The situation bears comparison with the USSR. The outside world had little or no idea how weak that "Evil" Empire was, and it is probable that neither did most of the people running the empire. Our CIA for all its surveillance arts and magical probing devices was caught napping.

We kept on bankrupting ourselves with crazy military expenses long after the threat from the USSR was over. Gorbachev had in effect to sue for peace before we tumbled to the truth.

As for me, while I had some sense of what was going on in Russia, I missed what was happening right here at home to our steel industry, and indeed to much of our manufacturing might.

My gradual enlightenment was helped by a scholarly individual who was working by choice in a machine shop when he looked me up—shortly after he arrived in Pittsburgh. Charles McCollester is a world traveller of the backpack persuasion, who has a Ph.D. from Louvain and an abiding fascination with the American worker and the American work experience.

To finance his education, he worked in manufacturing, retail and trucking jobs, and yet managed to do a great deal of traveling. His career is an unusual mix of teaching, research and working in industry. A career in management had no attraction for him, but unions did. At one plant, he was elected chief steward while working as a milling machine operator. This was in the Pittsburgh area.

It was natural that when Bishop Robert Appleyard, Episcopal, formed the Tri-State Conference on Steel to alert the community to the imminent danger of the loss of our basic industry, Charlie was enrolled as a participant. This was in 1979, and he has been active in keeping the conference alive.

At the opening session, he tossed an 18" chunk of steel rail on the floor with a reminder that we inhabitants of this steel center might one day have to look for the substance in museums rather than the work place.

It was after the opening session that Charlie drew me into the conference, and I am grateful that he did, because Tri-State has done important work in educating and agitating to catch the attention of the public and of the decision-makers.

There are clergymen of various denominations active, along with trade union officers and rank-and-filers, also a lawyer or two.

McCollester's aim has been renewal from below, with the workers and community active, not passive. The emphasis was on the practical always. Help the victims of steel's decline, save as much of the industry as possible, and pull in new industry. Tri-State has been a working and not a doctrinaire agglomeration of activists.

Although he has resumed his academic career—teaching and research in institutions of higher learning, and publishing—he remains the recruiter and activist for the Tri-State Conference. That conference, as part of its constructive work, tried in vain to save the big Dorothy 6 furnace at Duquesne and the LTV electric furnaces on the South Side.

The Steel Valley Authority, which is working to attract and finance new industry for our area, was spawned by the conference. So have charitable endeavors, food banks and the like.

The news is not all bad. USX Corporation gave the valley a continuous caster, which means steel will not vanish from our midst.

Where do we go from here? Our great steel industry was born in war, the Civil War, and nurtured by protective tariffs. War and preparation for war no longer chew up so much steel, so we may have to go the protection route. The free market did not create our steel industry, and unless it is tinkered with, will not serve to keep it alive.

PITTSBURGH CATHOLIC
February 12, 1993

The Triumph of Money

Rice remained true to his New Deal Irish Democratic ideals. He would publicly describe Catholic Republicans as "another cross in my old age." While he strongly opposed abortion, he argued forcefully against allowing that concern to define Catholic political life. The poor and their interests were given priority when it came to social analysis.

We Need a Two-Way Class War (1989)

Social Security, as an entitlement without a means test, was a noble concept whose aim was to preserve the dignity of the poor, but it has been hijacked to serve as a regressive general tax, supplementing the progressive income tax and, to an extent, supplanting it.

Good might come of this catastrophic insurance debacle in that the need for national health insurance, financed by general taxation, will become more obvious.

While that is being played out, direct assaults are launched to eliminate certain progressive features of the income tax and thus further enrich the rich.

Phony justifications are given for these handouts to those who already have too much. For instance, they claim that putting more money in the hands of the wealthy will increase productive investment. Actually most of it will continue to flow into speculation and financial games, while productive investment will continue to languish.

Some Democrats who had the moxie to oppose these giveaways were told by their Republican opponents that they were, horror of horrors, promoting class war. No one needs to promote class war, it is already raging, as witness the unremitting assault of the upper classes on the well-being of the rest of us, particularly those who fit the definition of financial lower class.

What is the ingrained hostility toward trade unions in nearly all the more fortunate and monied but a manifestation of class hostility?

What we really need in this country is a healthy and vigorous conviction in the bosoms of the lower class that the upper class is their enemy and is out to fleece and suppress them. We need working class solidarity and a sturdy recognition that the poor and almost poor have to stick together.

PITTSBURGH CATHOLIC
October 20, 1989

Trouble Ahead for the Newly Liberated (1990)

In our euphoria over the tattering of the Iron Curtain let us not forget the grim reality. Capitalism with its "free" markets is a cure with severe side effects. Among these is an increase in human suffering, and that is beginning to be felt in Poland.

What happened in Bolivia upon the unleashing of the global market is not reassuring. Through that wretched country we can look into the abyss. The few well-paid workers were reduced to poverty after their unions were smashed. In spite of total economic collapse the rich still thrive, but for the vast majority the result is excruciating pain. For the poor the merciless market adds to their wretchedness and their numbers. Unrest followed by vicious oppression is certain.

In Poland the scene was different. Elements of the communist nomenklatura were relatively wealthy but there were no super rich. That may change as capitalism and freedom move in and a truly rich entrepreneurial class emerges. Most Poles had it very hard but, unlike most Bolivians, they were not dirt poor. Workers in mass-subsidized industries, as in Bolivia, were relatively comfortable. As was never the case in Bolivia, family farmers were prospering.

These farmers will continue to get along tolerably, at least until capitalism's version of the collective farm takes over. But the workers, those who inspired the splendid counter revolution, are sure to lose. They preserved their status by strikes against the ruling communist powers. It is almost certain that they will have to strike again, this time against the ruling democratic powers and with much less chance of success. Dire poverty for many, perhaps most Poles, looms.

Nearly all of Latin America, under the sway of global markets and international money, has become a virtual basket case. Some of the newly-liberated Warsaw Pact nations may not fare any better.

Socialists, including the ones with the perverse vision, the communists, abhor and abjure private ownership of production because of the power it gives people over other people's lives, and the power it gives one class over another. Veritably the power riding with the class that possesses the money and controls its flow is fearsome, unless it be tempered by government intervention.

"Television can be cruel, tantalizing the poor with images of what they can't have and stimulating bitter envy of the rich, while, at the same time magnifying the power of money to dominate the political process and thus keep the rich rich and, in consequence the poor poor."

In our country, a half century ago in a time of trouble, the government under President Franklin Roosevelt developed the will to curtail the absolute power of money and to ameliorate the lot of the disadvantaged. That was the essence of the New Deal. President Ronald Reagan, although he had the brass to invoke Roosevelt, undid most, but not all, of what Roosevelt wrought.

The will of our government to fight poverty and promote justice eroded. Safeguards for the weak and the poor, along with restraints on the rich, crumbled and continue to crumble, so that, as Goldsmith lamented in the England of 200 years ago, "wealth accumulates and men decay."

"Money makes the mare go" and it does so in our democracy, now more than ever because of its swollen power to influence elections through television. As election campaigns cost more and more, those who control the flow of money increase their political control alarmingly. Money corrupts virtually everyone who is serious about achieving political position.

Television can be cruel, tantalizing the poor with images of what they can't have and stimulating bitter envy of the rich, while, at the same time magnifying the power of money to dominate the political process and thus keep the rich rich and, in consequence the poor poor.

Our government's will to enforce distributive justice is progressively sapped with each electronic election. Here, as always, unfettered money is power. Would-be reformers work under water submerged in an ocean of money.

But there is a poetic justice at work. We who worship money are running out of it at the moment of its triumph. We squandered it to build military strength. Now, our strength is weakness, holding us captive, bleeding us, inhibiting the good we might do at home and abroad, tempting us to use it crassly because we have it.

PITTSBURGH CATHOLIC
January 12, 1990

Homelessness in U.S. Scandalous (1989)

I am haunted by the homeless and the shortage in this rich country of places where they could abide. To my way of thinking a major cause of the increase in the numbers of homeless is the destruction of their habitat, that is, the type of old houses in which poor people can manage after some fashion. One way or another so many of these have been demolished.

In a shrinking city such as ours that demolition had to be horrendous because we have lost population. Less people should have meant that more, rather than less, habitable dwellings would be available. Animal species are wiped out when their habitat is destroyed; but that human species, which is made up of our homeless, multiplies when its habitat is destroyed. We now have two possible solutions: one, kill the homeless; two, restore their habitat.

Good intentions destroyed dwellings. Subsidized public housing was intended to increase the supply of decent, affordable houses but it began with tearing some down. Shacks were bulldozed, but so were adequate structures.

Developers of all sorts are the worst habitat destroyers; highway builders are a close sec-

ond. Consider the East Street Valley Expressway now gloriously triumphant. It flattened and paved over a solid community of several thousand settled and contented City residents in order that others who wanted to desert the City could do so painlessly.

Our Pittsburgh renaissance wiped out a lively and ethnically varied community in the Lower Hill, and for what? A Civic Arena, an unnecessary hospital, an apartment house, some highway spaghetti and parking lots.

The Lower Hill is gone and the rest is in danger. Walk or drive around it and you will be struck by the vacant stretches where homes used to stand.

Examples abound of civic and political blunders — Manchester on the North Side presents a wasteland where people once lived in some comfort.

In the years I lived in Homewood, I saw the housing stock decrease and the empty lots increase. Every time you heard of a fire, you could mourn one more irreparable diminution of habitat.

As a child in Ireland I remember the sad sight of abandoned rural houses — the roofs fallen, just the gables standing, gardens grown over and given to the weeds. Sometimes these were relics of the bad old days of evictions, most often of emigration. Families had given up and left the land of their ancestors.

PITTSBURGH CATHOLIC
January 6, 1989

French Revolution Was Unavoidable (1990)

Too bad the 200th Anniversary of the French Revolution came upon us at a time of resurgent conservatism, a time, also, when debacles of Communism are giving all revolutions a bad name.

One tires of pundits who claim that both the

French and Russian revolutions interrupted the course of a nice clean reform which would have resulted in calm, efficient market economies and democratic policies. Where exploitation of the weak would have been done gently, and wealth would have been accumulated decently. There would have been peace because capitalism never brings war, just Marxism does that.

In truth the Anciens Regimes of France and Russia were both rotten; they were corrupt and warlike; capriciously oppressive; also stagnant and ossified. There were solid reasons behind both upheavals.

I have had a more than passing interest in the French Revolution because I am Irish and have been marinated for 80 years in Irish poetry, folklore and prejudice. For one with these disabilities the French Revolution is notable and noble for having inspired both the modern Irish revolutionary tradition and the related Irish sense of national identity. Let me add defensively that my marination has been flavored with English poetry and English cultural prejudice.

Three national heroes, all Protestant and all influenced by French Revolutionary example and rhetoric, laid the philosophical foundation for the long Irish struggle against British domination.

Each one acted in revolutionary fashion and each gave his life. Wolfe Tone started it in 1798. The two others were Robert Emmet and Lord Edward Fitzgerald. The "rising" these three risked, and lost their all for, was ill-fated and put down brutally. The Anglo-Irish ruling class was merciless toward the Catholic peasantry who dared to raise their heads.

Was it worthwhile? I say, all in all, yes.

Another facet: France's Ancien Regime played a vital role in the survival of Catholicity in Ireland. Irish priests were trained in France during the long, often full-scale, persecution conducted by England. So the virulent persecution of the Church in France by the Revolution, and the execution of bishops, priests and nuns during the Terror, horrified the Irish clergy, and explains their pretty consistent opposition to Revolution even when it was for Irish freedom and directed against the nation's ancient oppressor.

PITTSBURGH CATHOLIC
July 21, 1989

A Warmonger's Dream

Rice consistently opposed military intervention abroad during the 1980s. He was harsh on American involvement in Panama and Grenada, but showed exceptional anger over the Iraq episode. These positions were quite unpopular to many readers of the Pittsburgh Catholic, *but Rice welcomed the controversy that ensued.*

Persian Gulf War Is Not Just (1991)

The United States has been hammering Iraq for four days and four nights. We have encountered little resistance and suffered hardly any casualties. We hit either from the air or from a distance. So far, the action has been an exercise rather than a battle.

We have trotted out and tested every deadly device in our possession, from the antique battleship to the latest electronic marvel. This phase of the war has been a munition maker's dream—it also has been a warmonger's dream.

Predictably with the first boom boom, the American public snapped to attention and saluted. Likewise the media and, with a few honorable exceptions, the Congress. In the tiresome parade of experts and commentators, contrary voices have been virtually absent. President Bush's popularity has zoomed. In the general euphoria, there have been some expressions of concern in the standard media about the aftermath, unaccompanied however by criticism of what is being done or how it is being done.

If there is any bad news, it has been suppressed and we have not heard it. Everything comes from the official well. That is due, in slight measure, to the nature of the present hostilities, but chiefly to censorship. We hear of, and are shown, successful raids, beautiful coordination, brave men and women, smart generals, great weapons and systems.

The word "censorship" is being replaced by the term "information management," but it is the same old thing. It is intriguing that our reporters have been able to ship more fact from Baghdad than from Washington or the field.

We must not let ourselves be induced to forget that Iraq did not attack us, we attacked her. In the negotiations before the attack, our president was every bit as unyielding as President Hussein.

As you try to see things in perspective, keep in mind that for all the talk of a coalition being involved, militarily, the effort is ours and the glory or shame will be ours. There is a coalition, of course, but it is of American technological prowess and Arab oil money.

PITTSBURGH CATHOLIC
February 1, 1991

End of the Battle, Not the Last Act (1991)

I became sick while on vacation, in Barbados and the malady lingered on after I came home, causing me to miss two columns.

My problem was not the usual tourist complaint but more serious. I had written about it in some detail to satisfy your curiosity, but President Bush's ground invasion led me to postpone my account.

When I arrived in Barbados, Bush was already pulverizing Iraq, and Schwartzkopf was boasting and strutting. Add to this that official spokesmen and women in and out of uniform were telling nothing, but telling it in careful and upbeat officialese.

Our perfect mobilization of forces and our president's super-perfect assembling of a coalition were acclaimed ad nauseam. We were getting pictures of our super high-tech weapons doing incredible things, but no pictures of them messing up. Bush, Cheney and Powell were sounding tough, grave, determined and so, so righteous.

There was only one TV set in our resort and it picked up CNN. Tourism was way down, but there were some Americans about. They did not watch much television and were not affected by the pro-war propaganda barrage. I heard almost no fire-breathing patriotism. These American tourists were not rich but were the comfortable sort, not many of whose children or grandchildren were in our volunteer army.

Not surprisingly, English tourists abounded. Barbados is part of the British Commonwealth. The Brits were more keen for the war than the Americans, and were cheered by their ally taking up the White Man's Burden, as Kipling called it. Perhaps it would turn out to be a last-ditch colonial effort to keep the Wogs in their place, but it was a mighty endeavor that was going well, a superb demonstration of the colonists' technological superiority.

I would go to the TV room after dinner and find a few people looking at CNN. One evening, there was a goodly crowd, more Americans than usual, who were watching something else. I was dressed in a sportshirt and jacket. Not really thinking that anything more important than the war might be going on, I went to the set and turned it to CNN. A couple of husky younger chaps came up in obvious agitation to stay my hand.

It developed that something called the Super Bowl was going to come on and they wanted the sports channel. They were rather tense, and if I had been younger, things might have turned nasty. I stood my ground, discovered that it was not even the usual pregame garbage, but pre-garbage garbage and after I heard the usual official pro-war, anti-Hussein garbage, I returned the set to sports and left.

You know, I should have profited as much from watching the Super Bowl and hearing the cliche-ridden game and pre-game chatter, as I did from listening to the war commentators and seeing the military show-and-tell video. At least there would have been an element of spontaneity in the game.

My feeling then and now is that this is not our quarrel. As I saw our state-of-the-art war machines commanding the skies, overwhelming the smaller and less technically proficient Iraqis, reducing the land to rubble, terrifying the people and smashing their infrastructure at will, I was not proud of my country.

PITTSBURGH CATHOLIC
March 1, 1991

Saddam Hussein: Bum of the Month (1991)

When Joe Louis was at his peak, he ran out of worthy opponents, so for awhile, he had a fight about once a month with some stumblebum. Sportswriters quickly coined the phrase the "Bum-of-the-Month Club." We can understand Saddam Hussein as America's current Bum-of-the-Month. His predecessors were Manuel Noriega and that stiff in Grenada.

How quickly our official propaganda machine made him into the evil one, at the same time touting him and his military as a formidable force. Bush and his Pentagon said the villain was tough and wily and his soldiers battle-hardened. So it is that when we bowled him over, euphoria followed. Please note that all the boring and repetitive analysts and experts missed the point that the guy was not even close to our class in military power or skill. Either those sages went along slavishly with the Pentagon propagandists or they were plumb ignorant of the facts.

Iraq was modernized enough to be dependent on certain modern infrastructures and amenities, which we destroyed utterly. We did not spare the ancient irrigation system which had functioned from time immemorial.

Iraq was particularly vulnerable as we dumped on it all the high-tech stuff we had amassed to battle the Soviets. Saddam's half-modern force was useless because we blinded it by taking out its air force. We beat up a blind man.

In Vietnam, we confronted the jungle. In Afghanistan, the Soviets confronted the mountains and wild, primitive, fanatical forces that did not need modern eyes or tactics.

What have we to be proud of? Licking a nation of less than 19 million people and a tired army that had not mastered modern military science? Its real soldiers were outnumbered three or four to one.

That was not a war but a punitive expedition against an outmatched foe. But it pleased George Bush, who likes the idea of being a war president á la FDR and Wilson, and our warlike people for the most part, enjoy the excitement and pumped-up tension of war, especially one against a tin horn "strong" man. Remember, we have never tasted firsthand here at home the horror of a modern war.

PITTSBURGH CATHOLIC
March 8, 1991

Make Me a Channel of Your Bombs (1991)

I could not watch a lot of the television presentation of Desert Storm. It was sickening to realize that those magic machines of ours were killing helpless people and that all that talk of precision bombing and minimum casualties and collateral damage was horse feathers.

When the "Storm" was over, I caught some post-game musing while I "grazed" during commercials and war talk. My grazing was rewarded with one priceless quote that popped out of the cherubic countenance of Gen. Norman Schwartzkopf. An interviewer, Dick Cavett, was plumbing Norman's spiritual depths, and the good general confessed that he hits the Bible.

Inevitably, he was asked what was his favorite Scriptural passage. It was, he said, some words of St. Francis. Now I was not aware that Francis was one of the authors of Scripture, but the prodigious and prestigious general may know something I don't.

I'm glad I caught the bit because of what followed. With a straight face, the general volunteered that he was sustained in his professional life by — you won't believe this — the Prayer of St. Francis which begins: "Lord make me a channel of your peace."

Cavett, who has intellectual credentials, far from dissolving in laughter or recoiling in horror, nodded respectfully. No doubt he was so grateful to the general for coming on his modest show that he was not about to appear unappreciative. Actually, the general was in the throes of camera hunger. Having been overexposed on all the big shows, he would have gone on any show, however modest.

The episode was pure Americana. It had everything — confidence that God was with you and your country and that war is peace when we wage it; and for good measure, routine piety and standard hypocrisy were laid on. The usual assumptions surfaced: we are noble; our soldiers are brave; our might is right, etc. The bit might have qualified as a sort of last word on the Gulf caper, if only the caper had ended neatly and without horrid consequences.

President Bush has not been moved to action by the tragic by-products of his popular adventure. How easily he sloughs off any responsibility for the Kurd uprising. How "sincerely" he asserts that the de facto revolt was not what he had in mind and is none of his business, although he and his lieutenants clearly called for revolt and the overthrow of Saddam.

Too bad the Kurds misunderstood! The real "too bad" is that no one took the time to make it clear to them that they simply were not important to this great power.

One wonders — are those brave people expendable, a cipher in the cruel equations of realpolitik?

Seers in the White House were relieved that, according to public opinion polls, the American people were not bothered by the overkilling of Iraqis, nor do they seem to have been bothered by Kurds slaughtered while our magnificent military machine looked on. None of that lowers significantly the extraordinarily high approval rating of the president, nor does his inaction and seeming indifference to the hunger and cold that threaten Kurdish millions.

If the polls are correct, we Americans are not a good people, but are heartless and selfish. Now the God who, the self-same polls assure us, we believe in to the extent that His popularity rivals that of George Bush, will surely punish us and our children severely. It will go worse for us that we believe in Him and actually do much in His name which we invoke ad nauseam.

But I hope against hope that the polls are wrong because I love my country. I fear for her soul.

The president vehemently has assured us (the polls again) that no American mother wants one son or daughter to die in aid of the Kurds, yet apparently, they were willing to have sons or daughters die for oil and for the Emir of Kuwait. Are we really that evil?

PITTSBURGH CATHOLIC
April 12, 1991

It Is Not Burning That Dishonors Flag (1990)

Depending on your point of view, the ritual burning of the American flag may be regarded as heinous or noble or trivial, but under no logic may it be regarded as stupid. To be stupid it would have to serve no purpose and present a pointless risk for the perpetrators.

Actually it is rewarding for them and serves their purpose. The risks entailed are minor in proportion to the payout. How else could one so effortlessly produce an uproar and draw attention? Incidentally, the furious foes of flag incineration magnify the payout with every bellow of outrage. So it is that the rewards far outweigh the punishment, and would, even if the Bill of Rights were amended. Sensible America was thinking of itself, not of protesters, when it nixed the amending.

Those who ritually burn the American flag do so for reasons that make sense to them. Some out of defiance, others to attract attention to themselves. For both types it works beautifully. They are happy as clams at the indignation they

provoke. Then there are those who burn to call attention to a cause or to protest a real injustice. These may not win supporters but they certainly plead their case dramatically.

Veterans of World War II are the engine powering the push for flag reverence. They are many and they are sincere. I am filled with disgust as I behold their honest patriotism exploited callously by demagogues.

Undoubtedly this is the beginning of the end of heavy political clout for war veterans. There was a huge crop of them after the Civil War and, for decades, they dominated politics North and South and were appreciated. Then there came a sizeable crop after the First World War, but these did not fare so well because the depression hit just as they began to need help, and they were treated heartlessly until the New Deal arrived.

Our post World War II crop was huge, and a prosperous America was good to them with the GI bill, which meant housing and college (at least for the white majority), and a Veterans Administration that was generous to all.

There will not be another large crop because old-fashioned wars are over. War itself is not over, and the world may generate another evil genius like Hitler along with a third world war, in which case we shall not have proud veterans worrying about incinerated flags, just incinerated people worrying about nothing or, if there are survivors, all in the same boat worrying about everything.

Why, at the moment, are WWII veterans so touchy? America's prosperity has faded as they are in their middle years. Worthwhile blue-collar jobs have virtually vanished, and the middle class into which many of them rose is pinched and jittery. So they worry how their kids will fare; they worry about the pensions they had counted on; and the VA has gotten a bit stingy.

I hold these veterans in high esteem even as I despise those who manipulate their sensitivities. I understand their feelings for the flag although I do not share them. As they call for respect for it they are really calling for respect for themselves and they deserve it.

I respect the flag of the United States but I do not revere it, much less worship it (I reverence the holy not the secular), and I do not accept that it has always stood for freedom and justice.

For nearly 100 years it stood for a nation which legalized slavery. Our cavalry flew it as they massacred and dispossessed our native Americans. And it has fluttered proudly in the breeze as our military have done unspeakable things in this century in the Philippines and Vietnam. Did it proudly wave over the comic opera invasion of Grenada? Or the destructive Panama fiasco?

Our flag is dishonored, not by those who burn it, but by those in power who invoke it piously in cloaking dishonorable deeds.

PITTSBURGH CATHOLIC
June 29, 1990

The Community of Catholics

Whether writing about Ireland, Poland, or Haiti, Rice was always concerned with the Catholic role if there was one. He also was involved with many issues such as the plight of AIDS sufferers and the fate of criminals and prisoners because of concerns rooted in his Christian pastoral identity.

Father Aristide Is My Kind of Guy (1991)

Father Jean-Bernard Aristide is, or soon will be, the new president of Haiti, elected as such in the first free and honest election ever in that unfortunate land. That the election was permitted to run its course was due to the extraordinary corps of observers headed by former president Jimmy Carter.

"Titid," as those who love him call Fr. Jean-Bernard, is an amazing man, small of stature but of boundless courage, hypnotic oratory, charisma and vision. In the election, he was not the candidate of the United States, or, I regret, of the Catholic hierarchy, the Protestant leadership or of any power bloc, but he was the candidate of the poor, of whom Haiti has masses upon masses. Since some of the poor are controlled by money or fear or both, the fact that 66 percent of the votes were counted as having been cast for Titid is astounding.

Fr. Aristide has been a firebrand for years. He refused to knuckle under to the fearsome "Papa Doc," Dr. Francois Duvalier, and when the monster died, he agitated for the dethronement and exile of the monster's bloated and nasty son.

The Tontons Macoutes, the murderous and merciless enforcers of Papa Doc's regime, have survived; they threaten and are threatened by Fr. Aristide. They attacked his crowded parish church during Mass in 1988, killing 12 and wounding nearly 100. He had to go on the run.

It was then that his superiors began to get uneasy — understandably so. Fr. Aristide is a native, not a foreign missionary, but he was a member of and educated by the Salesians, the great Italian missionaries who were founded by Don Bosco, one of our modern saints. His superiors and he did not see eye to eye. Mind you, the superiors were opposed to tyranny and were sincerely concerned about the poor, but they were nervous about one of their men being an ace, if peaceful, revolutionary and rabble-rouser, hip-deep in politics.

Catholic authorities are inclined to be leery of any charged-up priest, and not just for bureaucratic reasons. A priest has special clout. In the broad Catholic tradition, by reason of ordination, he has a sacramental power and is by definition more than preacher or teacher. (Protestantism is a revolt against this.) The temptation for all religious leaders is the cult of personality, the temptation to enrich oneself in money or power. Any person who observes or reads critically must realize how gullible all sorts of people are, and that neither intelligence nor education confers immunity.

When I was being trained for the priesthood at St. Vincent, we were warned over and over against the lure of self, the thinking that it was you who made the difference — your gifts or personality were doing the job.

In the course of two thousand years, the Catholic Church saw many priests get carried away. Thus the hierarchy takes the long view and favors a tight rein.

But the hierarchy has its own temptation, its own besetting sin — the temptation to follow St. Paul too literally and respect authority too much. Also, from the psalms, the rebels are bad and disorder is the great evil.

Today, we realize that the devil can appear in the guise of order. Order can mean keeping the poor quiet. The most insidious temptation for the priest or bishop or preacher is to accept inequality as the nature of things, or, worst of all, the Will of God.

Inequality and injustice are not the Will of God. It all is a cursed spite, and we were born to set it right.

Antiracism march ends peacefully, prayerfully, on Stanton Avenue in Morningside; Rice in center, September 30, 1987

Fr. Jean-Bernard Aristide is no longer a Salesian — shame on them. He is no longer permitted to offer Holy Mass — shame on someone.

He is trouble; he is explosive and fearless, but this ancient Church of ours, which is subtle and suffused with tribal memory, certainly can find a way to grasp this modern-day John the Baptist to its bosom and trust him — trust him — as he cries for justice and charity and goes full-speed ahead. I say and he says, "Damn the torpedoes."

PITTSBURGH CATHOLIC
January 4, 1991

Let Us Grieve for the AIDS Sufferers (1989)

Just the other day I ran across striking phrases from Allen Ginsberg's talk to a poetry symposium early this year.

If you remember Ginsberg at all, it may be merely as a star of the "Beat" Generation and as, later on, a guru of what it is now the fashion to dismiss as the purely emotional and randy youth rebellion of 20 years ago. If so, you have the whole thing wrong.

Those young people of the late '60s were deadly serious, and Ginsberg caught their essence. He appreciated them and they appreciated him as what he is, a prophet deserving honor.

At the symposium, while discussing its theme, "Poetry in the Next Society," Ginsberg reflected on the sad subject of AIDS. He spoke of the "karmic shadow of slavery" in our inner cities and of the constant knell of AIDS, and, as Klawans reports, "the justifiable fear that the planet itself might now have a kind of AIDS, caused by the tainting of its earth and air and water and fire."

The poet spoke of a failure to recognize our enormous grief. "The destruction of the environment and of human trust have not yet been addressed with sincerity of heart." Ginsberg called for poetry "to localize our grief."

Grief certainly was part of what I felt as I took a small part in the "Names Project" that brought "The Quilt" to Pittsburgh. That huge actual quilt with its thousands and thousands of panels bearing the names of those who died from AIDS. Grief, quiet and deep, was palpable among the living victims and the friends and relatives of all the victims, living and dead.

Grief rather than smug condemnation is what the religious person should feel in contemplating AIDS' monstrous swathe. Righteousness is the moral pitfall for the righteous.

It was beautiful that our Bishop Donald Wuerl joined us in the reading of the names. He was barely recovered from back surgery and was in pain, but there he was. There were many of prominence who cared enough to join the reading, but he stood out.

I know how consoling that was, and how sincerely appreciated because of an incident the evening before. We were at the downtown Episcopal cathedral, Trinity, for talks and reflection. Dean Werner told of his dealings with sufferers and how much it meant to them to be simply touched by another human being.

A healthy looking man with AIDS spoke simply, nothing maudlin, and there were others whom the disease had affected directly and indirectly.

My part was a brief introductory prayer. A woman came up to me, she said quietly that she had lost a son to the disease; she added that she was a Catholic and was most grateful that one of her priests was taking part. You can imagine how much it meant to her and others, the next day, when her bishop openly displayed his concern.

Some normally kind people find it hard to avoid judging where AIDS is involved, and are sorely tempted to think of the epidemic as a punishment by God. Of course there are those who are only too happy to think of it that way. And then there are the ones who have an unreasoning fear of infection.

As you look at these people you have a temptation of your own to judge them as simply narrow-minded and mean. It is hard to have a calm public evaluation of the issue. Undercurrents run deep.

Let us grieve, then, grieve for the people, not condemn but help and sympathize. Let us grieve for the planet, and condemn because here our condemnation can be fruitful; we can force action and restrain the guilty.

PITTSBURGH CATHOLIC
August 25, 1989

Fr. Greeley, a Study in Arrogance (1981)

Father Andrew Greeley, with his ineluctable bad taste and bad timing, has chosen these sad days to intensify his attacks on his chosen vocation. My half taboo, which I now break, was not to use columnar linage on his case because writing about writers is too much like reporters interviewing reporters when there is no news.

However, the right honorable and clerical gentleman saw fit to refer to me recently, releasing me temporarily from my self-imposed restriction. Now, I do not care, I honestly do not, what anyone says about me, unless he were to accuse me of a shameful crime of which I happen to be innocent. To bother me, the crime would have to be shameful and the accusation false. Father Greeley does not accuse me of anything shameful and his accusation could be true.

Arrogance, he states, is my offense, but he does not prove it. It is not arrogant to pronounce judgment on a book or a study which

you may not have read, but which has been widely publicized as was the study on schools, written by Professor James S. Coleman and produced by Father Greeley's outfit, NORC. These studies — and there have been many of them — are padded bores, as interesting as counting the bugs in the parking lot; verbiage and charts wrapped around a couple of controversial, eye-catching assertions; often, as in the instant case, the methods are shoddy and the conclusions wrong. One does not have to read the book to make this judgment, any more than one would have to eat an egg to know that it was rotten. The smell can tell.

Father Greeley is himself a study in arrogance. To present dubious science time after time and to accuse those who expose it of being anti-Catholic, is arrogance. To whine constantly that priests and bishops do not appreciate one's talent and superior knowledge is arrogance. To claim that priests are uncharitable to one another because they, he states, vent scandalous tales about their brother priests, and to relate one of these tales, giving it wide and titillating currency, is worse than arrogance. It is waspishly vicious to the living and the dead.

The deceased accused, by the way, was a real scientist. The accuser has the arrogance to think that his gossip mongering will not be seen as such, by the device of saying, after he gives the story, that he does not believe in it. This is a classic case of old biddy gossip: "Have you heard the latest? Not that I believe a word of it but . . ."

There are a couple of theories to explain Andrew. One is that he is cynical and bats out carelessly what will sell. I am inclined to the more charitable view: The lad is brooding over insults, real or imagined, that he suffered when he was a young priest and some rough and ready mates jived him unmercifully. In any all-male company, that is apt to happen to one who is different or a hot dog. Athletes are notorious offenders. Sensitive souls, of which there are more among priests than athletes, may take it hard. It is not jealousy, although the sensitive soul may think so. Myself, I experienced this, but it did not throw me, although I am not the athletic type — scrawnier far more than Greeley if one can trust photos.

My career has been controversial and I have met opposition and heavy teasing from my fellow priests, and why not? But I could dish it out as well as take it. Still can, if anyone wants to try anything. Yet I have received support and understanding from the most unlikely clerical quarters during the toughest days.

Never did I feel abandoned or persecuted by the fraternity which I love, the priesthood with all its human imperfections.

Frankly I am worried about the Reverend Andrew, as the saving virtue of restraint drains from him. Has he slipped his cable, or has his bitterness insensitized him totally? Poor man, he is the opposite of Lord Cranbrook, an English statesman of the last century, who is said to have commanded respect without generating excitement.

PITTSBURGH CATHOLIC
September 25, 1981

🕿 Fighting the Good Fights

As Pittsburgh's mighty industries shut down or moved out, unionism itself came under sustained attack on both a national and local level. Rice was called on to support many of these union struggles as well as to analyze the antiunion phenomenon for his readers. With labor under siege, Rice moved to support institutions which, though flawed, he believed were essential for the health of a democratic society.

Airline Pilots Versus Predators (1989)

In August of 1981 it was easy for Ronald Reagan to break a strike of the air traffic controllers because they were Federal employees and forbidden by law from striking. Not content with breaking the strike Reagan outlawed the union, PATCO, fired the strikers, barred them for life and prosecuted their leaders. Talk about shooting the wounded!

The poor guys would not have struck if they had not thought Reagan was their friend. They naively assumed they had earned his friendship, just the year before, by breaking ranks with the rest of labor to support him.

They were a cocky bunch and very good at

what they did, but overconfidence made them careless. They should have consulted the other aviation unions before they jumped. They also should have known their own people better, and known that some would not stand up.

A crucial minority were born again Christians who would not strike against the gov'mint; the mix of these with military personnel and supervisors destroyed the strike's effectiveness and doomed the little union.

This was a blow to all labor and could not have come at a worse time. It exaggerated the perceptions of labor's weakness and Reagan's strength. We can't blame labor, even the aviation sector, for not saving PATCO. Reagan had all the cards and the rescue would have required an industry wide shut down, which simply could not have been organized in time.

The strike of the machinists, now in progress, has managed to shut down one big airline only because of years of expensive preparation and of heavy consultation with the other unions. It is no accident that the strikers are getting a decent press, and are holding their own in the law and politics.

In today's anti-labor climate unions are natural targets of ambitious entrepreneurs. If you get a position in a unionized industry and knock out your unions, you should be able to undercut the unionized competition and get bigger and richer.

Enter Frank Lorenzo, who by legerdemain, perfectly legal in our system, got a position in aviation. He acquired three airlines, one small and two big. The big ones were in debt and losing money and he used their financial difficulties to build his empire and battle his unions.

In a brilliant move he took one of his big airlines, Continental, into Chapter 11 Bankruptcy and was allowed to cancel his labor contracts and go non-union, and, of course, slash wages. Now he is working on his other big debt-laden company, Eastern, hence the machinists' strike, but this time it is not a walkover.

The unions learned from the PATCO strike they had to be prepared, and from the Continental demarche they were all vulnerable. Frank Lorenzo would not rest until he swept them off his properties and they must unite. They also persuaded Congress to defuse the Bankruptcy Code as a union-busting device.

The Pilots are obviously the key to the success of any job action in aviation; in the Eastern strike they are not flying and the airline is almost totally shut down.

Lorenzo had burned them along with the others at Continental and he was not totally magnificent in calculating they would forget this, take a generous offer, fly his planes and shatter the strike. However, he is not finished

and is not to be underestimated. Once again he tries bankruptcy but with mixed effect; the unions were ready.

By passivity Bush helps Lorenzo a little but he cannot pull a Reagan since the strikers are not Federal employees. Congress is an uncertain quantity in spite of its Democratic majorities; it can be spooked by massive strikes. The Federal Courts? After all those Reagan appointees they are not to be trusted.

The unions and their members are to be commended for their courage and sagacity in standing up to a ruthless predator. They are doing us all a favor.

PITTSBURGH CATHOLIC
March 17, 1989

Coal Miners in Fight to the End (1989)

In both communist and capitalist countries coal miners are being treated badly. A difference is that the communist system is in violation of its principles, while the capitalist system is doing what comes naturally.

In Soviet Russia the coal miner theoretically is to be favored because his work is so essential and so dangerous. Unlike the hated exploiter who extracts and accumulates for himself, the worker contributes to the welfare of the state and his fellow men. But his unions are to serve not only him but also the state. What is ideal on paper, in practice is flawed. The interests of the miner and of the state can be far from identical.

If Russia and Poland and the other communist nations were prosperous, the miner would do very well indeed, relatively better than he does in the "Free" world. As matters stand he is battered by hard times and contradictions in the system, so he is in revolt.

With us the miner and other workers theoretically have no particular status other than what they are deemed to be worth to an enterprise — the market rate. In practice it does not work out that badly but every deviation from the cold and heartless theory was wrung painfully from entrenched and privileged owners and renters.

Unions have made a difference, and so has politics. Together they improved the lot of the worker and redistributed wealth. With the New Deal there was humane legislation and a revival of trade unions which, in the prosperity following World War II, brought a sizeable proportion of blue collar workers into the middle class.

With manufacture faltering and Reaganism rampant, the retreat began. Union strength and repute ebbed. Politics was turned and the redistribution of wealth reversed its field, flowing from the poor and the lower middle class to the rich, to the manipulators and to the financiers.

In Thatcher's Britain miners were divided and defeated and their union emasculated. Other unions fared no better. The sort of legislation we have had for years has been enacted there to blunt trade union power.

In the United States slack enforcement of the few laws that assist labor, combined with anti-labor laws already on our books, along with the decline of our industrial base has sapped trade union strength.

As the United Mine Workers union valiantly strives to save the day for their members whose work by nature is dirty, harsh and perilous, it is confronted by new and improved employer strategy and tactics.

The UMW has committed itself totally in a virtual armageddon. Pittston Coal in Virginia refused to renew the contract, cancelled its benefits to the sick and retired, and declared war. The union resists and, in this fight to the death, uses peaceful tactics borrowed from the civil rights struggle.

Back in the '20s the UMW was in similar straits and was beaten to the ground. Anti-union tactics then were brutal: the club, the gun, the blacklist and hunger. The Coal and Iron police were a ruthless private army, the Baldwin Felts were hired thugs.

Today Pittston Coal and other owners in other instances are less physical but still brutal. Hunger and blacklist are back in favor, but instead of club and gun the new private armies, such as Asset Protection Team, intimidate and attack by surveillance and electronic spying. Pittston procured a $100 million credit from a bank consortium, and hired a law firm practiced in the art of union busting.

John L. Lewis and his UMW were counted out 60 years ago but they rose again. I may not live to see it but history will repeat itself under Richard Trumka. Brave men and women, God-fearing, patriotic and conscious of what they owe to their children will not be denied.

Trumka and his people must fight to the end lest the miners and other American workers be reduced to the level of the poorest paid in undeveloped nations.

PITTSBURGH CATHOLIC
August 18, 1989

Crucial Strike Involves Grocery Chain (1991)

There is a crucial management/labor struggle gathering momentum in our Pittsburgh area. The struggle pits Giant Eagle, our largest grocery chain, against Local 23 of the United Food and Commercial Workers. Although the union called the strike, it did so reluctantly. The company on the other hand seems to have welcomed the fray and to have prepared a very model of contemporary union busting.

A blitz-krieg appears to be part of the model. Right away a decision to hire scabs, replacements was conveyed. That means that if you dare to strike, you are out, you may be out forever, and you and your family can starve your fat off. The company now says that it was misunderstood.

I prefer the word "scab," to the phrase "replacement worker," because the phrase is threatening and does duty for the employer in frightening workers, while the word is honest proletarian usage and may buck up worker morale. Giant Eagle's early proclamations did more than threaten employees. They attempted to defame the union. I did not save the clipping but I know that some sort of spokesman said the union was "an outlaw" and I think, threw in "renegade" for good measure. Actually Local 23 and its parent, UFCW, are moderates of the moderate. That phase of the blitz should be counterproductive, particularly with media people who are on the story. Incidentally, the media, so far as I can see, are behaving admirably despite Giant Eagle's huge ad budget.

A friendly judge, with indecent haste, granted a restrictive injunction against the union, and did so, even though this has not been a violent strike and Local 23 has no history of violent behavior.

Let us consider my use of the word scab, rather than some euphemism. A scab is one who takes the job of a man or woman who is on strike. Years ago it was customary to hire permanent replacement workers during a strike, and the word scab was coined. Now it is becoming customary again, and the word again fits.

This Pittsburgh area was the heart of American manufacturing and mining, and therefore bitter, violent strikes are part of our history. Scabs broke many a strike but, beginning with Roosevelt and the New Deal, the playing field became more level, and we haven't see blatant use around here of strikebreakers until recently, and those uses were few and out of the way. The public was not able to play its part in them, but now we have a conflict in which the public is key.

An individual can make a difference by refusing to cross the picket line. Most are, and the company is beginning to soften its line, having lost 80 percent of its customers.

This is an important labor action that will have consequences reaching far beyond its participants, and the labor movement realizes that. The other night I attended a rally at which a broad spectrum of labor pledged its support and formed a coalition.

At the rally, I saw members of the United Mine Workers of America. Since July of '89 they have been conducting an unfair labor practice strike against the Aloe Coal Company to the southwest of us. Although they are in a fierce struggle themselves, the miners, characteristically, turned out to help other trade unionists in trouble.

Local 23 UFCW outlined for us a bushel of legitimate grievances. Concessions that were granted temporarily seven years ago are virtually permanent. The abuse of part-time labor is horrible. Some part-timers work well over 40 hours a week without overtime. More than half of Giant Eagle's workers are barely above the minimum wage.

Giant Eagle has been closing stores and turning them over to non-union no-benefit franchisers. Local 23 wants to stop or slow down that shuffle. What alarms the union is the increasing rate at which the company has been spinning off its stores in that fashion.

I hope there will be a settlement before permanent damage is done to the company and to the workers.

PITTSBURGH CATHOLIC
May 3, 1991

Don't Let Them Take It Away (1992)

A fortnight ago, on successive evenings, I made different kinds of public utterances in support of causes, which were themselves quite different, but both very worthy. The settings and moods were quite different.

On Sunday evening, it was a mobilization and candlelight memorial for those locally and worldwide who have to live with AIDS. I had been asked to read a brief statement, and after I read it, I joined the candlelight procession which concluded the solemn occasion.

The next evening, it was a labor rally. I kicked it off with a prayer and followed with what some would call a rabble-rouser of a speech. More on this in a moment.

At the AIDS observance, my tone was more somber but equally impassioned because I feel deeply on the matter. I began: "Nothing human is alien to me." A quotation from Terence that is written in Latin on the Rice coat of arms.

AIDS is a human tragedy, and it affects all of us and not just the segment of us who are personally involved as sufferers or loved ones. This is not a time to be self-righteous, but a time to assist and give sympathy to those who have to live with the affliction, and to influence others in that direction. It is a time to encourage researchers who labor to relieve pain and find a cure, and to pressure governments to do more. This colossal and heart rending tragedy does not call for condemnation, but for compassion and understanding; for grief and love and prayer.

I find in my heart pity and sorrow for those who have to live with AIDS, and admiration for the bravery and faith of those who look death in the eye without blinking — there are many such among the sufferers.

Now that the danger of infection from the blood supply grows, compassion and understanding will grow. This is a plague, and who knows where or how it will spread? Recrimination does not make sense, tenderness and mercy do.

Moved by the observance, I drove home in the night with sadness in my heart, but wonder at the human spirit and its capacity to hope and care.

The next evening, I took part in the labor rally, a different sort of mobilization in a different struggle against a different sort of foe. This large and feisty rally was in support of the members of Local 211, Teamsters, who had been forced into a work stoppage by an arbitrary, unilateral action of The Pittsburgh Press. We were outside the plant, whose presses stood idle because their operators were locked out when 211 was forced to strike.

After asking Almighty God to bless the workers in their struggle, I stated: "If you workers are crushed by The Pittsburgh Press, every trade unionist in the United States will die a little." That is a dramatic statement, but a true one, working America is under siege. Good jobs are disappearing and being replaced by low-wage jobs, or by part-time or contingent work.

One way or another, benefits are cut or eliminated. An economist of National Planning Association predicts that the proportion of American workers covered by pensions will decline from 50 to 40 percent next year. During the Reagan/Bush years, American earnings went down, so did our standard of living. Don't let anyone tell you this is the fault of the unions; it is the fault of the stupidity and greed of those on top.

Trade unions are precious and absolutely necessary for a free society, but ours are in mortal danger. Some have been destroyed to the detriment of all working people.

Unions, in this era, engage in work stoppages only as a very last resort; it is not the union's fault that you are paperless at the

Service for Pittsburgh Press *strikers at Śt. Pamphilus Church, June 30, 1992*

moment. Strong trade unions and good wages were the foundation of the prosperity we enjoyed before Reagan, and the whole country suffers from their decline.

My final word to all the workers at The Pittsburgh Press is the old Truman slogan, "Don't let them take it away!"

PITTSBURGH CATHOLIC
May 29, 1992

1892 Homestead Centennial

The Homestead Centennial was held during the bitter Pittsburgh Press *strike. The key issue at Homestead in 1892 concerned the right of workers to have an organization of their choosing to protect their interests as workers in a time of rapid technological change. To Rice and others, it was apparent that a century had brought little progress in the area of labor relations.*

A Bloody Homestead Centennial (1992)

We are commemorating a sad centenary this year as we recall the brutal smashing in 1892 of America's strongest trade union in a crucial industry at a crucial time. The union was not merely defeated in a dispute with a company, but utterly wiped out in an unprovoked civil war in which capitalists who owned the company were clearly the aggressors.

Homestead, a borough alongside Pittsburgh, was the site, and the union was the Amalgamated Association of Iron and Steel Workers, a powerful union of skilled workers. The evil, I mean that literally, capitalists were: the sly, unctuous Andrew Carnegie and his partner, the cold and frank Henry Clay Frick. Both were upright in private life, but amoral and ruthless in business.

Before the catastrophe, the people of Homestead had been blessed with a measure of prosperity and social amenity, unique for mill towns of the period. It was a good place for a worker to live and it might have served as a model. But that was just what the capitalist duo and their ilk did not want, which accounts for the ferocity of their assault on the Amalgamated.

Andrew Carnegie was a predator who had acquired other mills, one big one lay across the river. He lusted for the Homestead works and launched a merciless price war which knocked its owners onto the ropes. In 1883, he gobbled it up at a bargain price.

Whereupon he came face-to-face with a strong union, led by men who could not be bought or intimidated, and whose members were accustomed to playing a constructive role in operations. After five years of this, Carnegie teamed up with Henry Clay Frick and took him as a partner.

The attraction of Frick was his record in the Connellsville Coke fields, where by shrewd, tough methods he absorbed or crushed his competition and grabbed control of the fields. After that, he turned on the union and destroyed it totally, thus achieving absolute control of the workers. He used the Pinkerton National Detective Agency for that violent and bloody task.

In 1889, before Frick was fully in charge of the Homestead Works, a contract with the Amalgamated was signed in which, although there was give-and-take, the union did well. That was it, and when the contract was coming up for renewal on July 1, 1892, both Carnegie and Frick agreed the union must go.

The sanctimonious Andy went on vacation to Scotland and the vicious Henry was left to do what was required. As in the Coke fields, Frick acted coldly, effectively and without scruple or regret.

There were negotiations in the Spring and Summer of '92, but they were a sham, and the Amalgamated was presented with a set of non-negotiable demands that it could not accept. Meanwhile, Frick was preparing for war. A fence was erected around the mill and Pinkerton was awarded another dirty job. Then Frick said he would deal only with individual workers, no union. On June 29, he closed the mill and fired everyone.

The Amalgamated did not play dead and had prepared as best it could for what was coming. As a plus, it enjoyed the support of the wider community. As matters turned out, the union was no match in this capitalistic country for the power of money or for the solidarity of the upper class.

In a pitched battle on the shores of the Monongahela, Pinkerton's 400 well-armed strike breakers were defeated and forced to surrender. Three of them were killed but the resistance lost seven.

Then the state militia came in, busted the union, cowed the populace, and occupied the town for a year. Evil triumphed, and nightfall came to the steel mills and valleys, all of them. Organized labor in America was set back and its growth stunted for decades.

When I arrived here as a lad in 1920, this steel-dominated area was so in thrall to the power of industry and capital, that it was almost like one vast company town. . . .

PITTSBURGH CATHOLIC
July 3, 1992

Reflections on Carnegie and Frick (1992)

Andrew Carnegie got what he wanted out of life with one possible exception. In those days before income tax, he accumulated and accumulated until he was unbelievably rich. He was venerated worldwide by the people who — so far as he was concerned counted — the well-connected, the wealthy, the comfortable and the respectable. Also, come to think of it, many ordinary people.

The one thing he didn't get was children. I presume he wanted them, but I neither know nor care.

He gave lavishly and wisely so that his name became synonymous with enlightened patronage. Music halls, libraries, foundations, good works. Having subdued the steel towns and their workers, he gave them cultural and recreational facilities.

Characteristically, he did not permanently endow what he gave the workers and their communities, but arranged that posterity had to come up with the resources to continue what he started, keeping his name, of course, on the buildings. He seems to have pulled that off successfully and more or less permanently.

It is an irony of history that the scholarly commemorative lectures on the evils which Andy and his partner, Henry Clay Frick, visited upon Homestead and its workers will be given in the town's Carnegie Library.

Carnegie and Frick fell out, and it seems that, when Andy wanted to make up, Henry told him he would see him in Hell. I'm sure the quote has been doctored to make it seem that Frick regarded his smashing of unions and people as wrong, but there is no evidence to back that up. Frick went to his grave at peace with himself, as did the little Scotsman.

They were lucky that a flighty and attention-seeking anarchist, Alexander Berkman, made a clumsy assassination attempt on Frick, who played his wounds for all they were worth, and smeared the defeated union leaders who had nothing to do with the stupid attempt.

The simplest explanation for Berkman is, as Jimmy Durante used to say, "everybody wants ta get in tha act." I offer an Irish saying for Carnegie and Frick's public relations good fortune, "The devil's children have the devil's luck."

Carnegie at least tried to give the workers something in place of the freedom and dignity that he took from them. Frick? He did not give a tinker's dam for them. As he told a biographer, labor was a commodity like any other to be purchased as cheaply as possible. In that icy heart there was no compunction.

Up until a couple of decades ago, Carnegie Libraries tried to sanitize their holy founder's reputation by not carrying, or by hiding, damaging sources. Frick's daughter, Helen Clay Frick, used the power of the purse as long as she lived, which was very long, to prevent the truth from coming out. She died rather recently. The heiress threatened to sue publishers who planned books exposing her nasty papa, and they pulled back.

She uses her money from beyond the grave to maintain the Frick home in Pittsburgh as a sort of shrine with reproductions of great art and lectures and exhibits. It is significant that the Frick Museum, which houses the real treasures of art, is located in New York City, and not here where he made his rotten money.

History itself may well have been bought, and the reputations of the twin "malefactors of great wealth" may remain undimmed by their century old crime against humanity.

The American steel industry, which they fashioned in their own images, has not done so well. This industry elevated protectionism to a fine art and kept foreign competition at bay; meanwhile, it waxed fat and got stupid. The industry also suffered from the squelching of the worker initiative. So did most of American manufacturing, and now the country pays the price for that villainy and greed.

By the time you read this, the centenary observations will be over. The luck of those rascals having held, there is a Pittsburgh newspaper shutdown which prevents the details of the observance and its revelations.

PITTSBURGH CATHOLIC
July 10, 1992

Homestead Homily (1992)

Our great nation is not eternal, but while it lasts, let us hope that there will be those like us today, who will look beyond the monuments, and keep alive the memory of the defeated. More than that, strive lest the power of greed rot its heart. Let us pray that the spirit and idealism and solidarity of the poor, the discriminated-against will endure and their voices will be heard on earth as it surely is in heaven. . . .

We celebrate the birth of our nation's Freedom, this weekend. But here in Homestead we commemorate, not celebrate, because this is the centenary of a defeat of freedom; the waging of a civil war which decided whether money or the people, the workers, would prevail. Money won.

I heard the radio this morning saying this Mass would remember the 10 who died. All ten, even the three Pinkertons? Yes, they were human beings. Probably Appalachian whites, poor, mercenaries.

The seven others who died were workers or their supporters among the people. Some of them lay in unmarked graves and today when Mass is over, we will go to the cemetery to mark their graves and remember them and their sacrifice.

Carnegie and Frick, who prevailed and ruled over this valley unchecked, passed on their power and domination. They too died and went to judgment. Their power was evanescent. Sometimes it seems that the power of their money lives after them. They have left behind them great names and monuments, but they too will pass and crumble into dust.

HOMESTEAD CENTENNIAL MASS
July 6, 1992

Rice at a Mon Valley rally for Jesse Jackson, September 8, 1987

Rice at 87

Epilogue

⏢ Catholic with a Smile

Reflecting on his long and contentious career, Rice has few regrets. His priesthood gave him security and a platform from which he could exercise his talents. He consistently viewed the Church with humor and affection.

Ghosts, Demons In; Flying Saucers Out (1990)

Samuel Johnson said that when he was young he had been afraid of ghosts, but now that he was old he would like to see one. Same with me. As a small boy in Ireland, I was not only scared of ghosts, but felt they were plentiful. Now, like Doctor Johnson, I would be rather glad to see one. Not so for demons. Ghosts are not to be confused with demons, who are of the devil.

I had a lively belief in the existence of him and the possibilities of glimpsing him, or one of his associates. Still believe he exists and functions, but do not expect to run into him, at least not in this life. And in the next, I really want to avoid him.

That ghosts are being taken seriously again, as is the devil, was not expected. I recall an essayist writing some time ago that, when people believed in ghosts, there were a lot of reports of them being sighted, but in modern times the flaky see flying saucers. No one expected flying saucer stories to wane and ghost stories to wax.

Of course, there are ghosts and ghosts. Poltergeists, noisy ghosts, are different from the others, and these days there are more stories about them. Do I take them seriously? Naw. I don't think I would bother to exorcise one. Would be more likely to get psychological counseling for the seer. Not that I have not performed exorcisms.

In the old days with every Baptism there was an exorcism. I have not done a real one, although more than once, when some dear old soul, not necessarily a Catholic, was bothered by a ghost, I faked an exorcism. I would give a convincing performance; didn't see any ghosts scampering away but calmed a few worried minds.

Some priests and even a cardinal in New York are bothered about ghosts and are into exorcisms. The cardinal involved is a very nice man and I would not offend him for the world, but to me, ghost stories are for the birds, excluding cardinals.

A ghost is the soul of a human being that cannot rest, perhaps because of unfinished business. A very old rectory in the Greensburg diocese was supposed to harbor a ghost who would riffle the pages of a breviary presumably because a priest, who had lived there, missed his obligation too often.

I should like to meet that ghost and have a chat, but I would not exorcise him and spoil his fun. It might do some of our young priests good to encounter him and talk things over.

Bishop Wright was grumbling once about such old wives' tales, and I got a chuckle out of him by saying I rather enjoyed and half believed them. Catholic ghosts, by the way, reside in Purgatory. Others I hesitate to say.

A demon is a fallen angel and might be a nasty customer unless he were being nice and doing favors to get you on his side. If you meet one of these, remember the classic warning against making a pact with the devil. A bad idea, as Faustus discovered.

A visionary once reported on devils at work. At the gate of a very wicked city there was just one devil, and he was loafing. Nearby in the forest, around the hut of a holy hermit, thousands of devils were busy as hell.

PITTSBURGH CATHOLIC
March 30, 1990

Living Long May Be a Problem (1990)

Being old and subject to the aging process has not destroyed my enjoyment of life. Of course, I am in rather good health, thank God, having survived lots of stuff when I was younger, and come to think of it, older. I am mobile and can drive. Very importantly, I can read and write. My priesthood is a source of happiness. I have always enjoyed being a priest and am fortunate that, although I am retired, it is possible for me to keep a bit active in my beloved calling.

So, I am not ready to cash in my chips and leave the game of life, but I do not want to hang around indefinitely. That's not up to

me, of course, but depends on genes and the will of God. Be assured of one thing, I won't let "them" keep me ticking by extraordinary means, unless they sneak up on me when I'm unconscious and disregard my explicit instructions. A sick person is entitled to relief from pain, and also to die in peace.

PITTSBURGH CATHOLIC
November 16, 1990

Ex-Senator Tower Takes the Pledge (1988)

Seeing a Southern Baptist "take the pledge" — he calls it an oath — on TV was hilarious and it dredged up some old jokes about this Irish contribution to sobriety, also some political memories.

Seriously "the pledge" was a useful ingredient of the temperance movement that got under way in Ireland almost 150 years ago. An Irish-American Catholic temperance movement, pledge and all, flourished until it was killed by, of all things, Prohibition, something Catholics were generally opposed to. Strange that, when "don't drink, make or sell" became the law, although people still drank, fiery crusades against drunkenness ceased forever.

Booze was a huge political issue until Prohibition failed and, in 1933, was repealed. When Al Smith ran for President in 1928, he was defeated as much for his stance against Prohibition, as for his being a Catholic. The Southern Baptists might drink wet but they voted dry and the "Solid South" bolted the Democratic Party over Al.

Almost apropos of this, Dave Lawrence used to tell about a local Irish saloon keeper, Sean Hayes, who operated in the shadow of the Court House all during the Noble Experiment. Gradually over the years a body of useful laws and regulations governing places which sold drink (alcoholic beverages to you) had developed. With Prohibition all of them became moot, but Sean, as a pious and ethical man, would observe them as scrupulously as before. Curtains were drawn, and the place closed and opened according to the no longer prevailing prescriptions. No minors, no women. Of course, he was a law breaker, but who cared? A quiet, decent man, he was never busted.

As for the pledge, you "took" it from a priest and you could take it for varying periods. Some wise and tolerant old priests used to advocate short spans which were less of a strain on the periodical drinker.

Chap trying to get off the cause: "Father, I would like to take the pledge."

Father: "Fine, fine my dear man, now, for how long would you be takin' it?"

Dear Man: "Well Father, I generally take it for life."

PITTSBURGH CATHOLIC
March 10, 1988

Drawing the Line at Moving Statues (1989)

When Mary appeared along with St. John and a Lamb on the gable end of a house in the village of Knock, Co. Mayo, older Irish priests were, to put it mildly, skeptical. They had no trouble with apparitions or miracles but, in Ireland!

They were the greatest fans of Lourdes and when Fatima came along they went for that too. But Knock was different, not only was the Blessed Mother not alone in that appearance but there were rumors that the crowd, which witnessed it rather late in the evening, possibly was provided by the closing of the local pub.

I have not been to this site in the West of Ireland but it is a place of pilgrimage and the occasion of two miracles that I know of. The first miracle was the success of an old Monsignor, then pastor of Knock, in convincing the Republic of Ireland that an International Airport should be provided next door to his Church. The second miracle is that the bloomin' Airport is doing very well commercially. So much for the power of prayer and a shrewd old Monsignor.

Now I don't object to apparitions as such, it is when statues or pictures of Mary do things that I get uneasy. Sometime ago I was ready to take off on weeping pictures but, since our Orthodox Brothers are strong for weeping Icons, I shall forbear; my respect for them and their traditions overrides any smart-aleck American prejudices.

We have to draw the line at statues that shake. Fittingly enough it is in the town of Bally Spiddal (Ireland, where else?) that one of Mary's statues has been seen to move or shake. I simply can't believe that Mary goes about doing this sort of thing, even in the Irish mist.

Before we go any further, let me give my Marian credentials: I pray the Rosary every day, even if I am as sick as a dog and can't read my Breviary. The Memorare is my favorite prayer, and not only do I say the Hail Mary often, but always give it as penance in Confession. A very old-fashioned Catholic, you will agree.

This came from my grandmother and a sweet aunt in Ireland and from my father. Papa was a man of deep manly faith.

Miracles can happen because God can intervene in earthly affairs if He wants to, and He may want to, especially if His Mother pushes Him. I don't ask for Our Blessed Mother's assistance for myself. I simply don't pray for earthly personal favors; of course, I pray for peace, and for the poor and the sick and the troubled. Praying for the grace of a happy death doesn't count, anybody not a complete lunatic has sense enough to do that.

I used to say a Hail Mary to St. Anthony when I lost something, but at my age I have given that up because I lose and misplace so many things that I would drive the poor man crazy. Not that I disapprove of devotion to him, I revived his novena when I was pastor in St. Joseph's, Natrona.

Of Mary's apparitions, the only modern one I take seriously is Lourdes. The commercialization of the town of Lourdes does not bother me. Even if the Pope goes for Fatima, I don't. The people involved in Fatima quote Mary as saying the sort of gloom and doom stuff she wouldn't say. And they keep chattering and nattering with "messages" as long as they live.

Guadalupe, on the other hand, is great as is the whole legend and the beautiful peasant faith it inspires. All the Latin American Marian stories are credible because the peasants down there needed her desperately to soften their transition from paganism to the harsh side of Spain and Portugal. They need her more than ever today.

For much the same reason I shall not quarrel with Medjugorje in Yugoslavia, other than to wonder why she waited so long.

Let me make one thing perfectly clear, at my age and given the condition of my body and soul, I don't want any trouble with Mary — I need all the help I can get.

PITTSBURGH CATHOLIC
January 27, 1989

Fighter with a Heart

Looking back on his activities in the labor movement, Rice has had second thoughts about some of the Communist Party union leaders he fought so relentlessly. Opposing their objectives, he nevertheless now recognizes their contribution. Throughout his life, no matter the temper of the times, he has never abandoned the struggle for social change and has never stopped searching for a better understanding of the history that he helped to shape.

Steve Nelson: An Honorable Antagonist (1993)

At the age of 90, Steve Nelson died last week in a New York hospital. His passing got brief notice locally, but the New York Times carried a sizeable obituary.

In the heyday of the Communist Party in the United States, Steve was on the national board and was recognized as one of its most effective organizers.

The party grew strong in the Depression and New Deal days, but it really blossomed and attained a certain popularity during World War II, when the USSR was our ally and Stalin rallied his country to smash Hitler's invasion. At its peak, the CPUSA [Communist Party USA] had 70,000 members. As the Cold War developed, that began to change and membership dropped off.

It was at this point in 1948 that Nelson reluctantly returned to Pittsburgh to head up the local comrades. It was also at this point that anti-

Communist hysteria began to gather strength.

The Pittsburgh Press, of happy memory, laid down a barrage on Steve Nelson and painted his coming as a stepped up invasion of traitors.

The famed Honorable Michael Mussmanno, Justice of the Supreme Court of Pennsylvania, and justly acclaimed as a champion of the coal miners and a host of liberal causes, author of books, one of which became a great movie, prepared to roar into battle against the Communist Party and its new local leader.

What followed was Red-baiting of the loudest and most intensive sort and a travesty of justice. Mussmanno was a magnificent orator, colorful and a lover of the limelight.

He called Steve Nelson the prowling hand of Russia in our midst, a world revolutionary, a terrorist and the most dangerous man in America.

In 1949, the Communist Party held a legal convention at the North Side Carnegie Library, precipitating a riot. I was not part of this action. Mike Fitzpatrick of the United Electrical Workers, organized a counter-demonstration, parking a sound truck outside the hall. He gathered a crowd and worked them to a frenzy.

I was not going to be there, but a call came from Harvey Scott, superintendent of police: "you have to come down and see if you can quiet things." I did my best, but in vain. Finally Harvey said: "You have to help them out safely; only you can do it."

I then headed the police squad that brought the frightened Communists out of the danger zone. Still, I was blamed for starting the riot; even Nelson believed that.

I was anti-Communist and wanted to force them out of leadership in the trade union movement. I did not favor violence and kept my followers from it; besides, the CPUSA was a legal political party.

Steve Nelson resigned from the party in 1957 after Khrushchev told all, and related the evils perpetrated under Stalin. He did not do it flamboyantly and did not denounce his old comrades.

I have a copy of his autobiography and noted this morning that it has his autograph.

In his amazing career, he worked in China to assist the Communists there and get money to them during their revolution that overthrew Chiang Kai-shek. He attended the Leninist school in Moscow to improve his grasp of Marxist theory and tactics. In Spain he was a leader of the Abraham Lincoln Brigade, that is, the American contingent which fought against Franco and for the Loyalists. In America he was president of the Veterans of the Brigade.

An indication of his magnanimity is that a few years ago he invited me to speak at their annual banquet. He had forgiven my bygone hostility to all he once stood for, especially in the trade union struggle.

Mike Mussmanno acted as the prosecuting attorney in the trial he instigated. The presiding judge was a protege of his. Steve could not find a lawyer to represent him, and had to do the best he could. Steve was sentenced to 20 years under a Pennsylvania statute, and served hard time, often in the hole, until the stupid statute was declared unconstitutional by the U.S. Supreme Court. All sorts of illegalities and indignities were heaped upon him, but eventually he walked away a free man.

Interestingly enough, Steve in his book writes that many actions which I and my allies condemned the American Communist Party for, were its own grave mistakes.

All in all, an honorable man. May he rest in peace.

PITTSBURGH CATHOLIC
December 24, 1993

Enemies, I Have Known a Few (1990)

I have no lingering resentments, and do not brood over old enemies or injuries. No smoldering grievances. I am not angry at any of those old enemies, living or dead, thank God. Actually I did not bear hatred toward individuals, that is, after I grew up. And now I nurse no old wrongs or wounds.

Battles I have had aplenty, but in my adulthood they were never personal and, when I attacked people, it was over their actions or positions. I have lambasted employers and capitalists, Communists or their supporters, crooks in and out of unions, conservative politicians and the like. When they hit back, I did not take it personally. If you hit, you must expect to get hit.

I harbor more hostility toward recent presidents of the United States than toward any old antagonist. Reagan, because of what he did to the poor, and his casual cruelty to small, weak nations. Nixon also, over his bombing of Cambodia and his pointless prolongation of the Vietnam War. Johnson? He had a good and bad side and he paid for his sins. I don't think about him very often. Bush is earning my hostility, but I really don't think that worries him.

A former enemy died the other day. Harry Bridges, the feisty leader of the Longshoremen of the West coast. 'Arry, a native of Australia, probably was a Communist early in his career, although it was never proved, and he never admitted it. Why should he have? Regardless, he was a good trade unionist and an excellent leader. He survived my attacks and innumerable others. Having reached old age, he died at peace.

Let me add, I feel less bad over my violent assaults of 40 years ago on Stalinists in the American labor movement after the Soviet admission that Stalin had 15,000 Polish officers, prisoners of war, slaughtered in 1940. I knew stuff of that sort when I was conducting that battle. As for Harry, I am glad he won and that no one laid a glove on him. I've had a few laid on me, but no knockouts, perhaps, that is why I too am serene, more or less.

I never was crushed or felt crushed. I've been beaten but always got in my own licks. I laid low for a brief period but never kowtowed as men in authority in the diocese ran over me; I rolled with the punches, made a comeback and outlived them all.

God forgive me for that last sentiment!

PITTSBURGH CATHOLIC
April 20, 1990

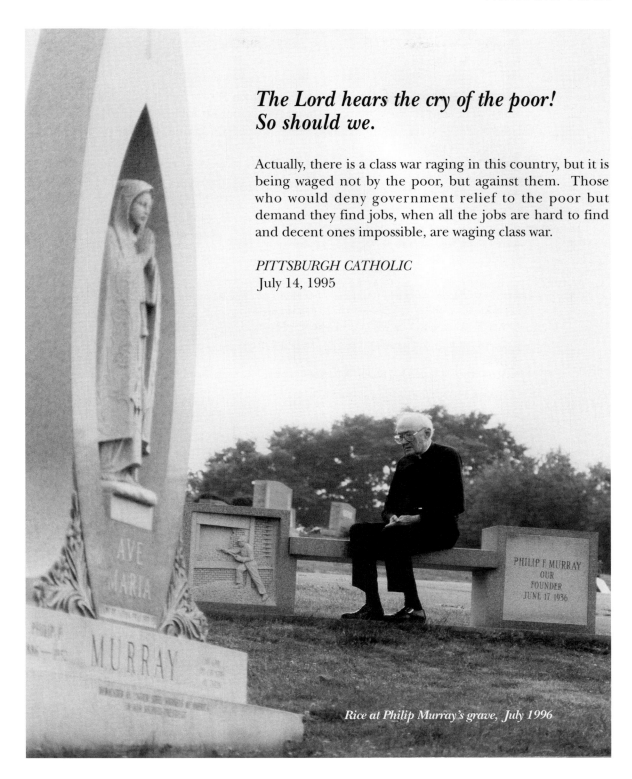

The Lord hears the cry of the poor! So should we.

Actually, there is a class war raging in this country, but it is being waged not by the poor, but against them. Those who would deny government relief to the poor but demand they find jobs, when all the jobs are hard to find and decent ones impossible, are waging class war.

PITTSBURGH CATHOLIC
July 14, 1995

Rice at Philip Murray's grave, July 1996

Photo Credits

Most of the photos used in this book are from Rice's extensive personal collection of photos. Many were sent to him by sympathetic news photographers and most have not been published before. Where the photographer, studio, or news agency is known, it is credited. Additional information or credits for photos are welcome and will be included in any future edition.

FRONTISPIECE:
Charles Owen Rice, 1937. Photo: Pittsburgh Press. Rice Collection.

REBEL ROOTS
Family portrait: Father Michael; Mother, Anna; and sons, Charles and Patrick, 1910. Rice Collection.

Patrick and Charles in Ireland, 1919. Rice Collection.

Patrick, his father Michael, and Charles on porch of Bailey Avenue home in Mt. Washington, Pittsburgh, 1921. Rice Collection.

Charles with neighbor boy, 1923. Rice Collection.

Duquesne University graduation photo, 1930. Rice Collection.

Fr. Peter Rice (uncle) and Charles, 1931. Rice Collection.

Fr. James Cox's unemployed army leaving Pittsburgh for Washington, D.C. Courtesy: Western Pennsylvania Room, Carnegie Library of Pittsburgh.

PICKET LINE
John L. Lewis and Rice at first convention of the CIO, November 14, 1938 (Photo Norman-Schmidt Studies). Rice Collection.

Rice, Fr. Carl Hensler, and Msgr. George Barry O'Toole at meeting of Local 325, Canning and Pickle Workers at H.J. Heinz Co., June 1937. Rice Collection.

Rice watches furniture loading on House of Hospitality truck, March 1939. Rice Collection.

Rice addresses Little Steel Strike rally at Youngstown Sheet and Tube plant, Struthers, Ohio, June 6, 1937. Photo: ACMEO. Rice Collection.

Rice and Clarence Hathaway, editor of the Daily Worker, after debate before more than 2,000 people on October, 10, 1938. Rice Collection.

Founding convention of the CIO in Pittsburgh, November 14, 1938. On stage: Cornelius D. Scully, Mayor of Pittsburgh; John L. Lewis, president of United Mine Workers, and the CIO; Sidney Hillman, president of Amalgamated Textile Workers, and Rice. Rice Collection.

Rice with two altar boys, Dukie Pratt and Willie Hyatt, at the House of Hospitality, circa 1941. Rice Collection.

At the House of Hospitality. To Rice's right is Alan Kistler who subsequently became organizing director for the AFL/CIO, October 1939.

REDS AND WORKERS
Anti-Communist Riot at Carnegie Hall, Northside, Pittsburgh, April 2, 1949. *Pittsburgh Post-Gazette.* Courtesy: Western Pennsylvania Room, Carnegie Library.

Franklin D. Roosevelt opens Terrace Village housing project in Pittsburgh, October 11, 1940. Rice looking on in upper left. Artone Studio, Rice Collection.

Pat Fagan, Rice, and Eleanor Roosevelt in 1940. Rice Collection.

Rice on picket line. West Penn Hospital Workers strike, 1941. Rice Collection.

Rice as union spokesman in steel strike, 1946. Rice Collection.

Rice doing national radio broadcast on ABC two days before nationwide steel strike, January 19, 1946. Rice Collection.

Mayor David Lawrence introduces President Harry Truman to Rice during a campaign whistle stop in October 1948. To Rice's right is Arthur Goldberg, steelworker attorney, and steelworker secretary David McDonald. Directly behind Rice is Jock Yablonsky. Rice Collection.

Mayor David Lawrence, Rev. Benjamin Mass, S.J., Philip Murray, and Rice at ACTU communion breakfast, 1952. Photo: Slantis, *Pittsburgh Post-Gazette.* Rice Collection.

Rice (seated at center) in labor school class for Braddock steel workers. Pat Hammil is the speaker. Rice Collection.

Phil Murray speaking to CIO convention during World War II. Caption: "Work, keep working. Produce, keep producing." Courtesy Russ Gibbons

Phil Murray leaving a Steel Working Organizing Committee meeting in 1937. To the right, union publicist, Vince Sweeney. Courtesy Gary Hubbard, USWA. Permission: AP/Wide World Photos.

Rice teaching at Braddock Labor School, 1950. Rice Collection.

PEACE AND JUSTICE

Leading Pittsburgh March for Peace and Justice, May 24, 1969. From left: Byrd Brown, Rennie Davis, Donna Allen, Rice. Rice Collection.

Black demonstrators confronting police in riot gear during construction jobs demonstration, August 1969. Byrd Brown in center. Courtesy: Western Pennsylvania Room, Carnegie Library.

Rice marching arm-in-arm with Dr. Martin Luther King, Jr., at spring mobilization march to the United Nations, April 15, 1967. Rice Collection.

Rice at press conference in New York City on August 29, 1967, announcing the march on the Pentagon. Speaking in center are Rap Brown and Jerry Rubin. Photo: *Newsday*. Rice Collection.

Rice, Corretta Scott King, Mr. and Mrs. Benjamin Spock, and Dick Gregory at the march on the Pentagon, October 21, 1967. Rice Collection.

Rice waiting to address a rally in Point State Park, May 24, 1969. Photo: Kevin Donavan. Rice Collection.

Rice speaking at Vietnam War protest in Boston, January 1968. Rice Collection.

Rice visiting with Billy Hines in prison. Rice Collection.

Rice addressing antiwar rally, 1969. Rice Collection.

Rice addressing antiwar teach-in at the University of Pittsburgh. Rice Collection.

Rice accepting draft cards, December 4, 1967. Rice Collection.

Rice leading picket line for Pittsburgh hospital workers organizing drive, early 1970s. Rice Collection.

Rice giving sermon at the funeral for United Mine Worker reformer Jock Yablonski, his wife and daughter. January 1970. Rice Collection.

Rice on picket line at Jefferson Memorial Cemetery. Rice Collection.

REFLECTIONS ON DECLINE

Rice marches with Methodist minister Charles Rawlings in Tri-State Conference on Steel protest of steel mill closures at U.S.Steel stockholders' meeting in Pittsburgh, May 1981. Mike Stout and

Matt Bartholomew carry coffin. Photo: The Daily News Publishing Co. Rice Collection.

George Becker and Lynn Williams lead support march for Pittsburgh Press strikers, September 1, 1992. Courtesy USWA.

Rice with mill worker at closed J&L steel mill in Pittsburgh. *New York Times*, June 7, 1982. Photo: John L. Alexandrowicz. Rice Collection.

Rice with Mon Valley dissident Ron Weisen, President USW Local 1397, in front of shut Homestead mill, August 13, 1986. Photo: Gene J. Puskar, permission: AP/Wide World Photos. Rice Collection.

Antiracism march ends peacefully, prayerfully, on Stanton Avenue in Morningside. Rice in center. September 30, 1987. Photo John Kaplan, Pittsburgh Press. Rice Collection.

Service for *Pittsburgh Press* strikers at St. Pamphilus Church, June 30, 1992. Rice Collection.

Rice at a Mon Valley rally for Jesse Jackson. September 8, 1987. Photo: *Pittsburgh Press*. Rice Collection.

EPILOGUE

Rice at 87. Photo: Richard Bobak.

Rice at Phillip Murray's grave, July 1996. Photo: Charles McCollester

CREDITS

Charles McCollester and Monsignor Rice at the commemoration of the sixtieth anniversary of his ordination to the priesthood, June 17, 1994. Photo: Salvador Portugal.

Book Project Committee

Purpose / The committee rasied funds to cover the editing, design, photographs, and other production costs of this book. A part of the funds will be used to purchase copies of the book for schools, libraries, seminaries, and union halls. A portion of the proceeds will go to establish the Charles Owen Rice Labor Education and Social Justice Fund (COR Fund, Foundation for IUP).

PROJECT DIRECTOR
Dr. Charles McCollester: Pennsylvania Center for the Study of Labor Relations, IUP

CHAIR
Lynn Williams: President, USWA (retired)
Co-Chairs
George Becker: President, USWA
Bill George: President, Pennsylvania AFL-CIO
Monsignor George Higgins: Catholic University of America
Cecil Roberts: President, UMWA
Andy Stern: President, SEIU
John Sweeney: President, AFL-CIO
Richard Trumka: Secretary-Treasurer, AFL-CIO
Rosemary Trump: President, SEIU Local 585

VICE-CHAIRS
Robert Argentine: Carpenter's District Council
Clifton Caldwell: UFCW Local 23
Memory of Alfred "Andy" Johnson: IBEW, Local 5
David Levdansky: PA State Representative
Martin Morand: PA Center for Study of Labor Relations
John Murray: President, Duquesne University
Andrew "Lefty" Palm: District 10, USWA
Lawrence Pettit: President, IUP
Tony Rinaldi: District 20, USWA
John Vento, Pennsylvania AFL-CIO
Bishop Donald Wuerl: Catholic Diocese of Pittsburgh

MEMBERS
Gary Batykefer: Sheetmetal Workers Local #12
Sam H. Beglar: Laundry and Dry Cleaning International Union
Meyer Berger: M. Berger Company
William Bywater: President IUE
William Coyne: US Congress
Tom DeBruin: Hospital Workers, 1199 SEIU
John DiTolla: Branch 84, Letter Carriers
Al Fondy: Pittsburgh Federation of Teachers
Ted Kirsh: Pennsylvania Federation of Teachers
Sol Hoffman: Vice President, ILGWU
Bishop John B. McDowell: Catholic Diocese of Pittsburgh
Joe Molinero: Teamsters, Local 211
Nick Molnar: District 2, UMWA
Tom Murphy: Mayor of Pittsburgh
Jack Shea: Region #1, IUE
Ed Yankovich: District 4, UMWA
Jack Yoedt: SEIU, Local 29

SUPPORTERS
Robert Ewanco, Teamsters 636; Judy Heh, AFSCME District Council 90; Representative Herman Mihalich; Samuel J. and Helen P. Papa; Pennsylvania Labor History Society; Paul Stackhouse, Allegheny Country Labor Council; Rich Stanizzo, Pittsburgh Building Trades Council; Teamsters Local 211; UFCW Local 23; Rose Trump.

CONTRIBUTORS
AFSCME Local 763; ABGWU Region 4; Albert Onda; Alice Hoffman; Amy Ballinger; Ancient Order of Hibernians South Hills Division #1; Andrew J. Kocerka; Armstrong-Clarion Central Labor Council; Bernard Kleiman; Butler County United Labor Council; Capuchin Friars Province of St. Augustine; Carl L. Bectol; David and Joanne Docchio, USWA; Desmond J. Nevrohr; Domenic Papalia; Ed Ghearing, USWA; Edward J. Wekler; Father Weithorn, Province of St. Augustine; Fred Heinhold, Jr. ; Gary and Ann Hubbard; Glen Plummer; Glenn Eastley, IBEW Local 149; Great Steel Strike Committee; Hotel and Restaurant Employees Local 57; Howard Brandt; IBEW Local 5; James M. Maslanka; James A. Young; Jamie D. Wright; Janet Zerick; Jeanette Stump; Joe Oxenreiter; John Seidman; John A. Remark; John Edward White; John L. Haer; Johnstown Regional Labor Council; Joseph D. Miller and John McIntyre, IBEW Local 5; Judith Douds; Kathryn "Kitty" Knight; Laborers District Council of Western PA; LDCIU Local 141; Local 1342 District 10 USWA; Local 13640 District 10 USWA; Local 1016 District 10 USWA; Mary Bartley, Memory of Rev. Thomas R. Bartley; Mary Anne Gorman; Maurice Goyette; Mayor James Joyce; Memory of Mrs. Berton; Memory of Alice Peurala, USWA Local 65; Memory of Frank G. Patemra; Memory of Deceased Members of Timczyk Family; Memory of Joseph P. Kujovsky; Meyer and Merle Berger Family Foundation; Michael C. Herman; Michelle Fagan; Molly Rush; Mr. and Mrs. James English; Mr. and Mrs. Charles Kennedy; Newspaper Guild of Pittsburgh; Parishoners of St. Anne Church; Patrick Fagan; Patrick P. Coyne; Paul A. Stackhouse, Sr.; Pittsburgh Metro Area Postal Workers Union; Representative Sara Steelman; Representative Tom Micholvic; Rev. David A. Boileau; Rev. James W. Garvey; Rich Gilardi; Robert Cunningham; Roy Schrenk, IAM Local 1060; Rudy Richtar; Russ Gibbons; Ruth King Grumblatt; Ruth E. Wilner; SEIU Local 585; Stephanie Gabor; Teamsters Local 211; Thomas and Georgeann Foerster; Thomas and Dee Murrin; Thomas P. O'Malley; Timonthy and Virginia Trant; UFCW Local 23; UFCW Local 1776; United Jewish Federation; USWA Local 1002; USWA Local 1082; USWA Local 1163; USWA Local 1187; USWA Local 1189; USWA Local 1408; USWA Local 1557; USWA Local 1869; USWA Local 1905; USWA Local 2227; USWA Local 2389; USWA Local 2632; USWA Local 3968; USWA Local 6189; USWA Local 7245; USWA Local 7487; USWA Local 7814; USWA Local 8047; USWA Local 8183; USWA Local 8302; USWA Local 8790; USWA Local 8790; USWA Local 9125; USWA Local 9204; USWA Local 12050; USWA Local 12050; USWA Local 13987; USWA Local 14659; USWA Local 14707

Suggested Readings

BIOGRAPHY

McGeever, Patrick J. **Rev. Charles Owen Rice: Apostle of Contradiction**. Pittsburgh, Pa.: Duquesne University Press, 1989. A seriously flawed but useful book. This biography has the facts straight, but the analysis is weak.

CATHOLICS AND UNIONS

Betten, Neil. **Catholic Activism and the Industrial Worker.** Gainsville, Florida: University Presses of Florida, 1976. An important study of the roots and evolution of Catholic social action during the past century in the United States. See especially the chapter "Labor Priests-The Contrasting Approaches of Charles Owen Rice and John P. Boland."

Heineman, Kenneth J. "A Catholic New Deal: Religion and Labor in 1930s Pittsburgh." **The Pennsylvania Magazine of History and Biography.** The Historical Society of Pennsylvania, 1994. A very focused and interesting article that effectively places Rice in the depression era Pittsburgh context.

Seaton, Douglas P. **Catholics and Radicals: The Association of Catholic Trade Unionists and the American Labor Movement from Depression to Cold War.** London and Tornoto: Associated University Press, 1981. This study places Rice's work in the broader context of the overall Catholic influence on the American labor movement.

COMMUNISTS AND UNIONS

Barrett, James R. and Rob Ruck. **Steve Nelson: American Radical**. Pittsburgh, Pa.: University of Pittsburgh Press, 1981. A powerful story of one of Rice's adversaries on the Communist side in Pittsburgh. In later years they would become reconciled.

Caute, David. **The Great Fear: The Anti-Communist Purge Under Truman and Eisenhower.** New York, N.Y.: Simon and Schuster, 1978. Classic account of Anticommunism and McCarthyism. See especially chapter 10, "Hell in Pittsburgh" and chapter 20, "United Electrical Workers on the Rack."

Filippelli, Ronald L., and Mark D. McColloch. **Cold War in the Working Class: The Rise and Decline of the United Electrical Workers**. Albany, N.Y.: State University of New York Press, 1995. A comprehensive history of the United Electrical Workers. Critical of Rice, but cognizant of his importance.

Levenstein, Harvey A. **Communism, Anticommunism, and the CIO.** Wesport, Conn.: Greenwood Press, 1981. A standard account of the communist issue inside the CIO with a good deal of information on both Rice and Phil Murray.

Rosswurm, Steve, et al., eds. **The CIO'S Left-Led Unions.** New Brunswick, N.J.: Rutgers University Press, 1992. Rosswurm

examines the internal failings of the Communist Party's relationship with the labor movement and makes an effort to understand the Catholic side. See the introduction and the chapter entitled "The Catholic Church and the Left-Led Unions."

Schatz, Ronald W. **The Electrical Workers: A History of Labor at General Electric and Westinghouse,1923–60**. Urbana and Chicago, Ill. University of Illinois Press, 1983. Still the most readable account of the anticommunist union struggle in western Pennsylvania. See especially chapter 8:" 'Red' Union or 'American' Union? Western Pennsylvania Workers Choose."

STEEL AND ITS DECLINE

Clark, Paul F., et al., eds. **Forging a Union of Steel**. Ithaca, N.Y.: ILR Press, 1987. An interesting collection of papers on Phil Murray's role in the steelworkers. See especially Melvyn Dubofsky's article, "Labor's Odd Couple: Philip Murray and John L. Lewis."

Herling, John. **Right to Challenge: People and Power in the Steelworkers Union.** New York: Harper & Row, 1972. The classic account of the evolution of the steelworkers union focusing on the election battle between I. W. Abel and David McDonald.

Hoerr, John P. **And the Wolf Finally Came: The Decline of the American Steel Industry.** Pittsburgh, Pa.: University of Pittsburgh Press, 1988. This account from a business and community viewpoint of the collapse of steel manufacturing in Pittsburgh is engrossing, though it only touches peripherally on the activist movements that engaged Rice in the 1980s.

Serrin, William. **Homestead: The Glory and Tragedy of an American Steel Town.** New York: Times Books, 1992. Serrin tells the dramatic story of the century-long rise and fall of the archetypal and even heroic milltown. This book also treats the issues that propelled "the Mon Valley insurgency" to resist plant closings so energetically.

Hathaway, Dale A. **Can Workers Have a Voice?: The Politics of Deindustrialization in Pittsburgh**. University Park, Pa.: The Pennsylvania State University Press, 1993. This book poses good questions and provides some useful information, although it has serious problems of fact and interpretation.

POLITICS

Weber, Michael P. **Don't Call Me Boss: David L. Lawrence**. Pittsburgh, Pa.: University of Pittsburgh Press, 1988. The best readily available account of the Irish Pittsburgh political milieu that spawned both Lawrence and Rice.

Text Credits

Reprinted by permission of Blueprint for Social Justice, Twomey Center, Loyola University, New Orleans: "The Tragic Purge of 1948," *Blueprint for the Christian Reshaping of Society*, February 1977.

Reprinted by permission of *Commonweal:* "A Company Union Finally Succeeds in Standing on Its Own Feet," November 8, 1946.

Reprinted by permission of Thomas More Association: "Irish and Catholic in the 1920's," *The CRITIC*, Spring 1987. "America's Darkest Decade," *The CRITIC*, Winter 1987.

Reprinted by permission of *Labor History:* "Confessions of an Anti-Communist," Summer 1989.

Reprinted by permission of *The Pittsburgh Catholic:* most of the material contained in this selection of Rice's writings.

Reprinted by permission of *Union Democracy Review:* "On the Eve of the Miner's Election," December 1972.

ARCHIVAL SOURCES

The papers of Charles Owen Rice are housed in the Archives of Industrial Society, Hillman Library, University of Pittsburgh. Much information on Rice's relation to the United Electrical Workers can be found in the UE Archives also in Hillman Library, University of Pittsburgh. The *Pittsburgh Catholic* is on microfilm at the Gumberg Library at Duquesne University, Pittsburgh, Pa.

Charles J. McCollester; associate director of the Pennsylvania Center for the Study of Labor relations, teaches Pittsburgh history and labor relations in the Department of Industrial and Labor Relations at Indiana University of Pennsylvania. With a doctorate in philosophy from the University of Louvain, Belgium, he worked for seven years as a machinist and was the chief steward of UE Local 610 at Union Switch and Signal in Swissvale, Pennsylvania.

Charles McCollester and Monsignor Rice at the commemoration of the sixtieth anniversary of his ordination to the priesthood, June 17, 1994.

INDEX